Orality
The Power of the Spoken Word

Graham Furniss
School of Oriental and African Studies, University of London

© Graham Furniss 2004

All rights reserved. No reproduction, copy or transmission of this publication may be made without written permission.

No paragraph of this publication may be reproduced, copied or transmitted save with written permission or in accordance with the provisions of the Copyright, Designs and Patents Act 1988, or under the terms of any licence permitting limited copying issued by the Copyright Licensing Agency, 90 Tottenham Court Road, London W1T 4LP.

Any person who does any unauthorized act in relation to this publication may be liable to criminal prosecution and civil claims for damages.

The author has asserted his right to be identified as the author of this work in accordance with the Copyright, Designs and Patents Act 1988.

First published 2004 by
PALGRAVE MACMILLAN
Houndmills, Basingstoke, Hampshire RG21 6XS and
175 Fifth Avenue, New York, N.Y. 10010
Companies and representatives throughout the world

PALGRAVE MACMILLAN is the global academic imprint of the Palgrave Macmillan division of St. Martin's Press, LLC and of Palgrave Macmillan Ltd. Macmillan® is a registered trademark in the United States, United Kingdom and other countries. Palgrave is registered trademark in the European Union and other countries.

ISBN 1-4039-3404-5

This book is printed on paper suitable for recycling and made from fully managed and sustained forest sources.

A catalogue record for this book is available from the British Library.

Library of Congress Cataloging-in-Publication Data
Furniss, Graham
   Orality : the power of the spoken word / Graham Furniss.
     p.cm.
   Includes bibliographical references and index.
   ISBN 1-4039-3404-5
   1. Oral communication. I. Title

P95.F87 2004
302.2'242—dc22   2004044736

10 9 8 7 6 5 4 3 2 1
13 12 11 10 09 08 07 06 05 04

Printed and bound in Great Britain by
Antony Rowe Ltd, Chippenham and Eastbourne

For Wendy, Eleanor, Jack and Katie

The play's the thing wherein I'll catch the conscience of the King

Hamlet Act 2, scene ii

Contents

List of Photographs and Figures — ix
Acknowledgements — x
Preface — xi

Introduction: The Power of the Spoken Word — 1
Chief Standing Bear and a writ of habeas corpus — 4

1 **The Oral Communicative Moment** — 12
   Orality as a nervous condition — 12
   Oral communication as model and ideal — 13
   On the concern with literacy — 15
   Power and the spoken word — 17
   Making the most of the moment — 19
   The anxiety of the moment: Marshal Mathers — 23
   Intentionality – the speaker or the text? — 25
   Memory and the making of the text — 27
   Making known – the private to the public — 27
   Mapping intention and effect in the oral
       communicative moment: Sir Geoffrey Howe in action — 29
   Concluding remarks — 42

2 **Cultural Parameters of Speech: Genre, Form, Aesthetics** — 43
   Attitudes to culture and to language — 43
   Genres — 46
   Genre and ways of speaking: the expectations of speaker
       and listener — 48
   Disputing the terms of verbal trade: the case of the northern
       Transvaal between the 1920s and 1950s — 54
   Notions of appropriate language: praising — 57
   Fixed and changing roles — 58
   Ambiguity versus clarity — 59
   Maintaining and disrupting the relation between form
       and content — 61
   Critical discourse about speaking and the aesthetics of speech — 64
   The aesthetics of speaking: two contrasting cultures — 65
   Concluding remarks — 70

viii Contents

3 **Insertion into the Social – Constituting Audiences, Audience Cultures and Moving from the Private to the Public** 72
   Social domains of cultural production: the performance and the audience 72
   The constituting of public culture 76
   Audiences and publics 84
   Audience cultures 87
   Concluding remarks 90

4 **Ideology and Orality** 92
   What ideology? 92
   Truth and values 95
   Ideology in process: typification and evaluation 100
   Evaluative/ethical discourses 102
   Evaluative language 110
   Alternative discourses: the advertiser's armoury 112
   From ideological process to ideology 117
   Stereotypes and the kaleidoscope of human speech and action 118
   Hubert Humphrey and the 1948 Democratic National Convention 124
   Concluding remarks 130

5 **Academic Approaches to Orality** 131
   Orality versus literacy: the Great Divide debate 131
   Poetics 141
   Rhetoric 144
   Pragmatics 149
   The ethnography of speaking 153
   Performance and political language 158
   Concluding remarks 161

6 **Concluding: On the Centrality of the Evanescent** 164

Appendix A: Sir Geoffrey Howe's Resignation Statement to the House of Commons, 13 November 1990 171

Appendix B: Speech by Hubert H. Humphrey to the Democratic National Convention, July 14, 1948 177

References 180

Index 183

List of Photographs and Figures

Photographs
1 Chief Standing Bear
   (courtesy of the National Anthropological Archives,
   Smithsonian Institution)   7
2 Sir Geoffrey Howe
   (courtesy of Glenn Ratcliffe)   30
3 Senator Hubert Humphrey
   (courtesy of the Lyndon Baines Johnson Library)   126

Figures
1.1 Pattern of kinetic emphasis (number of emphatic
     movements) in the resignation speech by
     Sir Geoffrey Howe   35
6.1 The oral communicative moment   168
6.2 Frames and the speech event   168
6.3 Contexts for the speech event and its frames   169

Acknowledgements

I thank those people who have kindly read through this book in draft and offered suggestions, hinted at discomforts and proffered support. To them all I am exceedingly grateful and I would like to mention their names, though they cannot be held to account in any way. They are Christine Allison, Karin Barber, Annette Czekelius, Kai Easton, Richard Fardon and Liz Gunner – a better band of sisters and brother I could not have wished for. It remains for me to thank my editors at Palgrave Macmillan and a diligent anonymous reviewer for their pertinent and constructive comments. Thanks are also due to the Research Committee of the School of Oriental and African Studies, University of London, to the British Academy, and to the A. G. Leventis Foundation for their financial support at various stages along the road. Earlier versions of sections of this book were presented for discussion at a number of institutions and I would like to express my gratitude to participants in those discussions for their comments and criticisms, in particular Bertrand Masquelier, Jean-Louis Siran and other members of LACITO in Paris; Jean Derive and colleagues at the Fourth International Conference of the International Society for Oral Literature in Africa (ISOLA), Chambery, July 2002; participants in the workshop on 'literature and performance' led by Drew Gerstle and Rosalind Thomas and held under the auspices of the SOAS/UCL AHRB Centre for the Literatures of Asia and Africa; and finally members of the Centre for Theoretical Studies in the Humanities and Social Sciences, University of Essex.

Preface

This is a book about being spoken to and speaking. While you read these words, my hope is that you will be spurred to reflect not on *this* experience of reading but on the daily experience of most of us – that of speaking and being spoken to. Since I will be 'talking' about such things as spontaneity, and the creativity and immediacy of the communicative moment it is perhaps inappropriate to use this medium (writing) in which you can go back, jump forward, re-read, skim, pore over, and 're-experience' without reference to what I am doing at all, in a way which would be quite impossible if I was speaking to you. Nevertheless, this does at least offer us a way to reflect upon the things we often take for granted about the spoken word, and come close to grasping the intangible elements within the oral communicative moment.

Why should the 'oral communicative moment' be of interest? As I will discuss in more detail later, lying at the heart of all human society is the experience of communicating and being communicated with, as an individual and as a member of a social organizational unit – be it family, firm or nation. At the same time, we are all aware that the communications that circulate among us can lead to a broad consensus of opinion among millions of people and can in themselves lead to the fall of regimes or the commercial success or failure of major corporations. Beyond the comprehension of the communication itself lies the world of perceived commonality and the experience of sensing a reality to shared views and perceptions. The emergence of broad consensus or fractured and polarized viewpoints maintained by large groups of people is a process of politics and ideology that is manifest in a multitude of forms – written texts, visual images, cinema, performances, and in coffee-shop discussion or individual exchange. The oral communicative moment is of interest because it is in understanding its dynamics that we can understand the how and the why of the transmission of ideas and values, information and identities. And we can see the differing cultural parameters within which the process operates from context to context and from society to society.

In the course of writing this book I have occasionally been asked whether it is a literary study or falls within the broad field of sociolinguistics. It does not, I think, fall into one specific disciplinary category as they are currently conceived. It has a central theme in the exploration of oral communication, but draws upon perspectives that are traditionally categorized as oral literary studies and rhetoric, linguistic anthropology, sociolinguistics, cultural studies and aspects of social anthropology. It owes its origins to the reading of the writings of F. W. Bailey and of Abner Cohen on symbolism and power relations, but its concerns are much closer to more contemporary work on the ethnography of speaking, the politics of language use and the broad field of oral literary studies. While my own earlier work has been concerned, in the main, with written and oral literary traditions of Hausa-speaking people in northern Nigeria, it has been the general issues of orality in contemporary cultures that has remained an abiding interest.

In gathering together some thoughts on the particularities of orality as I see it, I offer no special insights that relate to African as against western, Asian or other experience. Nevertheless, the issues of power and language use are central to an understanding of the postcolonial and fast-shrinking world of globalized communication in which the differences of economic fortune and political power become ever more stark. African oral literature is a field that has many specific and general issues that remain an abiding interest, but I have not tried to argue a case for special insight or special knowledge from that quarter. I remain firmly convinced that the issues I discuss remain at the heart of any investigation that seeks to follow the processes whereby human beings arrive at understanding and move onward to action, in whatever sphere. Few issues can be more general and yet more specific and varied in instantiation. Insofar as my own work has involved the consideration of aspects of African cultures, and more particularly the melting pot that is Nigeria, I have tried to provide a multicultural perspective upon the issues dealt with here. I draw upon aspects of my background and experience in the UK but also upon African, US and other examples from around the world in the hope that the issues are seen not to be confined to 'African cultures' or so-called 'oral societies' or indeed to the investigation of certain media of communication. As I argue in the opening chapter, the condition of orality is a ubiquitous condition of our waking lives, at least in most circumstances.

GRAHAM FURNISS

Introduction: The Power of the Spoken Word

The central theme running through this book is the nature and significance of the oral communicative moment and the situations in which such moments occur. This exploration pursues the 'magic of the moment' and the potentialities that lie in the necessary simultaneity of articulation and perception that is peculiar to all oral communication experienced unrecorded and unfilmed. It is that dimension to orality that this book focuses upon.

What is it about oral communication that means that people feel the need to come together to discuss rather than conduct their business by paper, by e-mail or by recorded message? With all the communications technology at our fingertips, why do business people fly halfway round the world to look each other in the eye as they make arrangements? Why do people meet in debating chambers to make rules and reach political positions when they could surely more easily handle the complexity of the issues and the large amount of relevant data by exchanging documents and be done with it? In this book, I explore related dimensions of these simple questions.

Is it about orality versus literacy? Only insofar as it focuses upon the communicative conditions of the co-presence of speaker and listener and the dynamics of the real-time events that occur in that oral situation. These do not constitute a separate class of event from those involving the written or recorded word. Time and again the oral communicative moment is intricately interwoven with the written word and the graphic image. So, while the focus is upon 'orality', the discussion will range across 'the written as spoken', 'the graphic encompassing the written and evoking the oral', 'the recorded spoken or sung', 'the spoken as then inscribed'. This discussion moves away from a view that contrasts the 'oral/spoken' with the 'written' – either as supposed characteristics of types of society, or as modes of communication which throw up contrasting limitations and possibilities relating to memory, thought processes, or the accumulation, durability and accessibility of 'knowledge'. Rather, the focus here is upon orality as sets of communicative conditions inherent in oral situations common to all human societies whether 'literacy' is absent, restricted or general. The emphasis here is on the 'oral' in the 'oral/literate mix' as outlined by Brian Street in his discussion of the 'autonomous' and 'ideological' models of literacy (Street 1984). In a way similar to Street's focus upon the cultural practices of reading and writing and the power relations in which such practices are embedded, this discussion looks at aspects of the cultural practice of speaking and being spoken to. Where Street argued against a model which established 'literacy' as a feature with inherent qualities having consequences for society (the autonomous model) and in favour of an approach which situated the activity of reading and writing in a variety of social and political contexts (the ideological model), so this discussion looks to explore aspects of 'oral communicative situations' without essentializing 'orality' as a set of a priori features contrary to those of 'literacy'.

A second general theme of this book is the dynamics of cultural production and the associated notions of private and public culture. The mercurial experience of the communicative moment is the site of a range of aspects of cultural production. Creativity and spontaneity of the moment building upon the power of the unexpected may lead to the creation of new perceptions and understandings in the listener/audience. A search for creativity can be a defining element in the performer's improvisation, or it can be manifest in the listener's response to a strictly 'scripted' performance. A search for creativity is, of course, only one aspect of the many and various processes of cultural production – which are frequently driven through the creation and distribution of the written word and the graphic and visual image. In the interplay between the written and the spoken, the parties to the communicative transaction move in and out of the private and public spheres, as is discussed later.

The third general theme, a dimension of the second, is the issue of the dynamics of persuasion. This is an issue that students of rhetoric have debated since before the time of Aristotle and which continues to exercise the minds of anthropologists, political scientists, philosophers and students of language and literature. In this discussion, persuasion is explored as a phenomenon that is not, of course, unique to the 'oral situation', since persuasion by text and by visual image is a predominant feature of much modern communication, but as a dimension of much oral communication – involving interaction between speaker and audience, intentionality, culturally specific genres of speech, genre expectations, notions of 'truth', the evaluative dimensions of language both lexically and contextually, and the aesthetics of language use.

As this book proceeds, we will begin by discussing aspects of the 'oral communicative moment' first as a ubiquitous condition of our social existence, then as the locus for the articulation of ideas and values where the act of articulation is a social act of sharing. Whether they are indeed shared, in the sense of believed rather than simply jointly perceived, depends upon the context of previous articulation, differing views among the listeners, and a whole range of other considerations relating to differential perceptions and experience. One important dimension to the discussion is the question of intention versus effect and the difficulties of drawing out evidence for the intentions of a speaker and the effect upon an audience during a single fleeting, but perhaps explosive, experience.

The next section of the discussion turns to the many different cultural parameters that surround the speech event in different societies. Each culture, or sub-culture, will have its own aesthetics of speaking and a wide variety of ways of speaking that are considered appropriate to different circumstances. These ways of speaking may be linked to temporary roles that people play, or be a marker of a category of people in society; they may be highly formalized, or loose and fuzzy styles that overlap and are the subject of play and humour. Ways of communicating can be the subject of dispute between people and thus intimately linked to contested power relations both between individuals and categories of people. Thus, from a discussion of the cultural parameters that surround the oral communicative moment, the book moves on to a consideration of the social contexts of orality, and the embedded nature of the event. Tape and video have allowed the retention of a record of live performance and thus the removal of the 'performance' from the event itself. But it was the event as the assemblage of people in real time that was the locus of articulation and perception in which notions of a group were constituted and identities forged, through the ways in which the speaker addressed the audience, through the co-presence of individuals, through common reactions commonly perceived. Intimately woven into the event are a range of other processes – creating knowledge, articulating values, and moving such ideas and information from the private sphere into the public with all the implications that can have for relations between people and groups. Articulating values and sketching out a characterization of people and events lead the discussion towards ideological processes, both in terms of notions of truth and knowledge, but also as consideration of the techniques of persuasion. One of the most illuminating and incisive discussions of the tactics adopted by people in oral communicative situations is to be found in F.G. Bailey's many writings and particularly in his discussion of universities and the myths academics live by (Bailey 1977). More recent volumes by him address a number of the issues under discussion here, in particular his book on the deployment of notions of truth (of which there are many), and the tactics of truth-telling and deception in public culture (Bailey 1991), and his work on the expression of emotion as a strategy in debate and argumentation (Bailey 1983).

The last part of this book examines some of the academic approaches to orality and the speech event, and discusses a range of disciplines and fields of enquiry which raise quite different issues around the topic under discussion here.

While the oral communicative moment can be one of the millions of interpersonal communications between individuals going on constantly around us, it can also be a single moment that is perceived to have momentous consequences for millions of people around our globe. Along the continuum between those two poles lie the range of examples discussed in this book, from historical moments where the oral dynamics are difficult to reconstruct, to imaginary illustrations of personal experience, to speculation on the communicative context of reified texts that are available to us.

Chief Standing Bear and a writ of habeas corpus

To illustrate some of the questions that this book is considering, I would like you to consider an event that took place in May 1879, in Omaha, Nebraska. Chief Standing Bear, a native American Chief of the Ponca people, appeared as the plaintiff before Judge Elmer S. Dundy, a US District Judge for Nebraska. At the conclusion of the case, Judge Dundy allowed Chief Standing Bear to address the court. An interested party, a journalist for the *Omaha Daily Herald*, Thomas Henry Tibbles, reported the event in the following terms (Tibbles 1972 [1880]: 93):

> The court room was at this time filled with leading citizens of the State, prominent officers of the army and their wives. Standing Bear's speech made a profound impression on all who heard it ... In spite of the orders of the court and the efforts of the bailiffs, he was greeted with continual rounds of applause.

And again (Tibbles 1957 [1905]: 202),

> No one who merely reads the speech can possibly imagine its effect on people who knew of the Poncas's sufferings when they heard it spoken by the sad old chief in his brilliant robes. I saw tears on Judge Dundy's face. General Crook sat leaning forward, covering his eyes with his hand. Except for the women's sobs there was absolute silence for a moment, then the whole room rose at once with a great shout. Among the first to reach Standing Bear was General Crook. The entire audience came crowding after him to shake the chief's hand.

The judgement handed down by Judge Dundy was portrayed as a 'brilliant essay on human rights' and a landmark civil rights case confirming the argument that 'an Indian was as much a person as any white man and could avail himself of the rights of freedom guaranteed by the US Constitution' (Brown 1991 [1970]: 360–2).

Clearly, then, the case and in particular the 'oral communicative moment' of Chief Standing Bear's speech would appear to have had a direct effect upon the fate not only of Chief Standing Bear and his people, but also of generations of native Americans in the ensuing years. But is it quite that clear and how do we know? Can we trust Thomas Henry Tibbles's account and what was it about the speech that had such a direct effect on all who were present? Can we ever know? That the case did have an effect upon the judge is confirmed by the opening lines of his written judgement (Tibbles 1972 [1880]: 95):

> During the fifteen years in which I have been engaged in administering the laws of my country, I have never been called upon to hear or decide a case that appealed so strongly to my sympathy as the one now under consideration.

And the effect of the representation of the position of the Ponca Indians is expressed later in the same judgement (104–5):

> They claim to be unable to see the justice, or reason, or wisdom, or necessity of removing them by force from their own native lands and blood relations to a far off country in which they can see little but new made graves opening for their reception. The land from which they fled in fear has no attractions for them. The love of home and native land was strong enough in the midst of these people to induce

them to brave every peril to return and live and die where they had been reared. The bones of the dead son of Standing Bear were not to repose in the land they hoped to be leaving forever, but were carefully preserved and protected, and formed a part of what was to them a melancholy procession homeward.

The bulk of the judgement delivered by Judge Elmer S. Dundy relates to jurisdiction, the application of the law, and the authorities in the case, but his confirmation, for the first time, that an Indian was a *person* in terms of the US Constitution led directly to the release from custody of Standing Bear and his party of Ponca Indians, allowing them to return to the lands from which they had been forcibly transferred to 'Indian Territory' hundreds of miles away in what is now Oklahoma.

From these excerpts from the judgement and the explicit descriptions of courtroom reaction by Thomas Henry Tibbles it would appear that there is a direct connection between the oral intervention of Chief Standing Bear and the future of the United States! But how to assess the relationship between the outcome and the different elements of the trial – what was the significance in the whole process of the force of the speech? Was the crucial issue the moral persona of the Chief (something of his persona can be gleaned from the transcript of the questioning during the trial that is presented in Chapter 8 of Tibbles (1972) and from the photographs that survive)? Was it the arguments of the attorneys who represented Chief Standing Bear – Poppleton and Webster? Was it the undisputed facts of the case that had their own moral logic? Was it the words of the final speech by Chief Standing Bear, despite the fact that, throughout the case, his words were being translated into English for the court by one Willie H. Hamilton (the identification of Willie H. Hamilton as the translator of Standing Bear's words comes from the transcripts given in Tibbles (1972: 79)), a 22-year-old store-hand who spoke Omaha, the language of both Omaha and Ponca Indians, and who also testified to the court? What weight can be given to the English rendering of Chief Standing Bear's words when there is doubt even about who the translator was? – other descriptions ('The Trial of Standing Bear' on www.nebraskastudies.org) indicate that the translator was Susette LaFlesche Tibbles also know as Bright Eyes, daughter of an Omaha Chief, who later went on to marry Thomas Henry Tibbles. She accompanied both Standing Bear and Tibbles on speaking tours on the eastern seaboard of the US and to Europe in the last two decades of the nineteenth century to speak of the injustices meted out to native Americans.

Photograph 1 Chief Standing Bear (courtesy of the National Anthropological Archives, Smithsonian Institution)

A further level of uncertainty remains around what produced the outcome. Kay Graber, in an introduction to Tibbles (1972), indicates that Thomas Henry Tibbles was somewhat prone to exaggeration and self-promotion, so how much store can we place on his evidence, particularly his memoirs, *Buckskin and Blanket Days*? Other writers also confirm that Tibbles was involved in the original moves to bring the matter to court and that there were others who were motivated to push the case and to select Judge Dundy to hear the case. Brown indicates that the arresting officer, General Crook, a very experienced military officer, having heard their story was unhappy at his orders from Washington to arrest Chief Standing Bear and his group of 30. Brown (1991 [1970]: 358–60) indicates that Crook contacted Tibbles to publicize the apparent injustice through the *Omaha Daily Herald* and more widely, and this then attracted the attorneys, Webster and Poppleton, who received the tacit support of General Crook in bringing a case against himself suing for release of his prisoners. Judge Dundy, back from a bear hunt, agreed to issue a writ of habeas corpus requiring Crook to produce the prisoners and justify why he was detaining them. The case turned on whether the Indians were to be seen as individuals who had detached themselves from their legal identity as tribespeople and thus were constituted as 'persons' under the Constitution. If they were persons they were being illegally detained. Crook was delighted to release them following the judgement of the court.

Central to the deliberations were those elements which convinced all present that Chief Standing Bear was indeed a 'person' both legally and in general. The legal argument hinged on whether these Indians had detached themselves from a 'tribe', but the criteria by which Standing Bear was adjudged more broadly a 'person' were of course framed by the perceptions and the morals of the day. And so, when Judge Dundy delivered his statement, quoted above, on the Ponca perception of what had happened to them and Standing Bear's desire to fulfill his promise to his dying son that he would inter his bones in their native land, he went on to say, 'Such instances of parental affection, and such love of home and native land may be *heathen* in origin, but it seems to me that they are not unlike *christian* in principle' (emphasis in original) (Tibbles 1972 [1880]: 105).

So what happened to Standing Bear and thirty of his people to bring them to this courtroom in Omaha, Nebraska in April and May 1897? Briefly, between 1800 and 1900 there were never more than 800 people known as Ponca. By 1874 there were 733 individuals living where the Niobrara river flows into the Missouri. Following a number of treaties agreeing to their occupation of this land, agents of the US government assigned the land to the Sioux in 1868. In 1875 the Indian agent, A.J. Carrier, sought permission to move the Ponca Indians to Indian Territory, hundreds of miles south in what is now Oklahoma. In 1877 a group of Ponca chiefs agreed to make a visit to the proposed land to see if they would be prepared to take their people to live there. On seeing the land they told the Indian agent they did not want to move. Furious, the Indian agent left them to fend for themselves, eventually making their way with great difficulty back to the Niobrara river. The US military were by this stage forcibly removing the Ponca people south. While travelling south and on arriving in Indian Territory, many Ponca died from illnesses, including Standing Bear's son, Bear Shield, who died in the harsh winter of 1878–79. Standing Bear and thirty of his people left the Indian Territory without permission from the government and made their way back through terrible hardships as far as Omaha, where their relatives the Omaha Indians took them in. They were arrested and detained at Fort Omaha by General Crook acting on the orders of the government. Chief Standing Bear described the experience of the Ponca Indians in Indian Territory as follows in his evidence to the court, translated by Hamilton (Tibbles 1972 [1880]: 81–2):

> When I got down there, I saw the land, and the land was not good to my eye; some places it looked good, but you kick up the soil a little, and you found lots of stones. It was not fit to farm. When we got down there we heard we were going to get clothing, and get money, and everything we wanted, but I have not seen it yet. When I was told to go down there, I thought, perhaps, the land was good, and I could make a living, but when I got down there it was entirely different from the land in my own home. I couldn't plow, I couldn't sow any wheat, and we all got sick, and couldn't do anything. It seemed as though I had no strength in my body at all. The hot climate didn't agree with me. But when I came back here I seemed to get strength every day. Instead of our tribe becoming prosperous, they died off every day during the time. From the time I went down there until I left, one hundred and fifty-eight of us died. I thought, God wants me to live, and I think if I come back to my old reservation he will let me live. I got back as far as the Omahas, and they brought me down here. I see you all here today. What have I done? I am brought here, but what have I done? I don't know. It seems as though I haven't a place in the world, no place to go, and no home to go to, but when I see your faces here, I think that some of you are trying to help me, so that

I can get a place sometime to live in, and when it comes my time to die, to die peacefully and happy.

The transcript goes on to indicate, 'this was spoken in a loud voice, and with much emphasis' and that the judge said, 'Tell the witness to keep cool'. Clearly, there were ways of speaking that were appropriate in the view of the court and some that were not.

When it came to the end of the case a multitude of experiences, memories and values lay latent in the articulation that Standing Bear was about to make. Interlinked social, legal and political interests represented in the parties present in the court formed the context that lay behind the moment when Standing Bear stood up to finally address the court. What did he say and how did he say it? Brown (1991 [1970]: 360) has a text derived from Addison Sheldon's *Nebraska, the Land and the People* (1931); Tibbles (1957 [1905]: 200–1) has quite another text. His way of speaking was not to argue the niceties of US legal practice, his way of speaking was, if Thomas Henry Tibbles can be believed, comprehensible in translation but full of imagery, personal and yet representative, imbued with a morality and trenchant recognition of the truth of his situation. Standing Bear was not alone in his approach to eloquence, he was part of a tradition summarized by R.D. Theisz in these terms (Theisz 2002):

> The heritage of eloquence in Native American oral tradition reflects the notion that selected individuals possess the gifts of thought, language, and moral courage to lead us to recognise the underlying meaning of human existence. Thus, life experience, historical circumstance, personal character, and oral rhetorical skill combine to allow speakers to share with their audience a moment of authentic understanding, the momentary recognition of the confluence of real events and their verbal interpretation.

It is a fair guess that the courtroom that day witnessed one of such moments. The best we can manage from this distance is to imagine through the description by Thomas Henry Tibbles:

> Standing Bear rose. Half facing the audience, he stretched his right hand out before him, holding it still so long that the audience grew tense. At last, looking at the judge, he spoke quietly.
> 'That hand is not the color of yours, but if I pierce it, I shall feel pain. If you pierce your hand, you also feel pain. The blood that will

flow from mine will be of the same color as yours. I am a man. The same God made us both.'

Half facing the audience again, he let his gaze drift far out through a window. His tone grew tense.

'I seem to stand on the bank of a river. My wife and little girl are beside me. In front the river is wide and impassable, and behind are perpendicular cliffs. No man of my race ever stood there before. There is no tradition to guide me.'

Then he described how a flood began to rise around them and how, looking despairingly at the great cliffs, he saw a steep, stony way leading upward. Grasping his child's hand, while his wife followed, he led the way up the sharp rocks while the waters still rose behind them. Finally he saw a rift in the rocks and felt the prairie breeze strike his cheek.

'I turn to my wife and child with a shout that we are saved. We will return to the Swift Running Water that pours down between the green islands [Niobrara]. There are the graves of my fathers. There again we will pitch our teepee and build our fires. But a man bars the passage. He is a thousand times more powerful than I. Behind him I see soldiers as numerous as the leaves of the trees. They will obey that man's orders. I too must obey his orders. If he says that I cannot pass, I cannot. The long struggle will have been in vain. My wife and child and I must return and sink beneath the flood. We are weak and faint and sick.'

He paused with bowed head. Then, gazing up into Judge Dundy's face with an indescribable look of pathos and suffering, he said in a low, intense tone:

'You are that man.'

Much of this book is concerned with the nature of such moments, their complexities, their conventions, their ubiquity, and their constitution across cultures. Their evanescent nature makes them difficult to grasp and represent, yet their traces in memory and in recording, and their power to move mountains make of them a subject of endless fascination.

1
The Oral Communicative Moment

Orality as a nervous condition

In the flow of daily life, each one of us lives in an ever-changing chain of experience in which thought, memory and perception interact with our immediate environment of other people and material conditions. Beyond the physical environment of our lives there lies the world of 'social' reality – people who have defined roles in relation to our freedom of action: parents, teachers, policemen, judges, tax collectors ... In all of these relationships, it is the nature of the interchanges between them and us that give reality to the social roles they play and the imagined structure that lies behind them – behind the policeman lies the idea of the laws and regulations that we must not break or we will be punished. The manifestation of these constructs is in the concrete utterances and behaviour of these categories of individuals; it is when the teacher says, 'Open your books' that you are inclined both to do what you are told and to understand something of the institution they represent. The flow of daily life is the succession of such moments of experiential interactions, manifested in words. In contrast with the words lying at rest and undiscovered between the covers of the book, or the relative permanence and immutability of objects, the spoken words in which we swim are always gone as soon as they arrive. The linearity of speech in time obviates the possibility of the constant gaze; while we can contemplate the crystal bowl from above or below, from front or back, the spoken word cannot be viewed from another perspective – it may be repeatable (play it again, Sam!), but in contrast to the written words on the page you cannot read them backwards or upwards; the paradigm can be 'read' upwards or downwards on the page, but the living syntagm of the flow of speech cannot be stilled, as no one can still the flow of the river from standing within it. The silence of aloneness is inhabited by the words of reflection, and few are the people whose life is dominated by silence. For most of us, the focus of our minds is the puzzle of understanding the intentions of others and determining the way to express our own perspectives, be they wants, needs, thoughts, reactions. This permanent, unavoidable presence at our elbow nudging us all the time, like a tic that won't go away, or a constant companion of which we are only occasionally aware, is not simply music in the background but the vehicle of our waking consciousness, a nervous condition with which we have to live.

We are surrounded by the spoken word and we are unable to shut it out, or deliberately invoke an ability to avoid understanding it. I may choose to ignore those words which were spoken in my hearing in a language I understand, but I cannot guard my mind from perceiving them and dealing with the meanings I have to take from them. The meanings I take may not be those which you intend, but it would be unusual for me to believe (in my usual state of mind) that when you say, 'The house is on fire!' you are saying that you have dropped a glass of milk. The conscious mind *must* deal with the perceptions that percolate through the sensory windows, and the conventions of language point to a range of available meanings – orality is the condition of so much of that process of perception that we have to deal with. And the perception of visual images of the constructed world around us often evoke words that are intimately associated, culture by culture, with those visual images. The clear blue water lapping the sand below the palm tree evokes both feelings and words.

Even the visual image of the written word plastered across the poster 'Your country needs you!!' shouts a deafening message of self-sacrifice and action. Orality, then, lies at the heart of our daily experience as individuals and as communicating beings within the social groups we inhabit. The condition of the spoken word has been the subject of much contemplation, from Aristotle's *Poetics* to the 'ethnography of speaking'. Philosophy and linguistics have pored over the nature of language, mind and meaning; linguistic anthropology, rhetoric and poetics have examined the condition of the spoken, and the contexts in which the action of speech effects a change in human relations. A number of these academic approaches to orality are discussed in Chapter 5.

Oral communication as model and ideal

As more and more of the messages we receive are lodged by their authors in the waiting rooms filled with now electronic and previously paper storage mechanisms, so we both become distanced from the human agent who produced the messages and yet seek a simulacrum of that human touch. Regardless of whether the message was fashioned with you the receiver in mind – 'Come back, John, all is forgiven', or was a general statement to all humankind – 'It is forbidden to smoke in the toilets of this aircraft', the letter or the sign retain the message for now, tomorrow and forever. You, the receiver, may choose to take in, or delay, or indeed to ignore – not simply to be aware yet feign no knowledge – but to remain blissfully ignorant because you have chosen not to become aware, to read or to hear. While advertisers may be battling to catch you off guard, to insinuate awareness into your daily experience, you may resolutely shut out all that is unwelcome, or at least you may think that you can. You can decide when to open that letter, slot in that videotape or read that book. The message is safely stored and available. And, of course, the mechanisms for the control of delay in receiving the message are not limited to physical media in our own control. Not only has the ansaphone in which the tape on your desk contains the message been supplanted by the message held who knows where in the labyrinth of telecommunications companies' computers, but the e-mail message with its delayable communication has further enabled us to regulate how and when we receive communication. The presence of the person or people who initiated the communication that lies before you is no longer inextricably linked with the message itself. Substituting for that presence, however, is sometimes an evocation, an imaginary speaker, 'written into' the message itself. The three-week-old e-mail message that starts with 'Hi!', the personalized mail shot letter, the question on the ansaphone tape still waiting for a reply. These are perhaps no more than extensions upon the time-honoured fictions of the 'Dear Reader' variety whether it be seventeenth-century novel or contemporary magazine advice columns. The willingness of the receiver of the communication to constitute himself or herself as a member of 'the reader' category or to acknowledge the greeting in the message, regardless of whether they accept the fiction that the sender intended specifically to speak to them, is of course intimately bound up with the receiver's recognition of what is happening. When you recognize the signs that someone is trying to communicate with you then you switch on the antennae. First the call signal, 'Hi!' then the category of communication, 'Will you buy?' and then the message itself, 'Who will buy my sweet red roses, two blooms for a penny?' You knew the sort of thing to expect and you were prepared to accept that the message was intended for you. If, however, you were gazing at the stars, it is less likely that you would expect to switch on the same antennae. A 'Hi!' from outer space you would not usually expect. Yet, were it to happen, your instinctive reaction would be to expect the communication to start with the simulacrum of presence, a 'Hi!' to simulate a moment of co-presence. Never mind the fact that the message was sent many light years previously. In a myriad different ways the estrangement between the sender and the receiver is covered, disguised, compensated for by the fictionalizing of a co-presence in the nature of the message itself.

The history of human culture has been the tracing of the inscription of the message into forms which can delay the moment of communication. The artefacts of recall and memory, the parchments, the books and the visual representations, have successfully allowed not only delayed understanding, but also the potential for repeated and infinitely variable reconstitution in the perceptions of each successive individual and generation. The notion of fixity inherent in the 'text' or the artefact from which the receiver of the message constructs an understanding is, of course, a common one. The 'death of the author' has led us to view the text as the kaleidoscope in which the 'free play' of meaning can dance through the mind of the receiver. This focus upon the text, whether viewed as imbued with fixity and recoverability or as infinitely variable in its reconstitutability, has dominated much of the discussion of western and non-western culture alike. The particular and peculiar features of literacy and the technologizing of the word have come to dominate the concerns of scholars in such a way that the transformations effected by the media of communication come to define the nature of communication itself. Yet so many of the styles and manners of communication within such media rely upon a fiction of direct 'here-and-now' communication. The newsreader is surely talking to me; the authorial voice in this novel is talking to *me*, surely; I could have sworn the playwright must have known about our family!

On the concern with literacy

The framework within which issues of 'orality' have been generally addressed has been made up of two rather separate domains. Orality has been a 'condition' in which the pre-modern world of classical and medieval society found itself – a world in which writing was the preserve of a very small number of individuals and a condition from which the vast majority of people were excluded. Therefore, orality was a pristine state, a homogeneous background against which the particular characteristics of literacy developed to revolutionize society – the accumulation of knowledge, a move from endless repetition to progress and the building up of layers of skill and expertise from one generation to the next, a process facilitated by the ability to record and recover earlier discoveries and reflections. Fundamental to this view is the idea of a progression from orality to literacy, a step upon the march of progress, a fundamental historical transition from one state of society to another, and one in which the focus of investigation was nearly invariably upon the changes wrought by the techniques available within the 'new/more modern' state. In relation to expressive culture either it was possible to peel away the 'literate' characteristics of an ancient text (Homer being the classic example) to reveal the original elements of orality manifest in formulae and other features considered to be typical of the 'oral' state out of which the text emerges to be inscribed, or the text maintains within itself elements that persist as residual features of 'orality'. The other domain in which orality has figured has been the concern with so-called 'oral societies' around our contemporary world. From New Guinea to Kamchatka there are societies in which 'writing' is not known (or at least was 'unknown' until very recently) and these must therefore be, by default, 'oral societies' whose ways of recording the past, of socializing the new generations, and of articulating their values and their norms must be 'oral'. A brief review of writing on orality will quickly demonstrate the way in which research on this subject has tended to fall into one of these two camps. Both camps tend to concentrate upon the significance of literacy, restricted literacy within 'oral' societies, or the effects of literacy upon education, upon the establishment of 'knowledge' and schools of thought, of science and of the development of those arts which are dependent upon the written word.

We will return to the academic debates about the so-called Great Divide between the oral and the written in Chapter 5, but there are two aspects to these approaches which bear further consideration at this point. The notion that there are usefully distinguishable categories 'literate societies' and 'oral societies' on the one hand and the notion of historical progression from orality to literacy on the other. In relation to the first issue it is clear that there are societies in which writing has not been known, and others in which writing has been either a restricted avenue for the acquisition and transmission of information or a generally taught skill intended to make available the resources of writing to as wide a part the population as possible. But does this mean that a literate society is any the less oral than a so-called 'oral society'? Surely not. The fact that the additional facility of recording language on paper has provided an important mechanism for communicating and storing information does not mean that all the oral mechanisms of communication are somehow less present, either by degree or by nature. If we look, for a moment, at a so-called 'literate society', that of twenty-first-century Britain, it is clear that down many a local street there will be many people who have the ability to read but whose daily lives are dominated by oral communication, people who have no books in their houses, who do not read a newspaper but live in a world of radio, film and television where they are constantly subject to the spoken word for information, opinion and comment as well as the massively varied world of entertainment. There may be many who cannot read at all, as well as those who can but are seldom called upon to do so. As many have commented before, while the Internet may bring us back to reading on the computer screens, the growth and spread of modern technologies of communication have moved us increasingly into a world of oral rather than literate communication as television, radio and telephones, tape and video recorders move us further and further from the written word. Rather than a passage from the oral to the written, we are seeing if anything a passage from the written to the oral. However, the notion that there is a historical progression under way is in itself a questionable way of looking at the issue. The issue is surely not the nature of so-called 'oral societies' and their transition to becoming 'literate societies', but rather the particularities of the communication processes that are underway in the various kinds of orality (direct dialogue between two people, verbal address by one person to many, recorded simulated interpersonal communication, etc.); this in contrast to the nature of communication and information storage and retrieval through writing. In this sense, therefore, orality and the dynamics of oral communication lie at the heart of *all* societies; orality is not a feature to be relegated to distant worlds, whether they be in time or in space, from the here and now of 'our' societies, whether we stand in London, Lagos, Lamu, Labuan or the banks of Lake Louise.

Power and the spoken word

Power, being my ability to make you do what I want, is vested in the capacity I have to shoot you if you don't respond, to take you before a process of assessment and judgement and punish you if you are found to have contravened a rule, or to control your action or freedom of action because you are in some way dependent upon me. The power of the spoken word which forms the subject of this discussion is intertwined within these relations of force, not to substitute for them but as relating to the world of representations and evaluations that envelop the exercise of force.

While much of the discussion here will focus upon the power of the word as spoken and therefore as agent of representation and communication, the particular contexts of power and authority within which the spoken word operates mean that we need to distinguish between the power of the word and the power relations between people involved in the communication process. It is by no means necessarily the case that those who speak are those who hold power. It may be that in one context, it is the powerless who are silent and deprived of 'a voice'; but equally in other societies and contexts it may be those who control who remain silent. Part of the authority of the king in Ashanti society, described by Yankah, lies in his public silent presence while his *okyeame*, his orator, speaks for him. In Mande society there is a saying translated in French as *parler c'est mourir* that carries an implication that to speak is to open oneself, to spill out and empty oneself in the course of speech, the power of knowledge and wisdom being vested in the quiet one rather than the loquacious and the eloquent person. Attitudes to speaking vary greatly and it is by no means inevitable that the power of speech goes along with the effective exercise of power.

Nevertheless, the field of enquiry with which we are concerned here – namely the process of oral articulation and perception of representation – is of relevance to a wide variety of disciplines. As political science considers, among other issues, changes in public opinion, moving to the right or to the left, or cynically disengaged, the question arises of how people's daily experience as individuals is articulated and evaluated, and then shared and amended or reinforced, until a growing force of common views emerges as an articulated combination of statements about how the world 'really' works, on a sliding scale from street to ward to quarter to town to city to region. Contested by others, at all the same levels, the set of views may become in time a political position that is apparent in elections, strikes, debates, and all the other manifestations that politics occupies itself with.

Similarly, while economists may deal only with the numbers that reflect cash flows around the world, savings ratios, and other 'economic data', if they are concerned at all with the microeconomic issues of how people behave in relation to economic activity then at the heart of that process lies the articulation of perceptions of 'reality' and the evaluations that accompany them. If people do things which in an ideal economic model world they would not do, then it is because there is some other motivation upon which people base their actions – actions, for example, that are based upon faith, hope and charity, and a myriad other motivations – social solidarity, jealousy, hatred, all of which are reactions predicated upon particular representations of self and other people, characterizations of who 'they' are, how 'they' are doing economically, how 'their' actions are affecting 'us'. On the one hand, to consider such issues may limit the discussion to individual economic motivation, on the other they may affect large portions of a national economy or indeed the international economic system. As the Japanese were exhorted in the 1990s to spend, spend, spend, both as individuals, as institutions and as a national government, in order to pull the East Asian economies out of a dangerous slump, so the attitudes to saving and to spending that are articulated in Japanese public life have had to to take account of the way in which people articulate the picture of their world and the values that they feel they must hold dear – a picture of the world forged out of the experience of the Second World War and the postwar period and the values both inherent in Japanese culture and in the 'cultural logic of late capitalism', to use Fredric Jameson's phrase.

Clearly the world of ritual and symbolic activity is the area in which the articulation of values, and the process of rendering comprehensible daily experience, is most apparent. Not only do we observe the repeated articulation of beliefs and values within institutions predicated upon their maintenance – religious organizations, schools, associative interest groups, all of which seek to maintain over time the 'living' presence of core values in the experience of spoken articulation – mosque on Friday, synagogue on Saturday, church on Sunday, Amnesty International local branch meeting on Monday, Oxfam on Tuesday, Resident's Committee on Wednesday, and round it goes again – we also see and experience the creative process whereby artists, dramatists, writers, as well as others, innovate through the articulation of new visions of the world, and rework old visions in the light of new circumstances. Chapter 4 will discuss further the issues that surround the articulation of values and thus the formulation of ideologies.

Making the most of the moment

Standing in the bar at the interval, anticipating the second half of the show, there is the sure and certain knowledge that if you weren't present to experience the moment, there is no way you could grasp what it was like. The magic of the moment when that cadence, that look, that aria, that speech, moved the audience, to a man or woman, to tears or to joyous bliss. Maybe you know the play more or less by heart, maybe the script has been in your hands as well as in the hands of the actors and director, but the experience of reading the script is a far cry from that moment of hilarity, tragedy or anger in which you were an eager participant. The moment is one in which the communication coming at you meshes with your own faculty of making meaning, your own experience and memories, your estimation of values and your vulnerabilities, to produce the reactive thought, the sense of pleasure or pain, and the judgement of the significance of the communication coming at you. While your colleagues in the bar may tell you that their array of reactions differs from yours, and their judgements are constructed differently, at least you can be confident that you know they saw the same thing on the stage as you did. The communication coming across was identical, it can only be the perception that is different. But was the communication identical? In an absolute sense, yes, in the limited sense that a book remains the same text whether you read it or I read it (assuming we both buy the same edition), but during the performance perhaps you watched one actor while I watched another, you sat with your eyes closed and only listened to the dialogue between the actors, while I, fixed upon the kaleidoscope of colour and movement, turned down my hearing aid, figuring that, since I know the storyline, I will have no difficulty in knowing where in the plot we are. The notion of shared experience is problematic. Nevertheless, while your and my perceptions may differ, we can at least argue with each other that, if we can agree that we both saw the expression on the actress's face and we both heard the tone in her voice, we beg to differ on our reactions rather than the experience itself. Our memories may filter out different elements of the experience, or we may have been watching different actors on the stage at the exact moment we are trying to recall, but there remains a unity in the notion that the event was one and the same. We can at least search for a commonality in something about the event, even if it was differently experienced.

But I begin by relating, not what I assume you experienced, but my own perceptions and reactions. In this it is the instantaneous simultaneity of the articulation by the actors and my own spontaneous reaction which I am trying to grasp and put into words. Not only my understanding of the layers, nuances, contradictions and importance of the meanings that I perceive to be inherent in the words spoken to me, but also my own feelings in reaction to my overall perception of the communication, both verbal and non-verbal, that is laid before me. Time for reflection comes later, delay and the possibility of, as it were, 're-reading' the experience through memory, are not in the forefront of my mind. As I grasp it now, that sets the framework for all subsequent action. Naturally, the moment of communication operates at many levels, the grasping of immediate meaning is complemented by my desire to make sense of the utterance within the framework of what has gone before and what I anticipate to be about to follow – how does it fit with the unfolding plot? How does it fit with or add to the nature of the person, or persons, I see before me? Not only do I note, classify and mark for recall, the utterance which is the focus of my attention, it may well be that I am nonplussed, I don't understand the significance of what has just been said. It seems to contradict what I thought I knew of this character, it doesn't fit with where I thought the plot was going, perhaps I simply couldn't understand the utterance itself. And so I am led to ponder, or to ask you what you thought of that particular comment. And between us we work out a way to make the words fit, not necessarily finally, but as an interim measure; we are, after all, still in the interval and the dénouement has yet to arrive. But the power of the play lies not in my ability to reflect afterwards and put all the pieces together, in the taxi on the way home or lying in bed looking up at the ceiling. The power of the play lies in the magic of the moment, the combination, in the same moment, of the articulation of the utterance, the falling of the scales from my eyes as I grasp the meaning, and the feelings in me that accompany, and are embedded in, that moment. Of course, I can be inspired, moved, educated by the reading of a book, and I can discuss all the same questions with my friend in the bar after reading it, nevertheless, the essential solitude of reading, the imaginary presence of the speaker/author, the imagined solidarity of other readers, and the potential discontinuity of the experience (when did you last sit down and read a book from cover to cover?), mean an estrangement from the reality of being confronted with, and incorporated into, a speech event.

Why is it that a speech event is of significance? Surely, the written word, albeit with the distancing of author, reader, and text, is equally significant in terms of both conveying meaning and evoking emotion? Is there any aspect of communication that cannot eventually be conveyed by writing? If, indeed, writing is sufficient, then why is it that so many of the decisive moments in our daily lives, both as individuals and as societies, remain firmly embedded in moments of orality? Surely it is not necessary in this day and age for the government of country upon country to require oral debate in parliaments of many different kinds. Surely, 'self-study' in the schools and universities of country after country can quite adequately substitute for the time, money and energy spent on putting teachers in front of groups of students and have them talk; if the students simply read the handouts in their own time and bury themselves in the silent libraries of the world, will we not arrive at a blessed state of enlightenment, hey presto!? The reason why we do not live in a reading world, be it from paper or from the computer screens of the Internet, is that there is an essential and inescapable social and individual need for the features of orality that are apparent in these forms of communication, quite apart from the obvious need for the interpersonal oral communication whereby we run our own individual lives.

Along with the army of civil servants who draft the laws and regulations which govern our social lives, time and again our politicians draft on paper (with or without speechwriters) the scripts from which they will work as they present the theatre of parliamentary debate. But even if they read the speech from a script held in the hand (and do we feel it unacceptable for the politician to do that, as we would if an actor walked on stage brandishing a script?), it is the oral presentation that is the focus of the occasion. The feature of orality which dominates the construction of the process is the notion of the commonality of experience, that all 350 members present heard and reacted to the same utterance, that they may have reacted separately and differently, but it was necessary that all should participate in/be exposed to the same event. Why? Because it is in the moment of simultaneous perception and judgement that the notion of consensus can best be constructed. If 350 people went into the debate believing in the necessity of capital punishment and 350 people come out opposed, then there was a commonality of experience and perception that must have been active and present for such an outcome to have arisen. That effect had to be derived from the simultaneous acceptance of the arguments presented by the opponents. But what was that effect? Here we must return to the nature of the moment of oral communication. Let us consider for a moment the classroom on a day when the students are listening, the teacher is on form and the omens are good (perhaps becoming rarer and rarer as class sizes increase and teachers are increasingly more stressed). Why teach a class on medieval history or the nature of Hausa prosodic systems when the students could just as easily read about it in a book? First and foremost, the student expects, within the circumscribed space and time of that class, to grasp the essentials of the subject being presented; not only that, the student (unless his or her mind has gone awandering) will, in following the teacher's train of thought, find that thoughts, questions, implications, arise in their own minds that lead them into new areas of experience that are their own. This uncontrollable process (uncontrollable in the sense that the student cannot at will 'pause' the speaker, 'run back the tape' and re-experience the utterance that induced the moment of perception) can be provocative and creative, or can be screened out by the student's well-honed ability to switch off and gaze into space. Either way, the student follows a train of thought and emotion either parallel to or in counterpoint with the articulation of the teacher. As is so often the case, most people switch in and out of what is being said on a regular basis. At the same time, the lecture notes may provide the teacher with a guide as to what issues to cover, but he or she may find that it is in the moment of creative articulation that a new way of putting it, a divergent spontaneous afterthought, creeps up onto familiar territory and displaces the speaker's own expectations. Flummoxed or stimulated, the teacher realizes that there was the same kind of originality in the moment of expression that he or she paid good money for when going to the theatre on the previous night – the words were familiar but the play was the thing with which to 'catch the conscience of the king'.

The anxiety of the moment: Marshal Mathers

A striking representation of the significance of the 'magic moment' of oral communication, the anticipation of such moments, the anxiety of anticipation, the borderline between success and failure in finding the words, and the centrality of co-presence is well summarized by the rapper, Marshall Mathers, 'Eminem', in the words he deploys in the film '8 Mile' about the experience of competitive aggressive speech in the rhythmic performances of rap. The words come from the 'song' *Lose Yourself*:

> Look, if you had one shot, one opportunity
> To seize everything you ever wanted, one moment
> Would you capture it or just let it slip?
>
> [He then describes the experience of being unable to perform a reply to being publicly attacked during a rap competition]
>
> His palms are sweaty, knees weak, arms are heavy
> There's vomit on his sweater already, mom's spaghetti
> He's nervous, but on the surface he looks calm and ready
> To drop bombs, but he keeps on forgettin
> What he wrote down, the whole crowd goes so loud

He opens his mouth, but the words won't come out
He's chokin, how everybody's jokin now
The clock's run out, time's up over, bloah!

The song describes the anger at his failure to speak and expresses a determination to find again the ability to take the plunge, 'he better go capture this moment and hope it don't pass him ... this opportunity comes once in a lifetime yo'. The degree to which his whole persona is wrapped up in that moment that provides the opportunity to speak, whether ex tempore or with a prepared script, is expressed in the line, 'the soul's escaping, through this hole that's gaping, this world's mine for the taking'. In the context of the rap competition that is the subject of the film, Eminem's lyrics focus upon exactly that 'oral communicative moment' when he as a performer is faced with the pressure to perform; in the heat of the moment before a baying audience his 'palms are sweaty ... arms are heavy' and words fail him. In his case it goes beyond the nervousness of the moment to a general commentary on his own life where his oral skills in keeping on rhyming have taken him from poverty to the riches to be had in the commercial success of US popular culture. The sense of urgency and the need to use the power of the rapped word to change his circumstances are elaborated in the latter part of the text where the transformative power of his success with words is contrasted with the bitterness of his view of where he came from.

The film '8 Mile' in which this particular song occurs is built around a competitive ability to extemporize insults addressed to another rapper up on stage in the presence of an audience quick to express its pleasure or displeasure, where each performer is given a minute to articulate a rap to a beat created by an MC in the background. The core events behind the film are summarized in Mathers's chorus line, 'the moment you own it, never let it go, you only got one shot, do not miss your chance to blow', and the moment is that same 'oral communicative moment' which this book is exploring.

The very unexpected, spontaneous and thus sometimes explosive nature of the articulation and simultaneous perception of an idea (such as Eminem describes as 'coming once in a lifetime') brings into question the nature of the aims and purposes that lie behind speech. Intentionality is an assumed correlate of most utterances, an intention to communicate to another person, or to express feelings, thoughts and emotions that are fighting to get out and to be articulated in a form that goes beyond the silence of meditation and into expressed words. But how do we read intention and where is it manifest? Does it require us to assign motives to the author/speaker or can we content ourselves with the manifestation of text?

Intentionality – the speaker or the text?

As scholars working in linguistics have moved closer and closer to an understanding of the universal principles that underlie the human capacity to create language in spite of the enormous variety of individual human languages, so also have other scholars focused on the social purposes to which language is put. When I say, 'Are you comfortable?', I am not only exercising my innate capacity to create a 'yes/no' question from an underlying propositional statement, a capacity manifested by millions of other people in a wide variety of ways in a large number of languages, I am expressing my concern for you and your current circumstance. In uttering these words I demonstrate my solicitousness, and I expect you to acknowledge that I am not abusing you or trying to sell you something, or indeed doing anything other than showing support for you and your position. The fact that my statement in context may have been sarcastic, ironic or inappropriate, does not take away from the fact that such transformations of the intention are based upon a recognition of that original, surface intention. My intention is read by you from the text I uttered. It may well have been supported by the tone of my voice, the look on my face or the gesture I made, but the interpretation stands, at least initially, on the meaning of the text as perceived. But as I see the quizzical look on your face, I sense that the key issue is not whether I intended the utterance at face value as an expression of sympathy, but rather that you are considering the text in the context of other texts that surround it, my previous statement that as far as I was concerned you could go to hell, your previous demand that I should have shown more sympathy when you had been in difficulty. Projected back onto me is your view that the only way to interpret my expression of sympathy is as a piece of unmitigated hypocrisy rather than a genuine change of heart. Outraged, I object to this misrepresentation of my motives. But you parade the evidence of the context, all that had gone before in support of your interpretation. Hapless and unhappy, I have to accept that my innocent and well-intentioned remark is reasonably interpretable in a way which was not my intention. So where is intention manifest? Certainly not solely in me as the speaker – my words themselves manifest the intention that is ascribed by you, the listener, instinctively to me. But freed from my control, my utterance is prey to all the vagaries that flesh is heir to: you may interpret my remarks in many different ways, both because my words may be inherently ambiguous, or because in the context of surrounding texts – texts that constitute the relationship between us – my words can mean the very opposite of what they purport to mean. Intentionality is thus a correlate of the utterance itself, but most particularly is it significant in oral communication, since it is the context of utterance and, with it, the presence of the speaker and the listener which is to the fore. Written communication may equally have intentionality manifest in its text – whether it is to set out the principles of life, liberty and the rule of law, or to incite racial hatred and a move to violence – but the absence of the author and the individuated, staggered stages of articulation and perception sets the intentionality adrift from the social constitution of simultaneous articulation and perception.

Context, then, is a framework for the ascription of intention in the utterance. So far we have considered context as the set of prior utterances that have transpired in the lead up to the articulation of the utterance under consideration, thus creating a set of expectations of one speaker by another. 'I know you're angry', so each of your statements needs to be seen as a manifestation of that anger, or a reaction to it. But equally important is an understanding of the conventions that limit and direct speech in any particular society. A culture is a toolbox offering ways of designing and effecting speech communication from which we pick and choose according to our understanding of what kinds of language must go with which kinds of speech event. Registers and genres of spoken language represent not only the equipment we must use when we seek to accomplish the serious business of living, whether it is while buying groceries at the corner-shop, or appearing before a magistrate on a charge of shop-lifting, they are also the playthings of our own humour and that of every bar room comic from London to Tokyo and back.

The genres of everyday speech live in the half-conscious practices of the switches we make depending upon circumstance. Family banter may not be appropriate for the schoolroom or the job interview; the private joke told in the inimitable way of the stand-up comic may contrast with the public sermon of the Sunday or Friday preacher. But, of course, the boundaries and expectations of genre are there to be played with and explored. The preacher may deliberately exploit the style of the private joke, and the banter of social equals may break through the social distance of the job interview. We recognize both the familiar boundaries we ourselves play with, and which place us in terms of class, gender, status, education and personality; we also occasionally come up against the unfamiliar – and occasionally perplexing – ways of other cultures and other conventions. Speech genres are embedded within all the familiar matrices of accent, dialect, and language, and have their own conventions and expectations among speakers and listeners. Such issues of the genres and ways of speech are the focus of the following chapter.

Memory and the making of the text

The simultaneous moment of articulation and perception discussed above arises often in the process of daily dialogue, a continuous flow of action and reaction that creates its own dynamic in the minds of speaker and listener. But for all of us, the dynamic that produces the narrative we set out for each other is one that derives from more than simple immediate response to the articulations of others. Experience resides in the memories we draw on. When I tell you what happened to me yesterday, it is not simply my response to your expression of irritation, it is the recollection of events and sequences of action as well as pieces of speech that I bring back and set out for you, trying as best I can to order them in some kind of way that allows for chronology, cause and effect, imputed motivation of others, and my own views and feelings. My narrative draws upon the sense perceptions of a previous time, reconstructed and described for the present, filtered, arranged and set out to relay those things which I remember as being important at the time: 'and do you know he even went so far as to say ...', 'I was just about to turn around when out from the other room came ...', 'and in the end I decided that, well, I just couldn't give a damn!' Perhaps I have told this story a hundred times before; perhaps it really is what happened yesterday. Not only do I have available to me in my memory all the little phrases that I use so much and enjoy using again and again, I have a latent string of moments, pictures of actions and speech, that I can recall and relive in my head either as I narrate or remember the events. The string is a necessary sequence, not always the same sequence, but at least a notional necessity that follows the one from the other on the basis of chronology or logic. I may break off for the flashback and the alternative perspective, but, in the main, recollection is re-collection as I weave my story with warp and weft, and with some sense of the overall pattern that I am working to.

Making known – the private to the public

The cynicism of contemporary life and the familiarity we have with the craft of the wordsmiths, the advertisers, the spin doctors, the satirists and the politicians should mean that we are immune from the disease of being taken in, of having our emotions and thoughts manipulated by doctors of spin, be they servants of totalitarian states, emissaries of multinational merchants of death, or so-called representatives of the free world. Surely, nobody will believe that smoking is good for you, that politicians are clean-living role models for all good citizens, that the state will protect and support you. As we have moved from a world in which the spoken word could only be heard by perhaps three or four hundred people at a time (as on the field of Agincourt) – the talking human voice being unable to carry further than perhaps 80 metres – to one in which millions can hear not only the shouted 'Heil Hitler' of the Nuremberg rallies, but the gentle murmur of the secretary-general of the United Nations, so also have we been able to magnify the effects of the power of the spoken word. The spoken word, not in dialogue with you personally, but listened to by you as if it were spoken to you, can be projected far and wide, and, of course, repeated again and again. Many are familiar with the cadences of Martin Luther King's 'I have a dream ...' or the defiance of Winston Churchill's 'We shall fight on the beaches ...'. Available styles range from the high oratory of political declamation to the simulated fireside chat. It is in part the success of the simulation of personal address in a style that is at once distinctive and redolent of the armchair conversation that kept Alastair Cooke riding the radio waves for many decades on the BBC; and the favoured format of so much media discourse is the spontaneous or rehearsed studio conversation in which the listener is invited to eavesdrop and side with one view or the other. But it is in the capacity for orality to mark transitions from the domains of the private to the public that we see its most explosive potential. In northern Nigerian Hausa social life there is a clear distinction between actions which *rufa asiri* 'cover over that which is secret', and those which *tona asiri* 'to dig out and expose that which is secret'. Things scandalous or embarrassing may be well known throughout the community on the gossip network, but they are 'officially' not known, and therefore do not exist. It is when a public articulation takes place, and is acknowledged as the 'outing' of that information, that a recognition of that 'social fact' takes place and produces approbation or condemnation. A clear example of the role of orality in creating that public articulation is to be seen in the circumstances surrounding the political demise of the former British prime minister, Margaret Thatcher. The parliamentary speech in November 1990 of Sir Geoffrey Howe that sealed the fate of Margaret Thatcher was seemingly devoid of oratorical flourishes or rhetorical persiflage – its effectiveness derived from the candid and dismissive simplicity of its depiction of how the prime minister's actions and words had, in his view, destroyed the basis upon which he and she, and others, had acted as a team and spoken 'with one voice'. The shock and power of the speech came from the expression in public of an entirely different and contradictory picture as compared with all previous utterances that had publicly passed his lips. For the audience of MPs and the general public his words conveyed an awareness irrevocable and decisive because it had been uttered publicly. With that 'truth' visible, the surrounding edifice of carefully constructed positions began to fall apart, leading to the end of Mrs Thatcher as prime minister. Persuasion in that case came through 'creating awareness' of an alternative 'truth' and not through the mere artifice of oratorical device.

In examining the nature and significance of the oral communicative moment we are faced with the seeming imponderables of determining the relationships between the words that were spoken, the intention of the speaker, the perceptions of the listeners, and the subsequent actions and/or change of thought and belief amongst those who 'shared' the experience. While we are most familiar with examining the words that were spoken for their available meanings and implications, intention is often derived by inference and effect is often imagined. Yet the relation between intention and effect lies at the heart of the problem and we need to consider ways of examining such relations.

In the remainder of this chapter I set out a way of looking at the observable pattern of stress placed upon certain parts of a speech as marking intention and the separate pattern of audible reaction to the same speech as marking effect. In this case the patterns don't quite match.

Mapping intention and effect in the oral communicative moment: Sir Geoffrey Howe in action

In November 1990 Sir Geoffrey Howe resigned from Mrs Thatcher's British government after some 18 years in Cabinet, or Shadow Cabinet, as one of her most trusted lieutenants, having served as Chancellor of the Exchequer, Foreign Secretary and then Leader of the House. At 4.30 in the afternoon of 13 November he made a statement to a packed House of Commons from the back benches. Reading from a written script on a series of small sheets of paper, he spoke for about twenty minutes. Nothing was *ad lib*, there was no composition in performance, indeed little in the content of the speech would lead one to think that it could not as well have been simply published first in one of the national newspapers, as it was the following day. Yet there had been growing criticism of Mrs Thatcher over some months and years printed and read in national newspapers, some of it also by other departed members of her Cabinet. None of that printed criticism had the devastating effect of Sir Geoffrey Howe's speech. Why? First, let it be said that the speech was made at a time when there was the prospect of a challenge to Mrs Thatcher's leadership of the Conservative Party at the yearly election of the leader. The previous year a challenger, Sir Anthony Meyer, had been soundly defeated. Speculation was rife that there might be a more politically heavyweight challenge this time around. After the speech, Michael Heseltine declared himself a candidate, and quickly a sequence of events developed which ended in the departure of Mrs Thatcher as prime minister. Immediately after the delivery of the speech, verbal comments were made to the BBC correspondent by members of

Photograph 2   Sir Geoffrey Howe (courtesy of Glenn Ratcliffe)

Parliament who had been present in the House of Commons to the effect that the speech was 'devastating', another termed it 'fatal damage' upon the Prime Minister. How and why? Sir Geoffrey Howe was not known for a capacity for such metaphorical murder with only his tongue as a weapon. The Labour politician, Denis Healey, had once famously dismissed his oratorical abilities by saying that, 'Being criticised by Sir Geoffrey was like being savaged by a dead sheep'. Yet in commenting upon televised extracts from Sir Geoffrey's speech, the BBC political correspondent, Nicholas Jones, said the following to camera:

> Yesterday Sir Geoffrey Howe delivered a devastating account of why he resigned from Mrs Thatcher's government. It was one of the most dramatic parliamentary occasions in years. Mrs Thatcher's Cabinet colleague for more than a decade bluntly and unequivocally set out his disagreement with her European policy, and appeared to put his weight behind a leadership challenge ... Sir Geoffrey's customary mildness was cast aside. Some of his comments brought gasps and whistles from MPs ... The former Labour Defence Secretary, Denis Healey, once said, 'being criticised by Sir Geoffrey was like being savaged by a dead sheep'. The strength of his remarks took backbenchers by surprise. A former minister, Jerry Wiggin said, 'no dead sheep about that performance. It was devastating.' Sir Denis Walters said, 'it was an indictment of the PM's conduct of European policy. There must now be a change of leadership.' Sir Anthony Meyer ... said it was a wonderful performance which had done her fatal damage. But Teddy Taylor said it was a vicious speech, 'If Sir Geoffrey's European policies were adopted, British Governments would have few real decisions to take', and Norman Tebbit, the former Conservative Party chairman, said the speech had not made Mrs Thatcher's leadership any easier but it would make no difference to the outcome of an election. And MPs now wait to see whether Michael Heseltine does decide to stand.

Where did the power lie in that *'performance'*? At first sight the speech seems remarkably devoid of firepower. Few fireworks, little imagery, no bombast, little hyperbole, and delivered in a seemingly deadpan way (so familiar from many of his previous speeches) reading from a script. The few hand gestures he does make are cramped, perhaps awkward, and constrained by his need to keep his place in the pages he is holding. Emphasis seems to be provided by a little extra stress on syllables here and there, and a curious forward movement of the head, a glance up and to left or right, or a momentary raising of the shoulders or bob down.

Never the flowing fire and style of a Lloyd George or a Winston Churchill, it seems, the growing crescendos and the lilting verbal music. But the speech has its cadences and its pattern. One of the distinctive characteristics of Sir Geoffrey Howe's delivery is a staccato effect produced by momentary pauses not only at the end of phrases, clauses and sentences – a natural correlation between grammar and speech – but also at regular intervals regardless of the clause and sentence boundaries. Within the sections bounded by these slightest of pauses, the regularity lies in the pattern of stresses placed within the section, rather than any notion of equivalence in section length. A lengthy section with three audible stresses is sometimes taken at speed:

> **on**ly **af**ter the then Chancellor of the Exchequer and my**self** as Foreign Secretary

or may be the shortest of equally stressed syllables:

> **I fear not**

The bulk of the speech is marked into sections by these pauses, marked in Appendix A by slashes, and the number of stresses in each section varies between one and a maximum of six, with the majority consisting of two, three or four stresses. The audible marking of this level of stress is sometimes reinforced by the visual markers of head or body movement or hand gesture. Emphasis is provided by these kinetics of the performance.

In one part of the speech, a pattern of two stresses in each of the three sections of a sentence are reinforced by the emphasis provided by visible head movement, marked by dotted underlining:

> As the **House** will no doubt have ob**served**, / **neither** member of that particular **part**nership / now re**mains** in **off**ice

In the example given above, the pattern is one observed from the actual performance on that afternoon in the House of Commons. It is not necessarily the pattern that is predictable from the written text on the page. Clearly, as soon as a text is upon a page there are two dimensions of the written word that may direct the reader into a rhythm. Words have their lexical stress positions, and any hint of regularity in the positioning of stress across a sequence of language creates the predictability of metre. From the moment you read, 'Nobody heard him, the dead man, but still he lay moaning', you know how to say, 'I was much further out than you thought and not waving but drowning.' Rhythm creates expectation of pattern. In the case of the observed oral performance, the stress patterns sometimes reinforce grammatical parallelism, and sometimes they appear unconnected with other dimensions of language use.

So what do the observed patterns of oral presentation tell us about the effectiveness of this particular speech? Have we learned the secret of the power of the speech? The patterns can only indicate the way in which the presentation was structured, that underneath the seeming lack of oratical flourish lie clear patterns of presentation that work to place emphasis in certain places and to give form to the way in which a sequence of meanings are orally presented. The speech was not presented as a long rambling series of unbroken continuous flows of language. Even the longest of sentences was, in presentation, broken into sections of between one and six stresses, more easily graspable and directing the listener's attention to certain components through the use of short, stressed, sections. But these are the necessary preliminaries to examining the framework of meaning which was conveyed by these features.

The introduction to the speech provided by the BBC correspondent, and the comments quoted from MPs who were present, would suggest that the 'devastating' effect of the speech was to be seen in those parts which related to European policy. Sir Denis Walters was quoted as saying that the speech was a 'an indictment of the Prime Minister's conduct of European policy. There must now be a change of leadership.' One way of assessing the effectiveness of the speech is to examine the pattern provided by the location of Sir Geoffrey Howe's own expressed emphasis. Where does he put most emphasis and does that provide us with clues as to where the 'devastating effect' comes from?

It is clear that there are two 'paragraphs' (each representing the text on a card in Sir Geoffrey Howe's hand) which display a high degree of emphasis through body movement to reinforce the points being made, the first being para. 27 in which Sir Geoffrey places great emphasis upon avoiding a simplified choice, a false antithesis, a bogus dilemma, indicating that there is a middle way between the two alternatives so often presented. The second strongly emphasized paragraph is 33 in which he hammers home his view that the danger is of isolation, not an imposition of will by other member states. But these two paragraphs, containing a high degree of emphasis, even for Sir Geoffrey with his downbeat style, are only the high points in a pattern that runs over the speech as a whole. The pattern can be illustrated by considering the number of emphatic movements in a paragraph and plotting the paragraphs with the highest number of body movements. This is illustrated in Figure 1.1. Figure 1.1 demonstrates an overall pattern of a low start, a middle to late crescendo and a later lower section with a final flourish. The graph presents the pattern of a growing level of animation as first Sir Geoffrey Howe talks of Lord Stockton (paras 22–4) and the first major crescendo, using hand movements for the first time in para. 26, as he leads up to his insistence that 'we' should not talk in terms of 'surrendering' and that there *is* a middle way. The pattern repeats itself between paras 29 and 33 as he cites Churchill's vision and contrasts it with Thatcher's, leading to his insistence that the risk is isolation from Europe not domination by it. A later section (paras 36 to 40) displays a declining level of kinetic emphasis as Sir Geoffrey talks of Mrs Thatcher's attitude and statements, finishing with his telling image of the batsmen with broken bats. The final flourish (para. 45) covers his talk of conflict of loyalty and decision to resign.

In so far as it is possible to examine the pattern of emphasis evident in the performance of Sir Geoffrey on the floor of the House that afternoon, it is possible to say that the focus of *his* attention was indeed upon the conduct of European policy. He emphasized constructive involvement in European affairs and the danger of thinking in terms of 'surrender', of enemies and of talking in terms of 'No! No! No!'; and all of this in the context of the history of Britain's involvement with the ERM and the prospect of Economic and Monetary Union. From this pattern it would appear that Sir Denis Walters was right, the speech was indeed an indictment of the prime minister's conduct of European policy. But was that what made it so devastating? Was it his indictment of policy that did 'fatal damage'? Was that what made his speech 'vicious', to use Teddy Taylor's term? Surely, the points made by Sir Geoffrey Howe on that afternoon about European policy had been made by many other people on numerous occasions both in the House, and *ad nauseam* in the press? Was it simply that the points were being made by one of the people, perhaps *the* person, who had stood side by side with Mrs Thatcher over so many years, and who had so effectively presented a united front with her – a team that had won election after election?

Another approach to examining what made the speech so 'devastating' is to examine, not the patterns in the oral performance by Sir Geoffrey but such responses as we are able to glean from the audience who were present at the time. The television recording cuts between a wide view of the Tory benches, an occasional shot of the Frontbench team, and a main focus upon Sir Geoffrey Howe with five Tory MPs visible around him, Nigel Lawson beside him, four others behind him including Jonathan

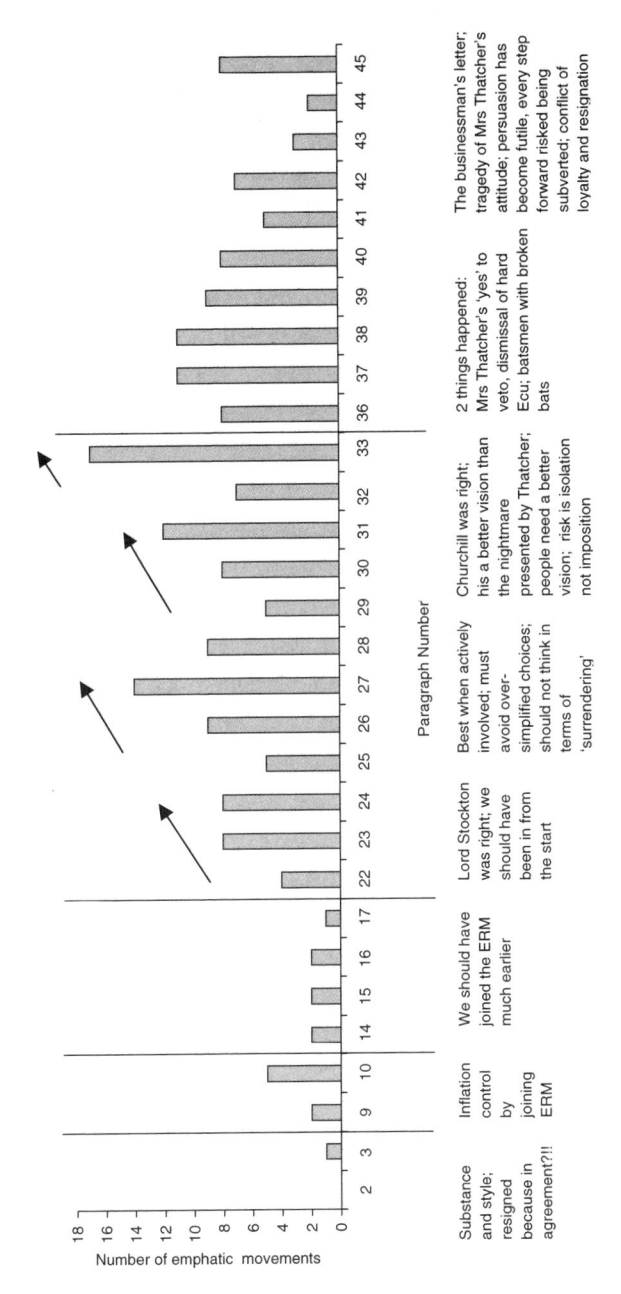

Figure 1.1 Pattern of kinetic emphasis (number of emphatic movements) in the resignation speech by Sir Geoffrey Howe (vertical black lines mark gaps in the video recording; arrows indicate apparent 'crescendos')

Aitken and Norman Fowler. For much of the speech there is rapt attention with little apparent expression on faces that look serious and unamused. Occasionally, Nigel Lawson nods in agreement, and Jonathan Aitken twice shakes his head in clear disagreement. The audible reactions include general laughter throughout the House, laughter from the Opposition and stony silence from the Government benches, and protestations as clearly someone remonstrates while others 'shush' the person who is distracting attention from what is being said. Most interestingly, and reflecting what Nicholas Jones must have been describing as 'gasps' (where the 'whistles' were is not so clear), there are audible expressions of dismay or shock at particular points, clearly immediate reactions from Tory colleagues taken aback by what had just been said. If the recorded performance is anything to go by, and the comments of the members of the audience subsequently, then it must surely have been these moments which most particularly made the speech 'devastating', 'fatal damage', and 'vicious'. In Appendix A, the use of square brackets and capitals marks the audible or visible reactions of the audience. Do those moments correspond with the high points of Sir Geoffrey's indictment of European policy or do they mark something else?

The first response of the audience is to the rather good joke made at the outset. As all good tellers of jokes contrive to do, Sir Geoffrey had softened up his audience by a gracious appeal to the 'generosity and tolerance' of the House as he says, 'I hope I may count on that today.' Thus the laughter is generous and tolerant on all sides as he makes his first joke at the expense of those in his own party who have sought to minimize the significance of his resignation (Nicholas Jones in his commentary ascribes the position to the prime minister). The portentous sounding 'I must be the first minister in history' is followed by the paradoxical 'to have resigned because he was in full agreement with Government policy'. The tolerance in the laughter of the Tory benches is of the sting in the exposure of the apparent nonsense of what 'former colleagues' have been saying. Of course, there was substance to his decision to resign. And the joke sets up the expectation that the substance is about to be revealed.

The expectation that there will be exposure of division is followed, however, in paras 4 to 8, by a summary of the length and strength of the unity that has been displayed in the past between Sir Geoffrey and the prime minister – their achievements and their record together. But the expectation of exposure of division is kept going by his statement that it had to be a matter of some substance that could rupture such a relationship. Furthermore, while praising the prime minister's role, he asserts his own claim to 'dry' credentials, and finishes on the pointed statement, relating to European policy, that they together managed Britain's signature of the Single European Act. In the ensuing parts of his speech until the end of para. 27, the responses consist for the most part of occasional murmurings of 'Hear! Hear!', occasional nods visible by Nigel Lawson and others, and even slight smiles from the prime minister and John Major when the Opposition hoot with laughter at Sir Geoffrey's comment that John Major had had to devote 'a deal of his considerable talent to demonstrating exactly how those Madrid conditions have been attained', a moment of laughter which Sir Geoffrey seems by his reaction not to have expected. This part of the speech is not uncontentious, but it represents a recognized pro-European assessment of the gains and losses of the timing and nature of Britain's involvement with the European Community over previous decades. The nods and comments come from other Tories who hold a similar position, and they particularly approve (audibly and visibly) when a figure of authority from the past, Harold Macmillan, is drafted in in support (paras 23–4). Anti-European Tories remain silent in the familiar routine of iterating and supporting the views of first one side and then the other. So far so usual.

It is in para. 30 that we encounter the first audible expression of shock or dismay from the Tory benches. In the remainder of the speech similar expressions are sometimes accompanied by derisive laughter from the Opposition, with no accompanying laughter apparent from the Government side. The sentences that produce such reactions are the following:

30. I find Winston Churchill's perception a good deal more convincing and encouraging for the interests of our nation than the nightmare image sometimes conjured up by my right honourable Friend, who seems ...

40. How on earth are the Chancellor and the Governor of the Bank of England, commending the hard Ecu as they strive to do, to be taken as serious participants in the debate against than kind of background noise? Mr Speaker ...

   It is rather like sending your opening batsmen to the crease only for them to find, the moment the first balls are bowled, that their bats have been broken before the game, by the team captain.

42. The tragedy is, and it is for me personally, for my party, and for our whole people, and for my right honourable friend herself, a very real tragedy, that the Prime Minister's perceived attitude towards Europe is running increasingly serious risks for the future of our nation.

44. But I realise now that the task has become futile, of trying to stretch the meaning of words beyond what was credible, of trying to pretend there was a common policy, when every step forward risked being subverted by some casual comment or impulsive answer.

In the above instances there are key phrases which induced the expressions of shock, expressions which followed immediately as they were uttered:

Nightmare image
Background noise
By the team captain
Casual comment or impulsive answer

In paragraph 42 the response consists not of an expression of shock but a shout of 'No!' by a Tory MP and the visible shaking of the head in disagreement by Jonathan Aitken. It is this sentence in paragraph 42 which perhaps best summarizes what Sir Geoffrey Howe was saying about the prime minister's conduct of European policy in his speech as a whole. The sentence is replete with resonances as it focuses upon the effect of words spoken by Mrs Thatcher in giving expression to an attitude which he has been at pains to describe through his speech. Those spoken words risk, as he puts it, tragedy. His personal 'tragedy' was real, as evidenced by his presence on the back benches; that of his party was to come in the fractious decline over the European issue, and, as some in the party would see it, in the very fact of this speech itself; the tragedy for 'our whole people' would be a potential decline in relation to other European countries; and the tragedy for the prime minister would be played out in her departure from power, induced in no small part by the effect of this speech itself.

But what of the significance of the other four sentences (and key phrases within them) in terms of the 'devastating effect' of the speech? These are the moments when, as Jerry Wiggin put it, there was 'no dead sheep about that performance'; these are the apparent 'crunch points' in 'a wonderful performance which had done her fatal damage', according to Sir Anthony Meyer.

A strong sub-theme which threads its way through the speech is about how you should operate when you are a member of a team. The groundwork is laid in the early part of the speech by the invocation of the record of joint achievement (paras 4–8). Acknowledging the role of the leader, Sir Geoffrey's first paragraphs outline 'our' achievements under 'her leadership'; for all present during that speech the remarkable record of 'teamwork' in which he and she had participated was well known. Time and again, members of the Cabinet had produced and reiterated the same line on any issue of significance. Rarely had it been possible to discern daylight between the public statements of the prime minister and her loyal chancellor, then foreign secretary, Sir Geoffrey Howe. Political correspondents had for years scoured public statements for any signs of a difference of nuance, or speculated upon differences of view behind the closed doors of the Cabinet room that would, however, not be reflected in what was understood to be the joint Cabinet public position. That was the norm. Rumours of dissent within the privacy of the Cabinet had for some time been rife, but the public ship still held together. The key term for Sir Geoffrey in representing the operation of a team is 'loyalty'. Loyalty is built upon an agreement about the rules of the game. He says, 'Cabinet government is all about trying to persuade one another from within. That was my commitment to government by persuasion, persuading colleagues and the nation.' The outcome of persuasion 'within' had been, and should be, agreement on a position for dissemination 'beyond'; loyalty was inextricably bound up with a commitment to arrive at, and to publicly present, agreed positions. This fundamental position was the basis of Sir Geoffrey's commitment to politics and to Mrs Thatcher's government in particular. His was not a position that the leader was always right, nor that the leader can change position without reference to his or her 'team'. The process of teamwork involved other members of the team supporting the leader in articulating an agreed view, and equally the leader supporting others in their articulation of an agreed position. That reciprocal obligation underlay all action, even if it required some elasticity in language to maintain the position. The central and crucial issue was the perception of the meaning of words, and in particular the power of the spoken word in its ability to destroy the coherence and credibility of other agreed words:

> I realise now that the task has become futile, of trying to stretch the meaning of words beyond what was credible, of trying to pretend there was a common policy, when every step forward risked being subverted by some casual comment or impulsive answer.

The intake of breath among Tory MPs at the idea that comments by the leader, Mrs Thatcher, could be termed 'casual' or 'impulsive' is audible.

It is the implication that her words were not weighty and significant, but frivolous and damaging that creates the shock of insult, as does 'nightmare image' and 'background noise'. The idea that the words of the prime minister could be called 'background noise' by someone of Sir Geoffrey's background and history was indeed shocking. Yet it reflected again his view of the role of others when a team member articulates an agreed position. Noises off stage are distracting and potentially dangerous to the operation of the team. The dismissive tone of 'background noise' is the culmination of a sequence (paras 38–9) of statements that the comments of Mrs Thatcher were 'disturbing', 'remarkable (in a negative sense)', 'tragic' and 'extraordinary'.

For the politician who rarely provided a graphic 'soundbite', let alone anything as cutting as Denis Healey's comment, the culmination of his sub-theme on the rules of the game and the loyalties that depend upon them lies in the memorable and devastating cricket metaphor. The metaphor is not about European policy, or any other public policy issue for that matter, it is about the values and conventions of teamwork as he perceives them. At the devastating heart of his speech lies his statement that he can no longer play the game. There were rules which he followed requiring unity from all members of the team on agreed positions. He loyally participated on the basis of those rules. The team captain betrayed those rules. The betrayal of the rules of the game can only be resolved by departure from the game, despite a sense of loyalty to the team captain. The source of the 'devastating effect' is the exposure in public of a naked truth, a truth about the moral basis of a relationship reinforced by the dismissive overtones of 'nightmare image', 'background noise', 'casual comment' and 'impulsive answer' – a relationship that previously had been repeatedly tested in the fire of political action. It was not a statement about European policy but a view of betrayal and loyalty, reciprocity and rules that lay at the heart of the devastation.

The evidence of the response of those who were present on that afternoon suggests that the effectiveness of the speech derived from the articulation of two parallel themes. The one was the conduct of European policy, a theme on which Sir Geoffrey himself placed most emphasis, the primary 'intentionality' of the speech, and which constituted the bulk of the speech. The other concerned the values and conventions which Sir Geoffrey articulated as underlying his participation in government, and which he presented as underlying teamwork generally, with the implication that the success of government, and of Mrs Thatcher's government in particular, was built upon adherence to those values and conventions. It was the statement of betrayal of those conventions by Mrs Thatcher herself, and in particular the significance of oral interventions by her which he characterized dismissively as 'casual comment and impulsive answer', which drew the most telling 'gasps and whistles' from the audience. It was the effect of the articulation of this second theme which was 'devastating', 'vicious' and 'fatal', if the audience reaction was anything to go by, and constituted something of a metacommentary upon the power of the spoken – or perhaps misspoken – word.

In examining a speech given by Sir Geoffrey Howe before a packed House of Commons at 4.30 in the afternoon of 13 November 1990, it is possible to set out in detail those elements of the oral performance – its patterns of sound, the body movements that accompanied it, and the reactions of those who were present – that allow the establishment of the pattern of intended emphasis on the part of Sir Geoffrey Howe, and, simultaneously, the pattern of greatest effect upon the audience. Sir Geoffrey Howe emphasized European policy, the audience reacted to what *he* had to say about the moral framework of the interpersonal relations within Mrs Thatcher's government. The power of Sir Geoffrey Howe's spoken words lay in the fact that it was *he*, of all people, who was speaking publicly, presenting a typification of Mrs Thatcher's behaviour (and her use of spoken words) that was radically different from anything he had ever *publicly* stated before. It was radical because it was clothed in an evaluative frame that was inescapably condemnatory and inescapably 'true'. As a verbal enactment of resignation it was simultaneously a declaration that Mrs Thatcher was finished as prime minister – close to being a declaration that became a fact by being enunciated. The group moment of cognition in that packed House was like the pebble tossed into a moving sub-zero sea. It is said that a strange phenomenon can occur when the sea remains liquid but has dropped below freezing point. A thrown pebble can start a crystallization on hitting the water such that ice quickly forms and spreads out rapidly from that spot. That afternoon Sir Geoffrey Howe threw in his pebble to devastating effect.

Of course, there were many, many other economic and political pressures and causes that led to the downfall of the Thatcher government. Nonetheless, the power of the oral performance remains a cardinal symbolic element in the political dynamic of rise and downfall. Reflection, judgement and assessment are all contemplative post hoc processes that hang upon the moment of articulation and of emotional reaction: the process of oral communication.

Concluding remarks

This chapter has presented a number of issues surrounding the 'oral communicative moment'. The co-presence of speaker(s) and listeners and the simultaneity of expression and perception in a form which is inescapably transient, and which surrounds us all for most of our waking lives, are features of orality that impact profoundly upon society. The dynamics of simultaneous articulation and perception affect many dimensions of social, political and economic behaviour. Co-presence is often simulated in the delayable communication of writing and recording and the experiential moment is one of potential angst and of success and failure. That same experiential moment is the site of match and mismatch between intention and effect and is the vehicle for the transition of knowledge from the private to the public – in itself a political process of sometimes apocalyptic import.

2
Cultural Parameters of Speech: Genre, Form, Aesthetics

Attitudes to culture and to language

In the newsroom of the Hausa language service of the BBC World Service, a service that has been broadcasting for over fifty years, there has long been a replaying of old debates that reflect an underlying tension between two broadly opposed attitudes to language and to culture. There are those whose first reaction, faced with the difficulties of translating a new concept into Hausa, is to search within the resources of the Hausa language for an image, a parallel, an association, that can be drafted in to serve as the new term for 'genetic modification' or 'quasar' or any of the other terms and associated ideas that pass through newsrooms all over the world. Combined with an explanation, the familiar Hausa word is given a new extension, a new set of connotations, to become the new standard term through repetition and the ripple effect of being taken up and used by others in similarly influential positions, in the Hausa language media in Nigeria and abroad – so *dan sama jannati*, 'the name for a particular type of religious zealot who wears a gown the sleeves of which were believed to act as wings that will transport the person to heaven on the Day of Judgement', is pressed into service to become the commonly used and standard term for 'astronaut'. These processes go on all the time, all over the world in many different languages. The attitudinal difference lies in the approach to how to proceed faced with the problem of the new concept and the necessity of cultural translation. The response of some is to insist upon the notion of the internal integrity of the language, a notion that is intimately bound up with a sense of purity, essence and correspondingly a danger of pollution, corruption and damage occasioned by the threat of outside forces. To use the English term, or the French term, or indeed a term perceived to be borrowed from any other language is to put the Hausa language and a notion of cultural identity bound to it, at serious risk. This notion of ill-intentioned outsiders attempting to subvert, through their attempted control of the terms of verbal trade, a core, a centre, a purity is deeply held and deeply conservative. It is linked to the need to classify cultural artefacts into categories based on us and them, our culture and its manifestations, be they anything from literature to housebuilding, and to demand allegiances through expression of knowledge of such forms. It is also a view which constructs culture in terms of a core, a centre of knowledge manifest in certain forms of cultural production. There are experts who know 'deep Hausa', areas of esoteric knowledge that require either birth within a certain community or years of cultural training to acquire. Values are seen to inhere in that cultural core. A set of such values overlap, in the case of Hausa, with perceived Islamic values that go well beyond the Hausa cultural world and are shared with many others. None of this is particular to the Hausa language or to Islam or to Nigeria. The Académie Française and the French state has perceived a danger in very similar terms in the spread of the English language around the world. Not only has the use of English in certain public contexts been legislated against, a plank of French foreign policy remains the protection and the expansion of *la francophonie* in the face of the danger of English. The representation of other cultures in terms of threat is one which is taken issue with in the speech by Sir Geoffrey Howe that was instrumental in the fall of the British prime minister, Margaret Thatcher, as we saw in the previous chapter.

There is another set of attitudes which starts from a different set of premises and leads to a different view of cultures and languages. In the newsroom debate there are those whose primary concern (shared with the other camp) remains to provide the necessary explanation of, for example, 'genetic modification', equally to fix upon a term, use it consistently, and try to ensure that the agreed term is maintained as the 'standard' term which will eventually find its way into the dictionary. But for them, the issue of whether the terms chosen are seen to be 'authentic' Hausa, or are borrowed from elsewhere, is not material. For them, the question is to know what is plausible, memorable, simple, and, most importantly, current. It may well be that a term is already in use, on the street corner, in the market, in the school playground. It is that term which it is appropriate to use. If the kids on the street look up into the sky and say that there is a *helikwafta* passing overhead, then that should be the term, not 'plane that lands like a vulture' – however picturesque or 'genuine' a purist would consider such a coinage for 'helicopter'. This attitude sees language as the currency of exchange, not the repository of core value. A libertarian cosmopolitanism underlies such an approach. A common assault upon this position is to label it as eclectic, without absolute standards, a relativist quagmire of decentredness. Yet, the essential difference between these two sets of attitudes lies not in the presence or absence of values and standards, but in the perception of cultural and language issues in terms of threat and defence, exclusivity and purity on the one hand, and a supposition of commonalities and shared values on the other.

Underlying the issues raised in the previous section is the fundamental question of the ways in which attitudes to self and others are worked out in practice. In the face of the hegemonic pressure of cultural production which is seen as originating elsewhere, even if it is manifest in cultural practices which are manifestly local, there can be a perception of threat – threat to self requiring the conscious establishment (usually articulated as rediscovery or revaluation) of an alternative, constructed as local and often 'traditional'. The reconstruction of the local is undertaken in contradistinction to, and in terms which are understandable to, the hegemonic presence in order to assert difference which can be acknowledged (to assert in language which is incomprehensible or invisible to the hegemonic centre is simply to create background noise). The empire has to write back in words that the emperor can understand. The assertion of difference or equality (the two alternative strategic positions to take to avoid inferiority) requires an agreement concerning cultural liberty. As the argument in immediately post-apartheid South Africa reflected an opposition between those who insisted on continued allegiance of cultural production to the 'cause' in contrast to those who saw the whole point of the struggle as having been to create liberty in a more absolute sense, so the attainment of broader, inclusive, federated political structures can release the potential for greater self-assertion as part of the process of finding a place in the greater whole. So, in the EU, regional political and cultural self-assertion goes hand in glove with the strengthening of a supra-statist framework. But, of course, one man's meat is another man's poison. The assertion of one cultural framework in one context as liberation is taken as a potential threat in another. Your ascendancy may be my downfall, and my culture may be under threat from the 'rise' of yours. At the same time, language and culture in so many parts of the world constitute a coat of many colours. Not only do the people in my street see themselves opposed to the next street in one context yet are united in opposition to another area of town in another context, such that, like the layers of the onion, we participate in a series of more inclusive identities depending upon context, but also we may change colour like the chameleon. As we shift from Paris and French to London and English we manifest in our language and our style not more inclusive identities but shifts and changes that are across boundaries of exclusivity rather than through greater levels of inclusivity. This is even more true for the daily lives of so many people in a country like Nigeria, where people shift gear between two, three and sometimes four languages and their cultural styles on a daily basis. It is this heterogeneity manifest in the individual and in the eclectic creativity of modern culture, whether it be in downtown Lagos or in the backstreets of Camden Town, that is one of the most striking forms of the liberty of identity available to more and more people. It is conscious choice, rather than the manifestation of that which is 'natural', that more and more marks that which is exclusive, jingoistic, or 'national'. It is the conscious choice of cleaving to the singular in the light of the confusing manifestations of the plural that dominates the manifestations of fundamentalism and traditionalism.

The dichotomies in attitude alluded to above inform reactions to many of the issues addressed in this chapter – maintenance of 'inherited traditions' versus eclectic mixing in the use of genres and ways of speaking, and an aesthetic of speaking that ranges from the restrictive and purist to the all-embracing celebration of diversity.

Genres

A central purpose behind the study of particular oral literatures is to present and understand the varied voices within such societies – voices of individuals and groups, professional wordsmiths making public statements, private musings by the young, by the old, by women, by men, and so the particular social and political contexts within which the speech act occurs must constitute the object of discussion along with the text. Performance aspects, from this point of view, are not only the kinetics and non-verbal processes surrounding the utterance, but the expectations and reactions of the audience and of the performer. Those expectations operate both at the level of the individual – performer, text, message and performance – and at the level of the speech genre. Each genre has its own intellectual history and history of its material conditions. It is the audience's familiarity, or lack of familiarity, with those which conditions and surrounds their response. If you know the praise genre, you know roughly what to expect from a performer as he or she starts to praise, in terms of style, of content, and of evaluatory frame.

The implications for the effectiveness of the utterance can vary depending upon the aesthetic criteria current within your culture and the degree to which you hold to those criteria. Your culture may place an aesthetic premium upon conformity with certain conventions – a sequencing of content, a language style, a declamatory tone – or it may decry conventionality and demand originality and innovation. Usually the tension between two contradictory sets of premises – 'adhere to the tradition' and 'be original' – underlies the dynamic of how a performer and an audience interact. The contradiction is inherent for all performers and audiences since a text can only be perceived as original or different against the backdrop of the genre to which it is believed to adhere. Nevertheless, the concept of an established genre out of which forays are made that slowly change the boundaries and perceptions of the genre is not necessarily the most appropriate model for the understanding of current cultural processes. African popular culture is replete with the explosive admixtures of expressive forms that create hybrid genres diverging and multiplying and losing any sense that they are simply variations upon a single original genre or source. This fluidity is perhaps one product of the evanescence and experiential nature of the oral performance. Oral literature exists only in the here and now. It is the moment that matters – who was there, what they saw and felt, and what they remember. Karin Barber, in a discussion of African popular culture, picks up Fabian's (1990) suggestion that the moment of performance is the moment when 'certain kinds of knowledge are generated',

> These texts and genres seem to be sites of emergent consciousness. The dance halls, shebeens, churches, community halls and taxis where they are produced and received are the meeting places of new kinds of crowd, engaged in the work of producing new kinds of self and collectivity ... Cultural expressions – whether paintings, songs, novels, plays, anecdotes, cartoons or slogans printed on cloth – are not seen by these authors as 'reflections' of an already-constituted 'world view'. Rather, they are part of the work of cultural production, a cultural production which produces consciousness. (Barber 1997: 6)

In the context of the 'work of cultural production' the discrete antithetical positions of the performer and the listener, necessary for the analysis of the speech event, begin, in the repeated event, to become a continuum on which the performer as initiator, as perceiver, as critic, as rememberer, merges with the role of others who can and do take up and manifest those same roles.

Genre and ways of speaking: the expectations of speaker and listener

The speaker's speech will is manifested primarily in the *choice of a particular speech genre*. This choice is determined by the specific nature of the given sphere of speech communication, semantic (thematic) considerations, the concrete situation of the speech communication, the personal composition of its participants, and so on. And when the speaker's speech plan with all its individuality and subjectivity is applied and adapted to a chosen genre, it is shaped and developed within a certain generic form. Such genres exist above all in the great and multifarious sphere of everyday oral communication, including the most familiar and the most intimate. (Bakhtin 1986: 78; my emphasis)

Let me illustrate the issues of speech genre and speech choice with a fictional anecdote: my computer has stopped working and my intention is to complain. In preparation and in advance of the action itself, an act which will involve me in both a verbal and a physical enactment, I contemplate my aim. I am angry, I need to express that anger and thereby attempt to remove it from me. I wish to explain my objection and have that explanation acknowledged as understood, I want certain responses – explanations, apologies, and the enactment of remorse. I remain in repose as I contemplate my options. In my head I run through the various scenarios in order to plan my alternative pathways through the forthcoming actions. If my interlocutor refuses to acknowledge the truth-value of my statements then I will need to repeat and rephrase with a higher degree of intensity; if he presents an alternative view of 'the reality' then I must be able to counter any such alternatives, and maybe I should think them through beforehand; if he acknowledges my view as being right, but refuses to show remorse, I must demand some form of statement of apology – what forms might they take and which would be acceptable?; if he and I do eventually reach an understanding we will need to find a way to acknowledge that the matter is now settled and a different mode of communication is now appropriate between us.

As I think my way through the maze of alternatives I am aware that the presentation of myself that I am about to undertake sits at an intersection between that which I feel to be my words, my personality, and my way of doing things, and a whole world of familiar techniques, modes and manners which I have seen and enacted in the past and which I expect my interlocutor also to be familiar with. I know that I want my interlocutor to recognize and acknowledge my position with the minimum of fuss and quickly too. Knowing that he is familiar with certain recognizable ways of talking, I can choose to employ or to avoid them according to whether I think they will help or hinder my purpose, both in order to express my anger and to arrive at the conclusion I desire. I will make my strategic choices but I know that when it comes to the moment itself, being an oral confrontation it will only be in the event itself that the outcome can be determined, perhaps I will be vanquished, humiliated, and even more angry. In assessing therefore my approach to the event I need to assess the balance between my need to express anger with a need to arrive at a satisfactory outcome; will my expression of anger induce remorse, or will it simply produce a rebuff that makes more unlikely the prospect of a settlement? But is my need to express anger so overwhelming that the rest does not matter?

My first step must be to assess what my alternative ways of speaking are. In this I have to assess not only those ways in which I know I can speak, I have to start with the ways of speaking that are familiar in relation to the social roles that my interlocutor and I will be in at the time of the exchange. We will not be friends meeting after work, or strangers on a train, he will be the salesman who sells computers and is therefore responsible for the quality and reliability of the product, and I will be the customer who has paid good money for a reliable and high-quality computer. I am not a schoolchild faced with a teacher, a parent talking to a teenage child, a CEO addressing his workforce, a teamworker with another member of the team, I am a buyer and he is the seller. There are standard expectations relating to the way in which we will deal with each other. I will ask for information, guidance, reach a decision; he will provide information, encourage me to buy his product, acknowledge that I have the freedom to decide one way or the other, and that 'the customer is always right'. These are expectations of the content of an initial purchase-oriented exchange. The way of speaking that is appropriate to the content of the exchange is one that is typified by the introductory remarks, 'Can I be of assistance? Please don't hesitate to ask if I can help you with any information on the capabilities of these machines, etc.' And those words are accompanied by all the body language of the polite and helpful salesman. My response is to assess the individual for their degree of fit with the type of person I wish to do business with, a type which is familiar from the myriad other occasions when I have looked to buy one thing or another. Yes, the words fit and I make an immediate assessment, 'Sounds like a reasonable salesman', or 'What a nice man!', or 'Don't think much of him!' But now the roles are the same, but the exchange is going to be different. I have not come to buy, I have come back to complain. As I stand ready to do battle, I am faced with a variety of ways of speaking that will pigeonhole me within certain 'type' categories in the mind of the salesman. The way I present myself physically and the way I speak will evoke classification: the 'bloody customer' whose unreasonable anger requires a decision between two responses, either to throw them out of the shop, or grovel and apologize and give them their money back (or somewhere in between); the polite and reasonable complainant whose just case can be fairly dealt with; the incompetent moaner who ought to be able to sort out the problem for themselves; the crook who is falsely claiming a problem with the machine in order to try and obtain a more up-to-date replacement. The assessment of 'type' of person will begin to happen on the basis of the way of speaking that I adopt. What is it that will go into marking the particular way of speaking that I adopt? Clearly, my tone of voice will be one of the first signals, and that will be matched with the content of what I say, and expectations will look for certain familiar correlations: a measured tone should accompany a proposition of sweet reasonableness, a tentative softness with a moderate request, a raised voice with angry retort; but, of course, sometimes it is the contravention of the familiar which is a means to surprise effect: to whisper sweetly 'This is a disgrace!' would be a violation of the normal expectation, and perhaps produce a change of heart (although unlikely), or at least a disconcerted moment! While there may be no fixed script that accompanies the familiar way of speaking, a world of cliché is available to mark the familiarity of the form: 'This is a disgrace!', 'I've never been so insulted in all my life', 'I shall be speaking to the manager!', 'I want my money back!', 'This is not fit for the purpose!', 'How dare you!', etc. This armoury of available and familiar phrases is part of what I bring to the strategic decision about how to speak, and simultaneously it is part of the panorama of marking mechanisms known to my interlocutor. We are both familiar with these well-trodden paths of oral communication. It is the very recognizability and the relative stability of such ways of speaking which constitutes them as types, as genres of speech:

> Language is realized in the form of individual concrete utterances (oral and written) by participants in the various areas of human activity. These utterances reflect the specific conditions and goals of each such area not only through their content (thematic) and linguistic style, that is, the selection of the lexical, phraseological, and grammatical resources of the language, but above all through their

compositional structure. All three of these aspects – thematic content, style, and compositional structure – are inseparably linked to the *whole* of the utterance and are equally determined by the specific nature of the particular sphere of communication. Each separate utterance is individual, of course, but each sphere in which language is used develops its own *relatively stable types* of these utterances. These we may call *speech genres*. (Bakhtin 1986: 60; my emphasis)

And so I march into the shop and up to the counter. 'I wish to complain. It is an absolute disgrace. This man here sold me a computer which he said would be able to handle all the things I said I wanted to do. Not only did he sell me inappropriate software, he sold me a machine that was incapable of doing half of what I needed, and the machine doesn't work anyway! I want my money back and an apology for all the time I have wasted and the trouble I have been caused! It's an absolute disgrace and I want to see the manager!' Holding my breath, feeling the anger burst forth, and hoping for complete capitulation, I wait as the manager approaches. I know that for everybody present, both sales personnel and other customers, I have hit most of the appropriate notes for the 'irate customer', using a speech genre that is well-recognized, through the tone of voice, the vocabulary and sequencing that is familiar. It is a speech genre appropriate to my purposes in the context of seller–buyer, and applicable to the computer purchase I have made, but it is not confined to either of those contexts, the one more encompassing than the other. I could have used the same speech genre with the newsagent, or the airline clerk, but also in contexts broader than that of buyer to seller: an adapted version of the same genre would perhaps help me to deal with a noisy neighbour, or an indolent employee.

As I rub my backside from the pain of hitting the edge of the pavement, I ruminate on whether I would have been better to have adopted a different approach. Perhaps by adopting the 'irate customer' route I gave the manager only two options – to completely capitulate before assembled customers and staff, or to throw me out on my ear. His adoption of the latter route accompanied by simple comment 'speak to my solicitor' in response was regrettable but perhaps inevitable. The assuaging of my anger had been only temporary and I had not attained my objective of having my computer replaced. Perhaps I should have avoided adopting such a marked genre, the less marked conversational mode might have been a better way in. But not so good at assuaging anger perhaps. I could not have brought myself to adopt an entirely duplicitous 'Hail fellow, well met!' genre of bonhomie, in view of what

I needed to get across, surely. There must be some congruence between speech genre and content, surely, to avoid the entirely justified charge of hypocrisy. A speech genre has its familiar correlates in terms of intention and context of relationships between the parties involved, these have to be taken into account.

It was only in the event, my action in the shop, that the intentionality of my communication came up against the countervailing will of another, a person whose perception of my actions provoked a counter-action. On the one hand my ultimate aim was to obtain a working computer, but I intended to get there by making a choice between a variety of speech genres whose effect would be to reach that ultimate goal. My deliberate choice of speech genre allowed me to fulfill my aim of venting my anger and getting across my view of what should happen next. It was only the ultimate instrumentality that was thwarted. I had succeeded and failed. Perhaps I would have been more ultimately successful if the manager had allowed me to finish. It seemed as if he had made up his mind after my first few sentences, and started advancing on me before he had heard me out. Clearly, he had picked up my tone of voice, my first few remarks and recognized the genre immediately. Rather than wait for the full content, he had determined his course of action on the basis of the very first words. Clearly, the choice of genre must have been the problem. Perhaps I should go back in and pick a different speech genre. On the other hand, perhaps I should not go straight back in. Should I change my accent, pick a different register, adopt a different tone? Rather than rely upon a recognizable form, perhaps I should try to be creative and surprise him. Be jocular, be threatening, be distant ... How far off expectations should I go? At what point would I get myself arrested under the Mental Health Act? Perhaps I am barking up the wrong tree. It is perhaps better to avoid surprises and genres that are marked or unusual. How can I make seamless the boundary between the content of my utterances and the form in which I express it, so that it seems the most natural thing in the world that I should say those things in that particular way? What is the standard way to get across the message I need to convey? But there are so many different ways in which I can reformulate the utterance:

> The generic forms in which we cast our speech, of course, differ essentially from language forms. The latter are stable and compulsory (normative) for the speaker, while generic forms are much more flexible, plastic and free. Speech genres are very diverse in this respect. A large number of genres that are widespread in everyday life are so standard that the speaker's individual speech will is manifested only in its

choice of a particular genre, and, perhaps, in its expressive intonation. Such, for example, are the various everyday genres of greetings, farewells, congratulations, all kinds of wishes, information about health, business and so forth. These genres are so diverse because they differ depending upon the situation, social position, and personal interrelations of the participants in the communication. These genres have high, strictly official, respectful forms as well as familiar ones. And there are forms with varying degrees of familiarity, as well as intimate forms ... These genres also require a certain tone; their structure includes a certain expressive intonation. These genres, particularly the high and official ones, are compulsory and extremely stable. The speech will is usually limited here to a choice of a particular genre. And only slight nuances of expressive intonation (one can take a drier or more respectful tone, a colder or a warmer one; one can introduce the intonation of joy, and so forth) can express the speaker's individuality (his emotional speech intent). ...

In addition to these standard genres, of course, freer and more creative genres of oral speech communication have existed and still exist: genres of salon conversations about everyday, social, aesthetic, and other subjects, genres of table conversation, intimate conversations among friends, intimate conversations within the family, and so on. (No list of oral speech genres yet exists, or even a principle on which such a list might be based.) The majority of these genres are subject to free creative reformulation (like artistic genres and some, perhaps, to a greater degree). But to use a genre freely and creatively is not the same as to create a genre from the beginning; genres must be fully mastered in order to be manipulated freely. (Bakhtin 1986: 79–80)

The creativity available to me in making my next intervention belies my calculations as to possible or probable effects. If I do it this way, will it work out the way I want? If that, then what are my chances of getting across my view sufficiently strongly? The key issue is to work out what his expectations are of the genres that I might employ. He knows I want to complain, what is the appropriate way to do that from his point of view? There must be an appropriate way, surely. I try this, I try that, in my mind. Eventually, I pluck up the courage to go back in. Having failed to decide upon a way of speaking that will be appropriate in this now more complicated situation in which I have already been thrown out once, my only recourse, as the manager bears down on me, is to ask, 'So what should I do?' After a moment's hesitation the reply comes, 'If you wish to complain then there's a way to do it! Follow me.' Now I realize that control of the means of communication was at the heart of matter from the beginning – not only was there an appropriate way of speaking, there was a formalized procedure of actions to be gone through, a routinization of the emotion and the exchanges that needed to take place. And in ceding control over the process I finally stood a chance of reaching my ultimate goal.

This anecdotal example has focused upon the choices and creative potential that lie in the styles of speech and ways of speaking that are available to us. While each culture will have its own ways of appropriately doing the same thing, such as complain, effectiveness in achieving the purpose (or failing lamentably) will depend upon the degree of skill and understanding displayed by the (in)competent speaker. Having approached the issue from the point of view of the individual, this discussion now goes on to consider other aspects of the 'toolbox' of language that is available as a shared resource among groups of people.

Genre as appropriateness conditions upon the delivery of particular kinds of communication was closely enmeshed with the issue of power over the process of communication. In ceding control, in the anecdote above, I had acknowledged a willingness to fulfill those conditions of speaking and acting that were deemed appropriate by the other party to the situation, and that released the block to progress towards an ultimate goal.

Struggle for power over the process of communication is carried on between factions, groups vying for dominance or pre-eminence within societies large and small, but is also manifest in the patterns of translation, and intercultural communication more broadly. For the purposes of this discussion one area of particular interest is the struggle that takes place to control the 'terms of trade' between oral communication and the written word.

Disputing the terms of verbal trade: the case of the northern Transvaal between the 1920s and 1950s

Isabel Hofmeyr has described the way in which, in the northern Transvaal between the 1920s and 1950s, officials of the Native Affairs Department attempted to insist upon the conventions of written communication and the significance of a written record in their dealings with native chiefs, while the communicative strategies of the chiefs was to press for oral communication in meetings (if they had to have communication at all) and the significance of oral agreements. In her work she discusses how the archival record shows the manifestations of this struggle. In 1923 the Native Commissioner of Potgietersrus was involved in a dispute with

Chief Alfred Masibi of Zebediela and wrote to him to say, 'I do not as a rule take verbal messages – you must get your secretary to write when transacting government business' (Hofmeyr 1995: 35). A later note of complaint about the behaviour of another chief refers to the need for a written statement or at least that any oral communication is undertaken in an environment of the official's choosing, namely the office, 'On the 16th inst. I attended the Local Council meeting at Zebediela, and there saw the young chief to whom I at once intimated that I was not there to receive his explanation which he could either submit in writing or personally at my office at Potgietersrust. Further that if I received no response to my letter within seven days of the last mentioned date I would submit the matter for further action by you [his superior officer] without his explanation' (Hofmeyr 1995: 35). In responding to these pressures, chiefs and others adopted a number of tactics to wrest back a victory for orality. They ignored the conventions of 'inst' and 'ult' and wrote as they spoke 'bathing documents in the stream of orality' (p. 38), oral address was combined with conversational explanation; picking up from apparent earlier conversations was supplemented with personal anecdote. They also would often send a person along with the letter and indicate that the accompanying person could explain the content of the written communication or answer any further questions. Spelling and language use deviated from the norms expected by the officials while translators and interpreters looked to fashion the texts into bureaucratically acceptable forms. Hofmeyr (p. 40) shows how a text that drew upon oral styles of speech and the performance language of the church,

> With respect Sir Amen
> I say that everybody at Kamola, they do not like the council and its power at all. Truly we do not like it. The entire *lekgotla* of Doorndraai they do not like it one little bit. You know that we do not like the Council. We are in a difficult position, we are in difficult position, we do not like the Council. You know that we do not like it.
> I remain
> Johannes Mashishi

was reworked by a translator as,

> Sir, with respect, Amen. The residents of the Kamola Area are very much against a Local Council. Every body at Dorrondrae. Sir I wish to tell you every body hates a Local Council in this area.
> I remain
> Johannes Mashishi

While these were strategies for appropriating the written form, the most direct response was sometimes to repudiate written agreements entirely as of no validity. In the 1930s a much-hated tax, a tribal levy, was resisted and Hofmeyr (p. 42) quotes an irritated Commissioner as follows,

> They flatly refused to pay the Levy, on the ground that their Headman, Lingana Mabusela, (since dead) did not inform them of it; I pointed out that Lingana actually signed the resolution of 6/9/1929 asking for the imposition thereof, but all argument was of no avail. Ultimately it became necessary to invoke the aid of the criminal law and some 100 were sent to prison for terms ranging from six weeks to two months.

Repeatedly in the confrontations between officials and chiefs the officials had to resort to spoken explanation of the supposedly authoritative documentation that was under discussion while for their interlocutors the remembered words of past chiefs, the words spoken in dreams, and the remembered exchanges from previous encounters were the elements drawn upon for authority and truth.

This example drawn from the work of Isabel Hofmeyr traces the struggle between opposing forces over the terms of verbal trade. William Hanks (Hanks 1999: ch. 5), in discussing Mayan texts (letters, chronicles, surveys) from sixteenth-century Yucatan, illustrates the emergence of ' "boundary genres" derived from a fusion of Spanish and Maya frameworks', a series of texts, on the one hand recognizable to the Spanish as belonging to familiar categories (letters, chronicles, etc.) while on the other being recognizable to Maya speakers in terms of their own familiar ways of speaking and categories of prose and verse – therefore 'doubly interpretable', as Hanks puts it. Hanks's focus in his study is upon the practice of writing in this intercultural context, the debates about discourse genres, and the sociohistorical context within which such a new and emergent practice took place.

Each culture has its own conventions about what are, and are not, appropriate ways of saying particular kinds of things. And in each case, those conventions are contested, revised, ignored, satirized and reiterated as people negotiate the power relations of speech and control of the terms of verbal trade. Each culture formalizes to a different degree and in different ways the mechanisms by which particular purposes are appropriately put into effect.

Notions of appropriate language: praising

Praising is a process which displays a variety of manifestations depending upon both the degree of praise to be articulated and the conventions that surround the verbal forms available. From the parental 'well done!' to the public display of praise and honour that goes with public awards, be they purple star, knighthood or Order of the Niger, or indeed the elegiac lament of pain and praise that is the obituary, the continuum of gradations in language are many and various. In Hausa there are particular genres that are deployed in the process of praising not only the good and the great, but hunters, thieves, wrestlers, farmers, butchers. As genres, they are recognized and named verbal forms displaying consistencies of form and language. The short epithet, assigned to an individual but deploying stock images and standard grammatical structures, can be incorporated into more extended utterances recognizable as other genres, each with its own name and expectations. Not only can the praiser, in the moment of praise, create and utter the individual's nomination and laudation, the phrases themselves may be well-known and articulated by a wide variety of people in a wide variety of contexts. This transition into the public domain, reinforced by recirculation, is manifest in two different ways. On the one hand, the particular praise-song by one particular singer may become popular and repeatedly heard on radio and on cassette where it is instantly recognized in ways with which we are familiar, as being the 'same thing' oft repeated; on the other hand, the epithet that has come to be associated with a particular person or place may not be repeated as if on a replayed cassette, but be re-articulated again and again with different nuances and surrounded by different interpretative contexts by many different people. Both these processes go on simultaneously but entail different relationships between speaker and listener, whereby the 'consumer culture' of the 'tape' listener is impinged upon by the active reformulation that goes on in the second. It is when I re-articulate the praise of person X that I become engaged with the message itself. Praising in Hausa as a public performance genre is usually articulated by professionals using a wide range of stock phrases and styles. In Yoruba *oriki*, a premium is placed upon the inventive juxtaposition of unconnected parts as the praiser builds a sequence of powerful and sometimes chaotic, yet allusive phrases. Not only does such verbal creativity take place on public occasions where well-known epithets for towns, clans or important individuals are articulated, the process also is carried on in private, for lesser-known individuals where the focus is upon the feelings and views of the praiser vis-à-vis the praised. In Zulu praising, the well-known tradition of royal praising is complemented by ordinary people's praising of each other; using similar techniques, styles of delivery and language, but not the well-known phrases which are specifically and exclusively associated with royalty, or other major public figures. In all these cultural forms, the spread of a genre across the glass walls of the private and the public, the individual and the group, the lowly and the famous, is marked by subtle shifts of language. The homely praising of a domestic partner's personal qualities of forbearance may be the limit of an individual's sphere of laudation, whereas the same articulation may take place in relation to a king, both literally or as a metaphor for his relation to the nation, but will be complemented by the wider dimensions of royal, national or other 'public sphere' qualities.

Depending upon the primary criteria of the purpose of the utterance and the social context of the speaker and the listener, participants in particular cultures are offered appropriate channels for the articulation of such a purpose. Certain words and phrases, certain grammatical and other structures, certain styles of performance are the building-blocks offered to the speaker contemplating speech. And most importantly, the speaker, in the context of oral communication, must be aware of the potential effects upon the relationship between himself or herself and the addressee. For the praiser, a positive reaction is awaited, an acknowledgement and a token of approval or gratitude, but not all communication can assume such a directly positive outcome.

Fixed and changing roles

Customer and salesman are a particular manifestation of temporary roles adopted for an interaction oriented at a financial transaction in which the unequal nature of the roles is integral to the nature of the event. A conversation between two friends meeting after work will usually imply a continuity to the roles and a different set of premises about the purpose of any verbal interaction. In other contexts, the roles may imply a difference of power between the parties which is manifest in the available verbal options for each party. As the headmaster may shout at the pupil without fear of retaliation, or the chief upbraid the villager in language that will not be reciprocated, a significant issue is whether the relationship is a temporary role-based one – the boss will be replaced by someone else at the end of his or her turn of office (or boss in one context is cousin in another) – or is one which is integral to the long-term status of the individual – the hereditary chief will always be chief until the day he dies. Re-negotiation of the relationship is often manifest in a re-negotiation of the verbal terms of trade. The transitions from one conjunction to another – patron and client become co-equal patrons, or child and parent become child and teacher ('Don't call me "mum" when we are in class!') – require adjustment to the management of speech genres. A culture will offer a range of subtle gradations in appropriate forms. Where criticism is the purpose behind a prospective verbal intervention the issue of how to do it can be highly problematic, particularly where the relationship is one between people of generally equal status and where a continuity of relationship is necessary or desirable. Face-to-face contexts, regardless of whether they are in so-called 'oral societies' or in supposedly 'literate' societies, present tricky prospects for the negotiation of criticism, and each society will have its own conventions and available armoury of possible ways forward.

Ambiguity versus clarity

Where the purpose is to criticize, the deployment of a particular speech genre will depend, as with praise, upon the degree of directness and vehemence which is appropriate. The judgement of what degree is in any particular context appropriate is always a fine one. In the anecdote given earlier, as I misjudged my intervention in the computer shop, allowing myself to prioritize my need to express anger over calculations about the instrumental effectiveness of my words, so I needed to find the speech genre that was appropriate to the context, the context of social relationships and the context of my intentions. Each culture has its own definitions of genres of critical discourse. In Hausa the most direct and forceful genre is *zagi* 'abuse', which has its own phrases and patterns ranging from the single word to the convoluted and rhetorically crafted lengthy utterance (see Furniss 2001). Moving along the two axes of more–less vehement speech and more–less direct speech, Hausa names another genre, that of *habaici* 'innuendo' which typically deploys imagery or other forms of language which require from the listener interpretative processes both to understand a 'hidden' level of meaning and to determine how to apply it. It is not clear from the direct meaning of the utterance what the significance of the words is and who to apply them to. When I deploy the proverb/innuendo/phrase *hadirin kasa maganin mai kabido* 'the dust storm that is the remedy for the one carrying protection against the rain', you are not sure either what the implication is or how to contextualize it. Your first step has to be to make an interpretative leap of imagination and abstraction, or to deploy your knowledge of Hausa proverbs, to conclude, approximately, that some thing or person which was considered invulnerable is not in fact so. In Chapter 3 we will return to the way in which proverbs deploy a movement from concrete to abstract in their insertion into moral discourse. But for the moment the issue is the variability of application. The interpretation given here is based upon the extraction from the image of certain features: the dust storm rises from the ground, the rain protector operates against a danger coming down from above, therefore the protection is ineffective. Other elements in the imagery are not material to this particular interpretation, although they go to make up the cohesion of the phrase itself: dryness, wetness, wind and movement, dustiness and washing clean, and other connotations of the image. The selection of the features that point to ineffective protection is the first step, the second is to examine the various contexts in which to apply this idea. Is it that I, the speaker, am indicating a danger to myself? – 'I thought I was well defended against Y but perhaps this is not the case.' Or am I commenting generally upon the vicissitudes of life? – the best-laid plans of mice can sometimes go awry. Or is it that I may be referring to person X, who has always thought themselves so wonderful, and yet, in view of what has recently occurred, has clearly suffered a severe setback? – How have the mighty fallen! Or am I making this veiled remark in the presence and hearing of the person to whom it might be being addressed? – You thought you were so wonderful but just look at you now!

Indirection may sharpen the nature of my attack, but allow me to legitimately claim that no such interpretation was intended or could possibly be appropriate. I was making a quite innocuous remark about life in general. In Hausa this way of speaking has a name and is a recognizable genre, *habaici*. Allusive diction is of course not confined to purposive contexts such as that characterized in my example above. The requirement that the listener make a leap of imagination and an interpretative foray is of course common to all uses of allusive diction, be it in lyric poetry, in innuendo, in political rhetoric or elsewhere, allusiveness is not a genre, it may be a feature of a genre where that genre requires indirection; the genre is characterized by a variety of features, prime among them is the purpose to which the communication is put, and along with that determination go the elements of form, lexis, patterning, diction and other features appropriate to the strategic aim of the communication. In terms of the Hausa categorization of speech forms, while there are labels for particular forms of speech (words for 'tale' or 'song' or 'proverb') certain labels relate to the purpose to which the words are being put – the phrase given above, generally termed a 'proverb' *karin magana* when deployed as a general comment upon life, can be used, as indicated above, as *habaici* 'innuendo', but could equally as well be deployed as 'praise' *kirari* in contexts where, for example, a boxer or his supporters might cry out, 'I am/he is as powerful as the dust storm, the remedy against those protected against the rain!!' This displays the same range of interpretation between (self-)praise, general comment and irony that was available in Muhammad Ali's famous phrase, 'Float like a butterfly, sting like a bee!'

Maintaining and disrupting the relation between form and content

There is often no clear boundary between genres of speech and other genres of artistic discourse, be they, in terms of the process of composition, oral or written. Intending to 'prognosticate' and to 'instruct', the available channels before me in Hausa include the option of composing on paper a didactic poem, amending and redrafting, replete with conventions about rhyme and metre, language and style. The genre of poetry is available to me because the tradition of poetry-writing is one which has been for two hundred years closely linked to moral and religious didacticism; everyone expects that if I deploy the first few words of an instantly recognizable genre then I will be putting forward a message of a certain kind. The 'tradition' tells me, as writer, and you, as listener, what to expect. There is a link between form and content that is usual and expected. Not that it is impossible to alter, revise and fail in meeting expectations, but revision is only possible because the norm is established, understood and expected. When a first volume of 'love' poetry in Hausa was published in the early 1980s, the criticism of it was often framed in terms of the departure from the expectations of what poetry was supposed to be. Poetry, certainly that which was to be published, should consist of the expression of didactic and religiously appropriate sentiments, appropriate for the public domain. A key factor in this debate was the apprehension that poetry was, and is, a public medium. Composed in writing it might be, circulated in manuscript or print it might be, but poetry was recited, listened to, appreciated and sensed for its aural rhythms and its chanted patterns of sound; the privacy of perception that goes with a genre that is deeply embedded in writing and reading, such as the novel, was not a perceived part of what constituted the practice and production of poetry. Being oral, and yet also written, the overriding issue was not that a poem could be perceived in the privacy of the eye and the page, but participating in the public processes of speech and its embeddedness in the relations between people. The genre of poetry in Hausa is one available genre of speech that has conventional correlates in terms of intention and content. The connections between speech genre and content are, of course, strengthened by constant repetition. When the lawyer addresses the witness and says, 'You say you saw my client enter the premises. Would you be so good as to tell the jury where you were standing when you say you saw ...', all those present understand from their experience of courtrooms and the roles that people play in them that there will ensue a series of questions and answers, phrased in a certain way, focused upon either demonstrating the reliability or the unreliability of the witness's statements concerning the truth of a particular narrative. All have witnessed these kinds of exchanges before, in fact or in fiction, or are familiar with the conventions that surround them. As a genre of discourse, there are rules that are enforced by the judge about the nature of questions and the requirement to provide answers. Switching to another speech genre – the bedtime story, the joke, or abuse – will bring the intervention of the judge to put the process back 'into genre'. Expectations are present because of the familiarity engendered in the participants through repetition. Verbal markers, 'my client ...', 'tell the jury ...', reinforce the salience of the genre. The case may change and the events and charges may change, but the framework of genre remains the same.

The more marked the genre, with its catchphrases, introductory and closing formulae, the more salient is its form. Introductory and closing formulae provide ways of agreeing between communicating parties on the transition into and out of the genre. When I say, 'Have you heard this one ...' I am asking you to acquiesce in a transition away from our continuing debate on the current state of the stock market into another genre, the 'joke', and when it is over and you have acknowledged the hearing and appreciation (or not) of the joke then we can return to the previous topic of discussion. In Hausa, to negotiate an agreed transition into an oral narrative, I offer you *Ga ta, ga ta nan* 'Here it is' and if you are prepared to allow the transition, you reply, *Ta zo mu ji ta* 'Let it come so we may hear it', and to indicate that I propose to exit from the story genre, I finish with *Kunkurus kan kusu* 'Off with its head'. Transition, in the continuous flow of discourse, requires acknowledgement of a mutual understanding of the terms of trade and an agreement to change tack, even if only briefly. Again, the issue of power relations is central to the question of whether the speaker can and will change the terms of trade unilaterally and without reference to the addressee(s) and listener(s). Power, politeness and the differential cultural understandings of the participants are all part of the impinging context. The marked elements of the genre are often those which make the transfer into the world of parody.

Familiarity with particular speech genres, and the expected content of the communication, leads to an effacement of the link between. Each Sunday morning I have a pretty clear idea of what the vicar is going to say when he gets up on his pulpit as he has done every Sunday for the last twenty years. I could practically recite the sermon off by heart – not any particular sermon, but a hybrid, typical version dredged out of my tedious memories. And what comes to mind? All the marking phrases that come every week without fail, 'My text for today is ..., brothers and sisters we are gathered together ..., we give thanks ..., will you please say after me ...' The connection between the genre and the plea for prayers for the destitute, finance for missionary activity, the improvement of behaviour, is a seamless and unnoticed one. It is only when the appropriate familiarity is broken that the connection is ruptured to create parody, irony or pastiche. There are, of course, two ways in which the rupture can take place. Where the content is repackaged in a new and unfamiliar genre, then we see new channels opening up for communication: the plea for finance for missionary activity has become the radio jingle, or the pop song, with all the attendant debate about whether the content has been damaged by being so repackaged or is now getting across to people who had not heard it before. Old wine in new bottles can produce differing reactions depending upon whether you like the old or the new bottles or indeed the wine. Parodic reworking entails often the faithful recreation of the genre, particularly those markers which acted as metonymic elements, but with wildly inappropriate content. It is the perfect reproduction of the bottle but with vinegar in it instead of wine which produces the sought-after reaction. The incongruity of the conjunction between genre and subject matter produces the laughter which is so undermining of the seamless link between serious content and serious form. The Hausa burlesque artist, Malam Ashana 'Mr Matches', has a particular performance routine in which he imitates a well-known, serious, speech act, the *tafsir*, which is performed particularly during the month of the fast and which involves a scholar providing an explanation in Hausa of verses in Arabic from the Holy Qur'an. He imitates all the features of the speech genre of such religious text exegesis – the interpellated phrase of Arabic and the Hausa gloss in the particular intonational styles so typical of serious exegesis before crowds of people – but substitutes the discussion of cooking and food for the religious subject matter of the original. The incongruity of the juxtaposition of food and exegesis comes about because of the expectations that go with the genre itself. Were the audience not familiar with the conjunction of form and content then there would be no force in the parody. In this case, the original model is part of the public culture of speech genres and the parody is also. However, the context of performance is very different. The exegesis occurs in meetings specifically called for the purpose of religious teaching and in the presence of learned and serious scholars, the parody is among villagers and ordinary people in the market. Part of the co-option and neutralization of the subversive power of parody is, of course, to bring the parody into the same performance context as the original. When the parody shares the bill with the object of its attentions, it moves into a grey area, in danger of becoming a canonical form ripe for a parodic interpretation of itself, or at least losing some of its effectiveness, as a seal of harmlessness is placed upon it. The prime minister who attends the show intended as a satire upon his or her government, helps to bless the performance as a harmless ritual of rebellion; the alternative is to send in the thought police to close it down.

Critical discourse about speaking and the aesthetics of speech

Perception and understanding are framed within the expectations that surround the many and varied genres of speech. Associated with each genre of speech are expectations of content, form and delivery. As soon as I hear the words, 'Brothers and sisters, we are gathered together in the name of ...' I am pretty much sure that I am about to hear a sermon and I know the kind of thing to expect and the kinds of ways in which it is probably going to be put. When I come out of the sermon, I hear my fellow parishioners murmuring, 'Wonderful sermon, vicar!' and we nod and grunt in general assent. In addition to all our expectations of content and form, there are qualities of this sermon, as against last week's sermon, or the sermon of the visiting vicar of the week before, which make us whisper, 'Outstanding!' But if you ask what it was about this week's sermon which made it so different, I will probably be hard put to find an answer, because I am not used to debating the aesthetics of the genre. I can talk about the content and whether I agreed or not, but not so easily about the rhetorics. Nevertheless, even if I can't put it into words, I can tell a good sermon when I hear one, and this was a good one! In addition, therefore, to there being a myriad different genres of speech, there are attendant gradations, both within particular cultures and as between cultures, in the degree to which there is overt articulation of critical discourse about effective speaking. There may be conscious debate about the terms of verbal trade, comment upon the performance of a poor speaker, whether it be a young novice story-teller or a deputy prime minister who falls over his verbal feet, as it were. On the other hand, there may be an unarticulated appreciation only refractively tangible through evidence of popularity, on the assumption that if the content was unappreciated and the oral delivery poor then that particular speaker and his or her speech would not be popular.

The degree of articulation of critical discourse may also correlate with the nature of the performance event. On the one hand, the performer may be physically separate from his or her audience with a clear spatial barrier and an immutable allocation of roles as between performer and audience. On the other, a person may be performer one minute and member of an audience the next, remaining separate from performer one minute, and audience participant the next. Critical articulation may then be a matter of discussion among co-equal members of the performer group/audience. And the nature of the discussion may be framed in terms of the observed performance of one particular person, or be framed in terms of general discussion of the performance of a particular genre in general, or of the performance of the 'typical' performer.

Besides these variable elements of considerable complexity, there is little apparent of a general nature in terms of a set of characteristics that are in some sense 'typical' of effective speaking. Not only is there variation as between the characteristics of different genres within the same culture, different cultures may themselves value characteristics very differently across a number of its own genres of speech. With reference to two African cultures I would like to illustrate such contrasting positions.

The aesthetics of speaking: two contrasting cultures

There is a rich and complex variety of oral traditions of song and speech in Yoruba, and among them *oriki* are a genre of pithy or elaborated appellations or attributions addressed to a subject, and as Barber (1991: 1) says, 'in the enormous wealth and ferment of Yoruba oral literature, they are probably the best-known of all forms'. The appreciation of performed *oriki* in Yoruba society is built upon an expectation that they will be dense, allusive, elliptical and hence 'difficult' to understand on the one hand, and deliberately disjunctive on the other, involving the juxtaposition of internally coherent sections into strings of contrastive and non-coherent sequences: 'An oriki chant is a form that aims at high

impact, high intensity, which it achieves through juxtaposing apparent opposites' (Barber 1991: 16).
Barber (1991: 17–19) gives the following example:

> This will not be the last festival you celebrate
> Eesade, son of Owolabi, it is I Abeni calling you
> Child of Mofomike, child of Moyosi, child of one who had a fine house in which to receive slaves as gifts
> Child of one whose corridors reverberated like rain
> Mofomike, magnificence is acquired with money, money has made your house its headquarters
> Native of Aran, child of one who gets rich on gifts
> Let us go to our house, Aran-Orin, child of 'The pepper leaf spreads'
> Child of Omiyode, child of Alari, one who taps the base of the wild mango tree and gets wine
> When you rise today pay homage to your father, Olugbede Otabilapo Ogun Ajagbe who got a *kowee* bird to make medicine
> He had nothing to give the visitor so he made a present of Fomike
> Native of Aran, child of One who gets rich on gifts, Ajagbe who found a *kowee* bird to make medicine
> Just make sure you pay homage to your father, you'll spend the rest of your money rearing children ...

In discussing this extract from a longer *oriki* addressed to Eesade, a title holder in the guild of hunters, Barber explains how behind each line are strings of connections and hidden references. For example, there are fragments of other *oriki* embedded within it: the references to Aran people mention the pepper-leaf which is a emblem of that town, while getting rich on gifts refers to their masquerading activities that are rewarded with gifts; to understand the reference to 'having nothing to give the visitor' requires knowledge of a narrative about a previous great man, and presupposed behind the reference to the *kowee* bird are allusions to the world of powerful medicines and the harbingers of death. These and other allusions are juxtaposed with no sense of there being a narrative sequence of beginning, middle and end to the text as a whole:

> The performer has at her disposal a corpus of textual elements. These elements may all have had separate origins. They may have been composed by different people, at different times and with reference to different incidents or situations. The corpus of oriki attributed to a given subject is made up of items which are largely genetically

separate. They therefore have no fixed or necessary relation to each other within the performance. (Barber 1991: 20)

The critical discourse surrounding the performance of this genre foregrounds the density and the disjuncture of its component meanings:

> The more skilled a performer is, the more she will produce conjunctions and juxtapositions which create tension. If too many lines resemble each other too strongly – if there is too much obvious parallelism and patterning – the performance is felt to be dull ... Skilful singers seemed deliberately to play on this fear (of stalling) throwing up gaps in the act of crossing them. The goal seems to be to maintain an intensity of disjunctiveness. From moment to moment, the performer extends slender threads of connection which are no sooner made than abandoned, one congruence no sooner proposed than left behind while the performer moves on to another. It is this which gives *oriki* chants their characteristic weaving, shifting, fragmenting and merging quality so fascinating to listen to. (Barber 1991: 270)

The aesthetics of this particular genre of Yoruba discourse focus upon complexity, allusiveness and a deliberate lack of narrative sequencing; the more the better. Other genres within the Yoruba cultural world present a somewhat different set of criteria, nevertheless, the richness of reference and allusion underlies many another genre.

In contrast, the aesthetic 'principles' underlying discourse among the Berba-speaking people of northern Benin are very different. In examining the articulation of three speech genres – oral narratives, proverb-speaking and local political debate – Annette Czekelius (1999) describes skills and criteria of judgement as they apply to all three contexts. In discussion with audiences and with performers she presents their views of effectiveness in speaking. In Berba society, an acephalous rural world of spread-out farming hamlets, there is extensive discussion of the aesthetics of speaking.

Story-telling is judged in terms of its 'authenticity' as a close rendering of the template well-known to the audience for any particular tale; 'clarity' in terms of being well-structured, economical, and easily comprehensible – without embellishment or redundancy; 'consistency' as between the events of the narrative and the moral that is derived from it. As Czekelius puts it:

> The notion of 'quality' in the tradition of storytelling is predicated essentially upon structural aspects, namely clarity and consistency.

Without them, it will be hard to procure an aesthetic experience, such as the enjoyment of the pattern of 'tension-release' or the cognitive satisfaction through an interesting plot or an insightful conclusion. The demands on the speaker and his narrative skills follow accordingly. They involve the memorizing and adequate (re)production of a tale template and a direct and lucid wording. (Czekelius 1999: 182)

Proverb-speaking, closer to *oriki* in the sense that it relies upon allusion and indirectness in its use of metaphor, is judged in terms of the relation between the proverb and the context of usage both situational and textual: its applicability to the situation, its explanatory value, its truth value, its appropriateness in being indirect in situations where to be direct would be socially unacceptable, its summative or introductory value. Czekelius again:

As far as the proverb tradition is concerned, the notion of quality centres around referential-functional aspects. A 'good' proverb is distinguished by its truth value on the literal and applied level and serves, on the functional level, the double exigency of elucidation and allusion. For the speaker's skills it follows that he has to dispose of an ample stock of proverbs, master the analogic mechanism and exhibit a certain degree of social competence, if he is to succeed in verbal interaction. (Czekelius 1999: 182–3)

Rhetorical failure in these two traditions within Berba society involves precisely the characteristics so prized within *oriki*: juxtaposition with little evident connection is viewed as enervating disordered discourse, a greater degree of density can be condemned as 'deliberate obscurity':

There are those kwankyama (proverbs) which are deliberately left unexplained. The flaw is evident: by abruptly switching code, the speaker has distracted the listener's mind from the main strand of thought, yet does not make any move to smooth over to the prose of the argument. In lacking the referential background, there is no way to decode the proverb's intended meaning. The audience is left confused, and will reject the proverb on both linguistic and moral grounds. Not only has the speaker disturbed the flow of conversation, he has also affronted the audience by offering them a saying which seems to convey an important truth, yet excludes them from its understanding. The reproach concerns hypocrisy and anti-social behaviour, for the speaker has abused the genre to boast of his intellectual superiority and withheld valuable insights – selfish and hence despicable behaviour. (Czekelius 1999: 161–2)

In relation to the aesthetics of speaking in the context of a Berba political debate, questions of verbal expression (speech act) are embedded in expectations that relate to the speech event: there is a specific reason why people have come together, there is an intention to resolve problems by the exchange of ideas and the arrival at a consensus and a decision. Each person has the right to speak and there are rules of conduct which ensure a lack of interruption and turn-taking between speakers. In terms of judging the speech act, a parallel set of criteria to those we have seen in the other two contexts comes into play. An effective intervention must be substantive and be seen to convey an element of truth, and contribute to the resolution of the problem; it must be coherent and clear; relevant and economical. After a lengthy discussion of Berba political debate, Czekelius makes the following comment:

> The evaluative discourse is anchored in Berba political ideology, featuring 'constructiveness' as its principal criterion. Respectively, contributions fostering the exchange of ideas and the solution of conflicts are acclaimed. The assessment concerns the textual and contextual level and compounds linguistic and moral aspects. On the textual level it is persuasive argumentation, lucid diction and a reconciliatory mode of speech which are most highly esteemed. On the contextual level, the approval is for those elements which serve to organize the course of debate, such as the presentation of a schedule, the employment of turn-taking markers and framing devices, and the contextualisation of the individual speech act through cross-references. The notion of rhetorical failure follows accordingly. The gravest objections are to those speeches which impede the exchange of ideas and thwart the decision-making process. 'Incoherence', 'redundancy' and insufficient explication' as well as 'counterproductive statements' and 'deliberate ridicule' are the main targets of critique. (Czekelius 1999: 243)

As Czekelius demonstrates, skills learnt in the context of one speech genre are deployable in another. The good storyteller and user of proverbs can be particularly effective in political debate. A general aesthetic binds all three genres of speaking in which a premium is placed upon clarity, relevance, cohesion and economy; principles which are in line with Grice's maxims of the co-operative principle in conversation (see chapter 5): 'make your contribution as informative, true, relevant, perspicuous as is required' (Czekelius 1999: 74). It is perhaps dangerous to suggest a general aesthetic for Berba verbal culture. Nevertheless, it is clear that there are spillovers and continuities in the appreciation of different genres of speech deployed in different contexts, and that the generalized characteristics of such an aesthetic stand in contrast to those which are in play in the appreciation of *oriki* in Yoruba society.

Striking as the contrast is between Berba verbal culture and the Yoruba appreciation of *oriki*, broader parallels can be seen depending upon the purposes and functions that lie behind similar speech events and social contexts. Appellation, whether in praise or in vilification, whether of a social superior or equal or self, can show the characteristic density and disjuncture that is visible in *oriki*. It is typical of Otjiherero praising in Namibia, Zulu praising in South Africa, Hausa praise-singing in Nigeria, and 'naming/praising' in many other cultures. Indirectness as a requirement dictated by the politics of face-to-face communication is negotiated by a variety of means, including proverbial usage, in many societies. The need to find mechanisms to move from a problem to a resolution where negotiation and consensus-forming are the only way (assuming there is no power that can impose a judgement) will always put a premium upon ensuring (though there may be many ways of doing so) that the audience does not become enervated, bored or antagonistic because what is being said is considered irrelevant, inappropriate, incomprehensible or downright wrong.

Concluding remarks

The oral communicative moment is embedded in a set of cultural conventions and attitudes about what it is appropriate to say and how this should be expressed. And the notion of cultural conventions is itself subject to a variety of attitudes, ranging from one which expects adherence to clear conventions, a purist notion of culture, to one which resists any such notion and in a more eclectic manner puts a premium upon bricolage and creativity. At the same time, different societies display differing aesthetics in relation to the act of speaking and to verbal art in particular. The choice of ways of speaking is bounded by norms of expectation between people about what are the appropriate ways of pursuing particular purposes, and misjudgements can have disastrous consequences. At the same time, each culture formalizes these ways of speaking in a different manner, certain purposes in one society may require highly formalized speech while that purpose may involve much less formally bounded ways in another. Within particular cultures there will be gradations not only of formality but also of intensity dependent upon the need to be discreet, to maintain relations beyond the speech event, or to mark irreparable rupture, each with their own ways of speaking. The nexus of appropriateness between purpose and ways of speaking is itself the subject of attention in the metadiscourse of humour, satire, parody and other mechanisms of counterdiscourse. The familiarity and therefore invisibility of the link between form and content is ruptured by the parodic rendering or the theatre of the absurd. Cultural conventions and expectations surround the oral communicative moment and in each instantiation provide an envelope of guidance for those involved in interpretation and articulation, the subject of the following chapter.

3
Insertion into the Social – Constituting Audiences, Audience Cultures and Moving from the Private to the Public

Social domains of cultural production: the performance and the audience

'My words have been taken out of context!' the politician cries, indignation on his brow and pain in his voice. Usually, of course, he means that, if you were aware of the words that came before or came after the quoted section, you would realize that he was not wholeheartedly endorsing euthanasia, or beef on the bone, or incarceration of minors, etc. The ability of tape-recorders and note-takers to freeze and repeat the spoken word means indeed that pieces can be extracted and in that sense 'taken out of context'. But there is a wider sense in which recording takes 'out of context'. The unrecorded speech act is always in a context and therefore surrounded by a time, a place, an event and an audience. No sooner is the unrecorded speech act articulated than it is embedded in a history, a real social and communicative context from which it cannot be extracted. It can be remembered and it can be reconstructed by those who were there using the fiction that the reconstruction matches the original, but it can never be reconstituted in its original context. A reified object like a printed text may have constant referential potential and observable presence, but lives only in its current reading, as has often been commented upon. The recorded speech act, like the printed text, has all the potential to evoke feelings, reactions, meanings, as had the original performance/reading. However, the repeated later performance is to a new audience in a new situation and with no inevitability about the evocation of the same reactions, thoughts or feelings as before. The existence of the recorded version alongside the continued presence of the speaker, produces complex sets of expectations among potential audiences. The jazz lover's delight in infinite difference and variation is reflected in an attitude towards the speaker that expects variety and difference from speech to speech, whereas the exact reproducibility available through recording can engender an attitude which demands exact similitude, often reinforced by the commercial pressures that go along with the saleability of the mass-produced object. As the rock singer may be under pressure to produce a stage performance that exactly mirrors the recorded version available on the popular CD, and under no circumstances to reproduce the song in an entirely different musical idiom, so also the speaker may be expected to repeat the earlier reading, recitation or narrative. Such attitudinal differences among audiences set the tone for the speaker, the genre of speech and the event itself.

The embeddedness of the unrecorded speech act, and therefore the historical specificity of the circumstances of who said what to whom, is nevertheless subject to frames of reference which are not specific to the event itself. Such frames of reference provide the link between the momentary instance and the notion of a social process that can repeatedly produce instances of cultural production on a continuing basis – for the want of a better word, a 'tradition'. On the one hand, there is a frame of reference, a categorization, for the event itself. From where we stand, and looking at the clothes of the people here present, I think we must be at a funeral, or a wedding, or a graduation ceremony, or a protest march. Knowing what has gone before – the death, the relationship between the parties, the years of study, or the rate of pay – I can confirm the appropriateness of the event to its antecedents. It would be odd to hold a funeral before a person dies, yet even that is not beyond the bounds of humour, mockery or intimidation. I recognize the scene before me as belonging to the general event category 'funeral', a category that I am familiar with as being oft repeated in my social world. As people tinker with the boundaries and nature of such categories, to shock, to amuse, to register a dissatisfaction with the frames themselves, so culture changes and the event category is redefined. 'Ah me! Funerals are not what they used to be!' bemoans an elderly relative.

Linked to this frame of reference, the event category, is the categorization of speech into appropriate forms, recognizable as relating to both the present instance and to a continuity of types of speech. 'Oh, it was a joke was it?' says your friend. 'Must be a farewell party going on at that table over there, from the way they're all remembering old times,

I'd say', says your colleague. If it is Friday prayer, or the church service then we must be listening to the sermon/homily, if it is a courtroom we must be listening to the summing up for the prosecution, if the royal court is in session then this must be the paean of praise. The genre itself may be inextricably linked to the event category and therefore to the purpose which is appropriate to the event. Poetry may be the form in which preaching and teaching is to be undertaken, the oral narrative may necessarily be to amuse, the proverb may be the cardinal way to make a summative moral statement. Each culture will deploy its own correlations between genre category, event category and the myriad purposes to which speech can be put.

The continuity of culture available in the knowledge of event and genre category is variably socially embedded in the sense not only of the differing degrees to which individuals are conscious of the issues, but particularly in relation to the permanence, fixity, or salience of the notion of speaker and audience, as we discussed briefly in Chapter 2. As I dispose of the propensity I may have to tell a good joke, no sooner have I finished than I relinquish the role of speaker to you as you take up the challenge and tell an even better joke in return. One minute I am the audience and the next minute I am the performer. As I muster my rhetorical skills to berate the market trader who, I believe, has cheated me, summoning my most extended and picturesque forms of abuse, so to my astonishment does a torrent of verbal fireworks return no sooner than I draw breath. A crowd has gathered, and I have supporters who join in to complain that they too were cheated. The roles of speaker, addressee and audience are passing round so fast, mayhem is about to ensue. The roles are transient and exchangeable. But here amongst us, all of a sudden, is a permanent professional. The Nigerian market is the domain of the market entertainer and here is a *dan gambara*, a specialist in banter and abuse, a man who earns his living from cadging and upbraiding. Within the context of the market, or any public place, he is a specialist in a particular verbal genre. As an actor dons the character in the play, when the 'dan gambara' steps out of the taxi, walks out of his house, picks up his drum, and people are around, then he is no longer the anonymous face of another individual on the street, but the living embodiment of that category. The exponent of the category is, when in 'public', never the audience, never anything other than that category, and therefore always on one side of the line which divides the speaker from the audience. As the king is only the king when he is seen in public, travelling incognito is no longer to be king, so the other end of the continuum from the ever-moving role is the permanent, professional exponent, linked inextricably to the genre and the event category. For the 'dan gambara' to be present is to create the event from which the flow of speech must follow. But, of course, there are many occasions when the fixed roles assigned to individuals are only manifest in the articulation of the speech genre when many different aspects of the event have been assembled. The marriage vows rely upon the co-presence of the couple, the officiating priest, an audience of witnesses, the co-ordination of time, place, clothing, decoration and many other things. Only when all these have been assembled and a set of events and actions have been gone through may the priest articulate the vows to be repeated out loud. The priest may be the priest wherever he or she goes, but the speech event needs special circumstances for its articulation.

An audience is, of course, all those present at the event. And yet the constitution of the audience has many elements to it. Not only may there be some physically present within sight or hearing distance of the speaker, but there are also, of course, audiences at the end of the loudspeaker, down the wire, and on the beach where radio waves break. They are also present at the speech event in the sense that they hear and cogitate at the same moment as those physically present. Clearly, however, the sense of reactive and counter-reactive potential that is present among the present is not available at the end of the wire. I may bay for your blood as you address me and my compatriots, but you and I will quickly be aware that I am either the sole lunatic in the crowd, or merely one among hundreds moving forward to tear you down from your perch. Bay as I may beside my radio set three thousand miles away, neither you nor I will ever be able to tell whether I could have affected the course of history had I been there in the crowd that day.

In another significant sense, however, the audience is 'constituted' in the process of the performance. Were Mark Antony to begin a speech today by saying, 'Friends, Romans, countrymen', he would not merely be appealing to the values of friendship, civic solidarity and nationalism, he would be constituting the nature of the people there present – inviting the individuals there present to put up their hands and say, 'I am a friend, I am a Roman, I am your fellow countryman.' Regardless of whether the people present actually do think of themselves in these or any other such terms, the speaker is constituting the identities of the audience through the speech event itself. We will return to this later in this chapter. And not only does this occur through the direct expression of identities, as in the above example, but it is also managed by the many resources of language. In Swahili, as in many other languages, there are particular ways of speaking for men and for women. To speak like a woman, in an unmarked way that is appropriate to talking to other women, is to constitute an audience as being other women. Markers may be required to indicate that the addressees are perceived to be men. There are a myriad ways in which audiences are constituted – as of higher status, of lower status, of close relationship, of distant relationship, as enemy, as friend – through the culturally specific resources of language.

The association between language resources and differences of status, gender, age and many other oppositional categories means that often the nature and control of particular genres of speech are contested and differently appropriated. There are oral literary genres (particular named forms of poetry, narrative, etc.) as well as speech genres (recognizable and choosable alternative forms of speech) and styles (recognizable elements of speech that are apparent whatever the form, content or purpose), that are the separate domains of groups, classes and categories of people, in which separate discussions go on in parallel. There are also genres which are deployed by categories in opposition to each other, either to reclaim the genre for themselves as the vehicle for their exclusive voice, or to contest the uses and meanings deployed by the 'other', and we considered in Chapter 2 the South African example of the competition for the control of the terms of verbal trade as described by Isabel Hofmeyr. Sa'id Babura Ahmad (1997), in his research on Hausa narratives, gives an example of the same narrative within the same oral literary genre being deployed by a man and then by a woman to present opposed and alternative interpretations of gender relations. The moral of the man's version of the story of 'the man and the dove' is to suggest that men should not listen to women, the moral of the woman's version is that a man should not marry a second wife if he has a reasonable relationship with his first. The speech genre constitutes the space within which the debate takes place for the constitution of competing world views, of which these two versions are only the smallest of manifestations.

The constituting of public culture

The individual utterance, bounded by the transitions from one speaker to another, regardless of its meaning and intention, is embedded within the frames that go to make up the communicative context: as I lie on my bed, talking to myself, I know that there is no one listening; as I offer up a prayer I hope there is someone listening; as I talk confidentially to my best friend I know that my words will go no further; as I talk in company it matters not to me whether everyone hears me at that moment when a pause in many conversations sends my voice out across the room; as I address the school I expect the assembled company to listen carefully to what I have to say; I may become a little nervous at the prospect that my words in the interview will perhaps be heard by millions of radio listeners. In all these contexts, and in a myriad variations upon them, a primary distinction lies in the notion of the private and the public, as we saw in our earlier discussion in Chapter 1. But the line of demarcation is not a fixed one: as far as I am concerned, for my best friend to know is on the one side of the divide, for those particular two schoolmates to have heard is to have blown the matter far and wide, 'you might as well have put a notice in the paper', say I. Known to hundreds of people, the details of the scandalous doings of a certain prime minister or president remain notionally 'private' until they appear in the gossip column of a national newspaper. And once the 'cat is out of the bag' a different set of judgements are made and a different set of consequences ensue. The endless debate about the relationship between private and public life feeds upon the appropriate response to knowledge and to articulation of that knowledge. 'Gossip' and 'rumour' remain the terms for the oral articulation of 'private' knowledge which may be widespread and widely believed, representing the insertion and infiltration into the 'public' domain of 'private' information which has not made the transition to 'public knowledge'. How, then, does that transition occur? It is the articulation, usually oral, of that information in an acknowledged 'public statement', that can then be retransmitted with the seal of 'official' status, and with the cachet of 'admitted truth'. This has now been admitted to by poor Mr X, by the Ministry of Truth, by the government, by the accused. The public admission that the government has been involved in torture requires a new departure in both attitude and action: an apology may be considered appropriate and the minister in charge for the security services may have to resign. A 'truth and reconciliation' commission is predicated upon the notion that the move from private knowledge to public knowledge is a precondition for 'reconciliation', without that transition there can be no 'reconciliation', with it there is the possibility. The transition from private to public (never the other way) is, of course, an entirely different issue from the establishment of 'truth' in any general sense. Fabrications and propaganda are the stuff of *public* discourse, and indeed black propaganda has always relied upon the effectiveness of the 'not yet public' world of gossip and rumour.

Public culture has its ways of doing things. Speech genres straddle the distinction between the private and the public. Some ways of speaking are indistinguishable regardless of whether examples occur in the public or the private domain: I may offer up a prayer alone on my bed that is in form and nature identical to that which is articulated by millions intoning the same words in time with the Pope addressing the crowds in St Peter's. But other genres may be intrinsically public because the bundle of expectations that go with them specify a 'public' that is notionally present. When the orator, the *okyeame*, in Akan society speaks for the chief, his way of speaking is predicated upon the notion that there is a public present to hear the 'public' utterance deriving from the chief (the question of whether the chief actually initiated the utterance is not material). The sermon is intended to be a public articulation, not a private musing. Even the simulated 'private conversation', in terms of the style of the dialogue, between interviewer and interviewee on radio news and current affairs programmes is recognized as a 'private style' acted out for the public domain. Addressivity, to use Bakhtin's (1986: 95) phrase, is inherent in all utterances, but certain genres of speech emphasize not only their orientation towards a listener but also the 'public' nature of their discourse.

A transition from the private to the public, then, entails the marking of a dialogic actual or potential dimension to an utterance, and thereby an embeddedness in a process of exchange and potential argumentation. The private musing becomes available for others to agree with, or disagree with, to counter or support, and thus becomes embedded in what Habermas called 'validity claims'. In Habermas's view, everyday discourse and the moral argumentation embedded within it that serves to co-ordinate action produces the public reflexivity that 'gives the participants the knowledge that they have collectively become convinced of something':

> Only an intersubjective process of reaching understanding can produce an agreement that is reflexive in nature; only it can give the participants the knowledge that they have collectively become convinced of something. (Habermas 1990: 67)

In arriving at an explicit common understanding that there is a 'common will' shared by a group, a necessary process has to be entered into willingly by the various participants that entails reflection either upon some disruption that has occurred to assumed common understandings with a view to restoring a pre-existing consensus or upon the formulation of a new articulation of a moral position.

While Habermas's focus is upon the process of consensus formation, repair and maintenance, the issue he addresses is also one of the transition of thought from the private to the public domain and the necessary correlates which attend that transition in terms of the insertion of the utterance into actual or potential dialogic relations, both between speakers and in intertexual relations.

A further dimension to this transition is the reformulation of the implications of the utterance in terms of its frame of reference. When I think to myself, 'I dropped a pound coin on the carpet just now and I mustn't forget to pick it up', I am operating at the most private end of the communicative continuum – I address no one else, I refer to a most specific moment in time and in space, and, I assume, I would be hard put to interpret my thought as having generalized metaphorical implications, although I might well go on from there to reflect that this illustrates again my general capacity for forgetfulness. Even when I utter the same sentence to someone else, I may have moved along the continuum towards the 'public' insofar as the statement is now available to be countered, scoffed at, responded to or ignored, yet the utterance itself remains the same. But I will argue later that a common ideological process to be observed in so much oral literature and oral discourse more generally is one that involves the establishment of a picture of the general derived from the outline of the particular – a process of 'typification' that can be seen as establishing a normative representation of person, action, event, circumstance, state or object. In addition to this process of typification, the deployment of evaluative language relies upon 'validity claims' that posit both a level of generalizability of the specific judgements made in such evaluations and a general applicability of norms. Part of the transition from private to public, or indeed of the articulation of public discourse, is the insertion of the utterance to a lesser or greater degree into a process of 'universalization'.

In considering the transitions that are effected as 'universalization' is applied to an utterance, the transition that Habermas has focused upon is the insertion of the utterance into moral discourse. One way to illustrate this process of transition is to consider the abstraction and 're-concretization' that goes on in the interpretative sequence that is required in understanding and applying some specific forms of speech, namely certain kinds of proverbs and riddles. There are many kinds of proverbs with certain commonly found characteristics such as a bipartite structure and a relative fixity in their shortness of form. Some may make generalized comments upon the moral make-up of society, 'No rest for the wicked', 'patience is a virtue', but many are constituted as simple, amoral descriptive statements of the world around us, and require us to find features within that image (with or without interpretative hints provided often in the second part of the proverb) that are open to abstraction such that, at the abstract level, generalization is available and thereby an insertion into the world of moral discourse. Let me illustrate. There is a proverb in Hausa which is constructed in two parts and the second part is itself split to provide a contrast and it goes as follows:

Kadangare a bakin tulu – a bar ka ka bata ruwa, a kashe ka a fasa tulu

There is a lizard on the lip of the water pot – leave you alone and you contaminate the water, kill you and break the pot

The core of the proverb is a simple descriptive statement which carries in itself no generalized comment or moral assertion of any kind, there is simply a lizard sitting on the lip of a water storage pot. There are many different features that could be abstracted from this image. The common (Nigerian) male lizard has typically a blue body and a yellow head, the lizard catches flies, a lizard likes to lie in the sun and absorb heat, a lizard is usually still but can move fast, it is a living creature, a lizard can cling to vertical surfaces, etc.; a water pot is stationary, a water pot is fragile, a water pot is usually brown in colour, transpiration through the wall of the pot keeps the water cool, there is a hole and a lip at the top for the removal and insertion of water, the water is for human consumption, etc. Which of these features is going to be relevant to a process of abstraction that is necessary for interpretation? Is this going to centre around the symbolic significance of blue and/or yellow versus brown? Is it heat versus coolness? In the event, the second part of the proverb directs us to certain elements in the image: 'leave you alone and you contaminate the water' immediately directs the listener's attention to the fact that the lizard as a living creature produces a contaminant through defecation and that it is the purity of the water for human consumption that is the contrasting element in that part of the image. So, not only does the second phrase point to the selection of certain elements in the image, it sets up a contrast between them at one level of abstraction:

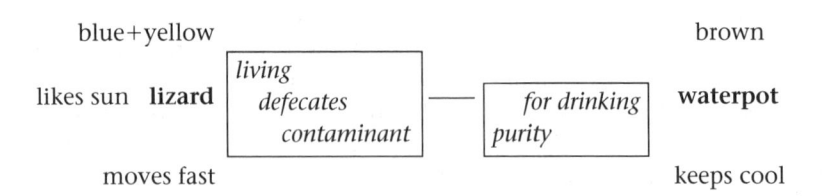

	blue+yellow				brown
likes sun	**lizard**	*living defecates contaminant*	—	*for drinking purity*	**waterpot**
	moves fast				keeps cool

The second following phrase, 'kill you and break the pot', relies upon the prior understanding of the above opposition as a conundrum such that the necessity of removal of the lizard to avoid the contamination of the water is contrasted with the risk of breaking the pot:

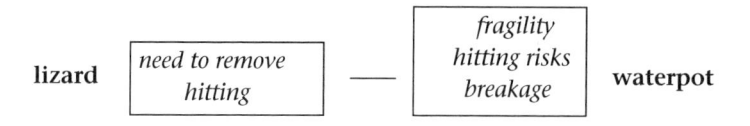

| lizard | need to remove hitting | — | fragility hitting risks breakage | waterpot |

By the process of following the directions provided by the latter part of the proverb certain potential features of the image are discarded and others are selected to be placed in a series of contrasting relationships. Colour is no longer relevant, heat and coolness are not relevant (at least in the conventional interpretation of this proverb), animate or inanimate are not relevant, and other potentially interpretable features have been left behind. What has been retained is the set of abstractions that are summarized as

potential contamination versus necessary purity = risk
acceptance of risk entails danger of loss
removal of risk entails danger of loss

It is at the level of abstracted features of a general nature, namely 'in a situation of risk and where there are two alternative courses of actions, either may equally lead to disaster', that the idea as a generality can be inserted into the world of moral discourse. The image itself of that rather attractive lizard sunning itself on the top of a large, shapely earthenware waterpot on a hot afternoon in the dry season contains no element of moral discourse until the process of generalization has been gone through in the mind of the human subject. And that process is not a unique one in the single mind of that single observer, it is repeated again and again across the collectivity of people who understand and use that proverb to discuss the moral conundrum that occurs again and again when people find themselves caught between the devil and the deep blue sea.

Whether it is from a bird in the hand or a stitch in time or, as Joel Sherzer reports from Texas (Sherzer 2002: 59), the fact that the skunk can't tell the buzzard he stinks, generalization of this kind entails insertion into the world of moral discourse and thus into the world of persuasion and rhetoric.

In contrast to the unidirectional process of moving from concrete features of an image to abstract characteristics that are amenable to general moral interpretation, the world of riddles (and some joking) deploys similar processes, but eschews the layer of moral interpretation by a process of re-concretization to find the parallel that is the answer. One brief illustration will perhaps suffice.

There is a riddle in Hausa (most Hausa riddles come as statements) that goes,

> Shanuna dubu madaurinsu daya
>
> My cattle are a thousand (but) their tethering rope is one

Recognized as a riddle, the person who is the 'riddlee' has to find another concrete circumstance which could be appropriately considered to display the same set of abstracted characteristics that have been taken from this image. Thus, the process is initially the same as we saw above. First, a series of features of the image have to be established and certain of them selected as abstractions, not for the purpose of generalization and insertion into another discourse, but for matching against abstractions appropriate to another image, 'the answer'. Cattle are animate, produce milk and meat that is food, provide hides for leatherworking, are usually brown/black/white, travel in herds, are cared for by people, constitute wealth and can be sold, are usually tethered individually, etc. The tethering rope has a similar range of potentially interpretable characteristics, but the riddle points to an opposition which in itself constitutes a question or a puzzle, a thousand versus one, reinforced by the notion of a thousand moving objects held by just one item. How can that be? asks the riddle.

The task of the riddlee is to find another alien image that displays characteristics derived from the original image. It is this re-concretization of the abstracted features that distinguishes the riddle from the proverb and removes it from the process of insertion into moral discourse as we have discussed above. So what is the answer to this riddle? As a conventional element within Hausa culture, there can be only one answer that is right; while I might be able to imagine a variety of other contexts in which features from this image had parallels, they would only be at best good guesses, they are not the 'right' answer. The right answer is 'tsintsiya', a broom. Not a broom with a wooden handle and a block of bristles, but a broom which is a bundle of parallel reeds or switches tied up with a retaining string around the bundle at the end where it is held in the hand. Why is it the right answer? Because the elements in the image of the cattle which are significant are the following, and only the following: cattle line up in parallel as they move through the bush, they form a group some side by side, some following on, they can be controlled by one herdsman, and the group are tethered together. Abstracted from these features are the characteristics that are re-applied to the broom: similar items – lying parallel – constituting a group – linked together – controlled by man. Here we see a process,

Concrete features – abstraction – re-concretization by analogy

Compared with the process in proverbs,

Concrete features – abstraction – generalization into moral discourse

In this discussion the issue is the link between processes of 'universalization', as illustrated here through the discussion of proverbial discourse, and an insertion into a world of moral discourse which in the next chapter we will pursue as an ideological process.

Again, Habermas has addressed the issue, but specifically in relation to the articulation of moral norms in discourse:

> In theoretical discourse the gap between particular observations and general hypotheses is bridged by some canon or other of induction. An analogous bridging principle is needed for practical discourse. Accordingly, all studies of the logic of moral argumentation end up having to introduce a moral principle as a rule of argumentation that has a function equivalent to the principle of induction in the discourse of the empirical sciences. (Habermas 1990: 63–5)

Generalization is intimately connected with both the process of typification inherent in the text and the epistemological status of the propositions put forward within the 'text'. Habermas's discussion focuses upon the status of the expressed norms and principles that are the subject of the process of generalization. Persuasive discourse may deploy such norms or principles either overtly or indirectly. Thus, when I attempt to persuade you to lend me your book I may overtly or covertly draw in issues of equality and reciprocity, of generosity, or of charity. Perelman (1969: 26–31) looks to distinguish between persuading and convincing. In the one case – convincing – the recourse to generalized norms and principles is combined with the 'rational character of adherence to an argument' (Perelman and Olbrechts-Tyteca 1969: 27), while persuading is a more encompassing notion that implies a tendency towards action in the light of a consideration of potential range of arguments, 'to the person concerned with results, persuading surpasses convincing, since conviction is merely the first stage in progression toward action' (Perelman and Olbrechts-Tyteca 1969: 27).

Audiences and publics

The notion of public has, of course, a whole other dimension to it in addition to the private–public dichotomy discussed above. Central to any consideration of orality as a mode of communication is the notion of audience, the assembly of participants present at the moment of the utterance, whether addressee(s) or hearer(s), who may also figure as referent or actor in the dialogic process in which the utterance is embedded. The notion of a 'public' carries broader implications that posit a continuity and an identification that goes beyond the temporary participative criteria that define an audience. When an entertainer talks of his or her 'public', the construct is built around all those who have, on different occasions, seen and adored. They might identify themselves as fans if they were asked, and could only be identified by others from their pattern of participation. They may be firmly convinced that there are millions more of them 'out there' and the entertainer may be able to point to the burgeoning postbag as an indicator, but the process of defining and determining the presentation of entertainer to 'public' is undertaken within the heads of the entertainer him- or herself, and of their publicity and marketing agents. In the same way, a radio station may have a postbag and a set of telephone lines from which the management gauges the strength and nature of its 'public'. Those sources may be able to confirm that the construct of 'target audience', chosen by the management in determining the nature of the programming, conforms with a 'real' audience. But, of course, that public is not able to identify itself as a bounded collectivity as an audience can. Nevertheless, action co-ordinated by the radio station may produce widespread public effects, as can be seen in the widespread participation in charity events, or with malign/beneficial effect in the mobilization of violence/resistance. The notion of an entity that lasts beyond the moment of performance, a collectivity of all those who repeatedly participate in audiences, is an important construct for the 'speaker', but is equally significant in the world of literate communication. The readership of the written word is an important construct, and my remarks here are not intended to convey ideas that are exclusive to oral forms of communication. Important because the presence of the 'public' is manifest in the message itself. When I say, 'John, I wanted to catch you before you go out, there is something I want to talk about', the addressee is present in the text. When the radio DJ of the 1960s says, 'Hi there, guys and gals!' he has a mental picture of the adolescents and young adults that he thinks he is addressing, no matter that it is quite possible that all his actual listeners are pensioners. Not only does the market research industry have its categories of people within society, and consciously look to manage the establishment of overt communicative signals to those categories within the nature of the communication, but the manifestations of mental maps in speech are everywhere: from the s/he pronouns in English, to the presumption in the political speech that there are critics in amongst the supporters in the audience and each category of position needs both acknowledgement and a specifically tailored message. The manifestations can be to varying degrees overt or covert, and can be more or less general or specific in their definitions. The text determines the elements that go to make up the public. If I say, 'We should build a school here if we have the money' then my main and conditional clause pattern posits not only that there will be an audience that will agree on the need for a school, but also that within that audience there will be a subset who will say 'We can't afford it!' My purported audience may be seen to be a personification of the most general category, 'the man on the Clapham omnibus' or 'Joe Public', or may be highly specific and exclusive, 'the people of this village say no to further development!' In this respect, then, the notion of public, as it is manifested in the communication itself, is intimately bound up with the patterning of the text of the communication in terms of the presence of alternative subject voices and alternative representations of the second and third persons. Not only 'who am I, speaking here?' but also 'you' and 'they'. For in representing who 'we' are and establishing a notion of who 'you' are, it is overwhelmingly the case that the definitional process involves contrastive representation of 'that lot over there!' Perelman sets out the issue and cites a description by Sterne of the ways in which a speaker constructs 'factions' of an audience by changes in the presentation of self:

> An orator does not have to be confronted with several organized factions to think of the composite nature of his audience. He is justified in visualizing each one of his listeners as simultaneously belonging to a number of disparate groups. Even when an orator stands before only a few auditors, or indeed, before a single auditor, it is possible that he will not be quite sure what arguments will appear most convincing to his audience. In such a case, he will, by a kind of fiction,

insert his audience into a series of different audiences. In *Tristram Shandy* ... Tristram describes an argument between his parents, in which his father wants to persuade his mother to have a midwife:

> He ... placed his arguments in all lights; argued the matter with her like a Christian, like a heathen, like a husband, like a father, like a patriot, like a man. My mother answered everything only like a woman, which was a little hard upon her, for, as she could not assume and fight it out behind such a variety of characters, 'twas no match: 'twas seven to one. (Sterne, *The Life and Opinions of Tristram Shandy*, bk. 1, ch. 18, p. 42)

Notice that it is not only the orator who so changes his mask: it is even more so his audience – his poor wife in this case – which his fancy transforms, as he seeks its most vulnerable point. However, as it is the speaker who takes the initiative in this 'breaking down' of the audience, it is to him that the terms 'like a Christian', 'like a heathen', and so on, are applied.

When a speaker stands before his audience, he can try to locate it in its social setting. He may ask himself if all the members fall within a single social group, or if he must spread his listeners over a number of different – perhaps even opposed – groups. If division is necessary, several ways of proceeding are always possible: he may divide his audience ideally in terms of the social groups – political, occupational, religious, for example – to which the individual members belong, or in terms of the values to which certain members of the audience adhere. These ideal divisions are not mutually independent; they can, however, lead to the formation of very different partial audiences. The breaking down of a gathering into sub-groups will also depend on the speaker's own position. If he holds extremist views on a question, there is nothing to restrain him from considering all his interlocutors as forming a single audience. On the other hand, if he holds a moderate view, he will see them as forming at least two distinct audiences.

Knowledge of an audience cannot be conceived independently of the knowledge of how to influence it. (Perelman and Olbrechts-Tyteca 1969: 22–3)

The constitution of an audience is thus a combination of the self-perceptions of those listening working in conjunction with the ability of the speaker to allocate identification to a 'virtual' audience, that which is constituted through the words and actions of the speaker, through address and reference. The construction of identities for audiences and the placing of the speaker in relation to those identities has profound implications for the broader political processes we will address in the next chapter. In commenting upon his study of speech play and verbal art around the world, Joel Sherzer (2002: 155) refers to such verbal art as expressions of social, cultural and personal identity and consciousness appreciated both for the 'sheer pleasure and creativity of play' and understood as the tools of resistance to threats and pressures,

> Speech play and verbal art emerge out of the heteroglossic and cultural diversity of the worlds we live in, out of the intertextual gaps that occur when languages, styles, genres, and cultures are in contact. They contribute to the imagined community and the invention of tradition, and they create and construct social and cultural identity. They express the political unconscious – but also the social, cultural, linguistic, individual and political unconscious and conscious of real people in real situations. They are forms of cultural resistance, ways minority groups deal with majority groups, and weapons of the weak as well as of the strong. (Sherzer 2002: 154)

Audience cultures

Different societies will have their own 'audience cultures' that relate to the way in which audiences tend to behave and, indeed, how speakers interact with audiences. In the Introduction, the case of the trial of Chief Standing Bear of the Poncas was discussed at some length in order to point to the central issue of the power of the oral communicative moment to change, in some cases, even the tide of human history! An assumption behind that discussion was that, in spite of the problems of cultural and literal translation that were involved in that moment of speaking before the court, nevertheless, a potential receptivity is inherent in any group of people towards basic human experience as articulated by Chief Standing Bear faced with his promise to his dying son. Yet the effectiveness of rhetorical force, or indeed attitudes to public speaking, are also themselves embedded in differing sociocultural norms. An audience culture may be predicated upon the rousing rhythms of the mixture of singing, call and response interactions between speaker and audience, or may be an individuated culture in which it is rare for large groups to come together, let alone for an interactive style of rhetoric to be the norm. Where a 'congregationalist' culture is very used to gatherings, whether religious or political, that involve participation and action by the audience, commonly call and response, then the salience of the congruence of the features discussed in this book are more often and more clearly apparent. A more 'reserved' cultural style may still have mechanisms for the articulation of commonly-held views and beliefs but by other means. In comparing the public presence of, for example, Mahatma Gandhi and Martin Luther King, there are apparent differences that relate both to the rhetorical traditions within which they were brought up and to the nature of their personalities and propensities. Anyone who has heard the speeches of Martin Luther King, such as are still available in recorded form, will recognize the rhetorical features that lay behind such powerful words. 'I have a dream ... ' has a patterning and cadence and a recursive structure that is both rhythmic and compelling. The African-American traditions of religious preaching, of church services, and of interleaving speech, chant and song are clearly audible in his language. It is that particular cultural background which potentiates the kind of effect that transcends one culture and is both comprehensible and powerful in another. Listening to a recording of the church leader, Charles D. Beck, and his congregation at the Church of God in Christ at Buffalo, New York during the night of 30–1 December 1956 (Beck 1957), or the French musicologist Herbert Pepper's recording of the Christmas Day service in a church in Harlem, New York, the cadences, the 'shout' tradition, the call and response, give a style to the event and the language of the preacher that have since become familiar in the moral and philosophical oratory that characterized Martin Luther King's civil rights message. Mahatma Gandhi was an equally significant leader with a message equally as powerful. Yet Gandhi was never considered to have the oratorical power or effectiveness that so characterized Martin Luther King. On the one hand, Gandhi, even though he would address sometimes vast crowds, was very downbeat in his style:

> Bombay had the largest industrial proletariat in the country, and much of the crowd was made up of workers. They hung on to every word. It was fascinating to feel the rapport between Gandhi and this massive audience. He resorted to no soaring oratory; of that he was incapable. He never raised his voice. But somehow, by the mystery of communication, his simple words got through to his listeners. They heard him out silently, and when he had finished, they broke into a roar of applause that seemed to reverberate far through the city. (Shirer 1981: 138)

William Shirer, who observed Gandhi closely while working as a journalist, drew a specific comparison with the orchestrated mass rallies of the Nazi Party and Hitler's oratory, which he had also observed, 'The Germans I saw in the Nazi time were deeply moved by the masterful oratory of Hitler. Gandhi was not an orator. He scarcely raised his voice and made no gestures. I doubt if the vast majority in the huge crowds I saw ever caught his words' (p. 76). Gandhi himself writes of his painful shyness in his early years. While in England to study he was elected to the Executive Committee of the Vegetarian Society and was upbraided for never saying anything in meetings; in a debate his prepared speech was read out by another. On the eve of his departure for home he invited vegetarian friends to dinner at a Holborn restaurant and was struck dumb when the time came for him to say a few words:

> When my turn for speaking came, I stood up to make a speech. I had with great care thought out one which would consist of a very few sentences ... My memory entirely failed me and in attempting a humorous speech I made myself ridiculous ... It was only in South Africa that I got over this shyness, though I never completely overcame it. (Gandhi 1982 [1927]: 71–2)

In commenting upon Shirer's remarks about Gandhi's apparent lack of oratorical skills David Arnold points to an aspect of the relationship between Gandhi and the crowds who came to see him, that it was their reverence for his presence, the physical sight of him, that was as significant as his spoken words. Referring to the situation in 1930, he wrote:

> Gandhi's personal reputation had never been higher, though something of his millenarian aura had dissipated since the high expectations of his semi-divine or magical powers at Champaran in 1917 or on his visit to Gorakhpur in 1921. His popularity remained nonetheless enormous and the march to Dandi and breaking of the salt laws had deeply stirred the public's imagination. Many thousands of people turned out to hear, or at least see, him. (Arnold 2001: 149)

Where Gandhi's natural shyness militated against his emergence as a fiery orator, the culture of his audiences was also one in which the physical presence of someone perceived to be a man of God was the key element inspiring devotion and attracting people to him. I would venture to suggest also that the comparative lack of a congregational tradition in Indian society, as compared with the culturally central and repeated presence of 'congregational' activity in our comparator here, African-American tradition in the US, is a factor both in the styles of these very different speakers and in the nature of the relationships between them and their audiences. Martin Luther King was able to call upon his audience, exhort his audience, and his audience would respond as he spoke because that was a familiar style from long practice, whereas Mahatma Gandhi explained, set out his criticisms, put forward his case as he would in a courtroom, and indeed had done on many occasions in a courtroom. Shirer writes of a moving courtroom speech from a man who was 'not an orator':

> In March 1922 ... Gandhi had been tried and convicted of sedition after one of the strangest and most eloquent pleas ever made in a courtroom – not in self-defense, for he pleaded guilty, but in defense of the right of India to be free – and sentenced to six years in prison. The trial and what Gandhi said at it launched him on the road he had followed to this day. His moving speech to the court constituted the most devastating indictment of British rule – and misrule – in India that had yet been heard in the land. (Shirer 1981: 82)

From the massed, regimented, and organized ranks of the audiences at the Nuremberg rallies, to the unorganized, disorderly, milling but huge crowds that came to see Mahatma Gandhi a whole variety of modes of 'audience' are constituted by the different cultures of speaking and listening across the world, audiences some large some small. But in all cases the traditions of speaking and listening combine with the specific skills and personalities of speakers to engender more or less effective persuasion and action, the subject of the next chapter.

Concluding remarks

In this chapter we have considered aspects of the insertion of the oral communicative moment into its immediate social context. The utterance is embedded within a speech event and such events fall within categories that are constructed and maintained by different cultures in different ways. Certain categories of event may be closely, or even exclusively, linked to particular speech styles or genres of speech, and particular groups within society may control or dispute the rights to certain genres. Continuums of greater or lesser fixity characterize the links between genre and event, the expectations of creativity or faithful reproduction within the 'tradition' of a speech genre, and the assignment of roles to people in relation to the speech event itself. In the case of the assignment of roles, one end of the continuum involves permanent and immutable assignment of the role to particular individuals; at the other end, roles may circulate between speakers emerging from and returning to the audience. The audience may be physically present and be conscious of common experience, or may be extended to include a range of hearers out of response range. Whichever they are, the speaker may construct, within the framework of the utterance, representations of who they are and how they relate to each other.

The oral communicative moment is also the occasion for the emergence of public knowledge, a transition from the private to the public, making the utterance available for others to consider and respond to, either to dispute or to constitute a basis for a collective awareness of consensus or agreement and thus insertion into the world of moral discourse and the process of persuasion. The private–public dichotomy, and transition between the two conditions, can mark very different modes of effectiveness. The public articulation of a 'private' knowledge, even if everyone already knows the 'private' information, may demand changes in social relations as when wrongdoing is publicly admitted and resignation follows, or when a hurtful remark once made cannot be withdrawn – it can only be compensated for. The public iteration of certain words may be an act that creates a new condition, as when a leader declares war or when a baby is baptized. A transition from private to public may be bounded by insertion into public genres of speech and may also constitute the transition from the 'amateur' to the commercial, and the commodification of language in commercial music, art and performance. And lastly, different cultures will display different audience cultures in the sense that expectations and conventions will vary about appropriate styles in the execution of the speech act.

4
Ideology and Orality

What ideology?

By what means, then, do ongoing power structures themselves influence their own legitimacy, or condition their own processes of legitimation? Two quite different accounts of this can be given. The first account concentrates on the *activity of the powerful* in influencing the beliefs of the subordinate, through their preferential access to the means of cultural development and the dissemination of ideas within society. In other words, among the powers any dominant group possesses will be the ability to influence the beliefs of others; and among the most important of such beliefs will be those that relate to the justification of their own power. The origin of such beliefs may be found in the first instance in the need of the powerful for self-justification; but their privileged access to the means of culture and ideological dissemination ensures that their ideas become widespread throughout society, whether as the result of conscious policy or not ... The above account is of course the familiar Marxist theory of ideology, which Marxists employ in the context of class relations. (Beetham 1991: 104)

The discussion of relations between social classes has, for Marxists at least, led to extensive theorizing of the notion that the ideas and beliefs that underpin the political and economic interests of the ruling class are transmitted to and adopted by subordinate classes, in many societies and at many times. This use of the term 'ideology' has many broad implications within political theory. However the discussion in this volume will use the term 'ideology' in a very much more restricted sense – focusing upon the dynamics of the articulation of values and viewpoints, whether those values and viewpoints represent the interests of one individual or can be viewed as belonging to a group or a whole class in society. In this sense, therefore, the present discussion is more about ideological processes than a broad class-related political science concept of 'ideology'. Nevertheless, at the heart of any discussion of ideology lies the problematic issue of individual and group. You or I may articulate sets of ideas in all sorts of contexts, but it is only when someone else listens and takes on those ideas themselves that we can think of the inception of a new 'ideology'. Yet the necessary link between ideology and group is underpinned by the fact that it is always individuals who articulate ideas to other individuals. A necessary precursor to a common recitation of a creed articulating not only your and my beliefs, but also the beliefs of all the others who wear the badge and stand with us, is the moment when I, as individual, listened to you and understood and accepted, and it surely doesn't matter whether you are my brother, a religious preacher, or the notional collectivity of the people who work for an advertising agency. Part of the articulation may, of course, rely upon the notion that the ideas are shared and venerated by ancestors, wise ones, decent people, democrats or divine beings, but it is individuals in the here and now who are making that articulation. Beetham, as political scientist, expresses the centrality of the ideological process in the following way:

> ... any explanation for the beliefs held by subordinate groups which confines itself to the processes of influence controlled by the powerful is open to a number of objections. Not only do the powerful not influence, let alone control, all the means of disseminating and reproducing ideas in any society; but even if they did, this could not of itself guarantee the acceptance of their ideas or justifications by others ...
> ... as much contemporary research indicates, people are never merely the passive recipients of ideas or messages to which they are exposed ... They are more like a sieve than a sponge. That is to say, they tend to be selective, assessing ideas and information in the light of their existing assumptions, and against their lived experience ... The power of ideas, unlike other forms of power, cannot be measured in terms of the *means* of power available to those who control their dissemination, but rather in terms of their credibility to the recipient. Any explanation for the ideas or beliefs that people hold, therefore, must be based upon an internal analysis of their plausibility or credibility to them in the context in which they are situated, rather than simply on an account of their means of dissemination. If all the

power of the medium cannot ensure the credibility of the message, we need to understand what makes some messages more credible than others. (Beetham 1991: 105–6)

The issue of plausibility and credibility, and more generally the process of persuasion, is central to the current discussion. Ideology has more recently come to be used in a way that moves away from the macropolitical focus upon class relations and ruling class cultural hegemony and turns instead to the questions of ideological discourse and its relation to cognition and society. Teun van Dijk (1998) foregrounds what Beetham calls the 'appearance of the socially constructed as natural' (Beetham 1991: 107) in saying that ideologies form 'the "axiomatic" basis of the shared social representations of a group and its members' (Van Dijk 1998: 126) and puts the link between group and ideology at the heart of his definition, focusing upon an ideology as a set of factual and evaluative beliefs, 'ideologies may be defined as the *basis of the social representations shared by members of a group*. This means that ideologies allow people, as group members, to organize the multitude of social beliefs about what is the case, good or bad, right or wrong, *for them*, and to act accordingly' (author's emphasis) (Van Dijk 1998: 8). For Van Dijk the link between the individual and the group is the 'mental model' where the interface between the two occurs through the presence in personal and 'episodic' memory of narratives, derived from others and from experience, that form the input into text and talk. Such individual articulations mesh with what he terms 'social beliefs', that is to say, general knowledge and abstractions that are shared with others:

> (models) ... not only consist of purely personal and individual beliefs, but also of situated instances of social beliefs. Thus, when being involved in a car accident we not only know about our personal experiences, or about the colour or the make of our car, and the unique circumstances of this accident, but in order to construct the model, we also need socially shared knowledge about cars, accidents, roads, and so forth, in general. (Van Dijk 1998: 84)

Integral to the individual and social dimensions of this mental modelling is the articulation of evaluative beliefs:

> Evaluative beliefs may instantiate socially shared beliefs, that is attitudes, for instance about car accidents, traffic or civil wars. The same processes of activation, instantiation and adaptation are at

work here, and again in both directions – personal opinions may be seen to be shared by others, and thus are generalized as social beliefs and attitudes. The acquisition and change of social representations may be similarly based on the generalization and abstraction of opinions in personal models. (Van Dijk 1998: 85)

In concentrating upon the discursive dimensions of ideology and ideological processes Van Dijk has moved on from the more classical socioeconomic approaches which could only be formulated 'in very general, abstract and often vague terms' towards a set of approaches and a theoretical framework that can examine the details of 'ideology in practice'. As he puts it, 'ideologies empirically only "show" in social interaction and discourse, as well as in their organizational and institutional structures, and hence they need to be empirically studied at those levels' (Van Dijk 1998: 319). The current discussion is pursued with such a view of 'ideology' in mind.

Truth and values

There is a particular genre of Hausa literature, called *waka*, which is a general term for, roughly speaking, rhythmically patterned language, as opposed to language which is not so patterned – prose, roughly speaking. Within the genre called *waka*, a distinction is usually drawn between instrumentally accompanied 'song' and an unaccompanied form 'poetry/verse'. I spent some time researching the latter of these two forms in particular. Such 'poetry' was usually orally performed in a chant-like style, and some of the salient features of its auditory manifestation were a number of rhythmical metrical patterns and a series of rhyme schemes. While oral performance was common, such poetry was usually composed in writing, in either the Arabic or the Roman script, and circulated in parts of northern Nigeria also in manuscript or printed form. I was particularly interested in the aesthetics of this art form. From the texts of poems printed in the main Hausa language newspaper and elsewhere since the 1930s, I could see the elements of form and structure, style and use of language that went to make up the genre. My further interest lay in how these features were perceived, what made for a good poem? I talked to poets, and I witnessed discussion among a circle of poets who met regularly to discuss their work in the early 1970s. At one point I had the opportunity to talk to one of the first writers of imaginative prose in Hausa, a man who was well known from the 1940s onwards in northern Nigeria and who had been the first Hausa editor of the main newspaper. He was the man who had selected poetry to publish in the newspaper. He was an accomplished writer and an important public figure in his own right. His name was Abubakar Imam and he was kind enough to grant me an interview.

After the usual round of cordial greetings, pleasantries and banter which makes so much social interaction in Nigeria so very enjoyable we got down to business. I began to ask Abubakar Imam about the characteristics that would make a poem publishable and interesting. I ran through the issues of consistency and recognizability of metrical pattern, the various styles of writing, the effect of the absence of voice and melody in the printed recension, and a whole host of matters concerning form and aesthetics. As the interview progressed, it became apparent that Abubakar Imam found the direction of my questioning more than a little tedious. It was clear that he was aware of the elements of textuality and patterning upon which I laid such emphasis, and, of course, he would not publish a poem that was essentially incompetent, but I was clearly missing the point. After a period of increasing discomfort he eventually brought the interview to an end with the concluding statement that 'the only real issue as far as I am concerned is whether what the poet says is the truth, the real truth!' I withdrew to lick my wounds.

Upon reflection, I was not sure what to make of his parting remark. Truth value hadn't been part of my aesthetic. Was truth value the summation of the convergence of form and content? Was this a matter of surface and centre, or periphery and core – was he meaning that 'underneath' the surface elements of form, the deceitful manifestations of style and rhetoric, there had to lie a fundamental element of truth and value? Or was it that a litmus test of truth value in the content of a poem, if failed, would obviate any appreciation of form and style? And whose truth was it anyway?

Clearly, however, Abubakar Imam was most directly drawing my attention to an omission in my conspectus of issues. If he were representing the general listenership for poetry then he was pointing to a fuller set of expectations that any practised audience brings to the experience of hearing or reading poetry. While that fuller set may well contain issues of rhyme and metre among other things, a core element was an assessment of 'truth value'. And, as far as I was concerned, the determination, by an individual, of the truth of any particular statement was beyond my frame of reference, I was more concerned with how the notion of 'truth-value' was deployed. I could certainly see a way to ask what the considerations were that went into determining that a particular poem 'spoke the truth' as against those elements that would lead to a judgement that a poem 'was nonsense', rather than trying to determine the validity of any claim to truth itself.

In considering what might lead Abubakar Imam to determine that a particular poem spoke 'the truth' there thus opened up a myriad potential directions to follow. What were the circumstances of his upbringing, what class within society did he come from? What was the influence of his western education, his Islamic faith, his membership of a northern elite, his membership of a conservative political party of the period? He was a man of great wit and humour, a Hausa cultural nationalist and someone who had quarrelled with local British administrators during the colonial period. Was I going to have to go back and try and explore the relationship between his assessments of 'truth-value' in particular poems and all these potential issues that surrounded him as audience member, critic and publisher?

An even more pressing issue was the nature of what he meant by 'truth'. One of the cardinal characteristics of the genre of Hausa poetry is that it has been, in the main, highly didactic. Born in the Islamic reform movement of the early years of the nineteenth century, written poetry was a primary medium through which the leaders of the 'struggle' (*Jihad*) had propagated the moral imperatives and religious practices of reformed Islam. Condemnation, exhortation, vilification, laudation – all these were integral to the genre itself as it developed through the nineteenth and into the twentieth century. Was Abubakar Imam implying that a sine qua non of a good poem was the presence of a moral, a message, an imperative? Could a pastoral idyll or an *angstvoll* introspection aspire to 'truth'? (Not that such a thing existed in Hausa poetry.) More likely, he was implying also that the message had to be the right one, that corruption should be eschewed and obedience to parents should be sacrosanct. In pointing to the moral foundation of the text itself, as well as the 'surface' elements of its particular didactic injunctions, Imam was echoing a notion that one of the primary engagements of the listener/viewer/reader in all art is with the moral categories that are deployed within it. This would chime with the line of thinking outlined by Antonio Gramsci in one of his prison notebooks,

> One will have to establish properly what is to be understood by the term 'interesting' in art in general and in narrative literature and the theatre in particular. The nature of what is 'interesting' changes according to individuals or social groups or the crowd in general: it is therefore an element of culture, not of art ... But is it therefore completely extraneous to art, completely separate from it? In any case art itself is

interesting, and interesting for its own sake, in that it satisfies a requirement of life. Besides this more intimate characteristic of art, that of being interesting for its own sake, what other elements of 'interest' can a work present, for example a novel or a poem or a play? ... The most stable element of 'interest' is undoubtedly the 'moral' one, both positive and negative, for and against. What is 'stable' here is the 'moral category', not a concrete moral content. Intimately linked to this is the 'technical' element, in the particular sense of a means of conveying the moral content, the moral conflict of the novel, poem or play in the most immediate and dramatic way. Thus, in drama we have the *coup de théâtre*, in the novel the dominant 'intrigue', etc. Not all of these elements are necessarily 'artistic', yet neither are they necessarily non-artistic. From the artistic point of view they are in a sense 'indifferent', that is, extra-artistic. They are facts of the history of culture and must be evaluated in this light. (Gramsci 1985: 346–7)

My chase after the 'technical' elements, and the assumption that they contribute to that which makes for the 'artistic' as determinants of the good poem, had clearly got under the skin of Abubakar Imam as they would have done to Antonio Gramsci.

But truth is recognized beyond the orbit of codes and moral precepts. A primary element in Imam's response was the intimation of 'awareness' inherent in the notion of the 'real'. The experience of 'recognition', an acknowledgement that the 'text' has been a party to a process of inducing a perception, an awareness, is wrapped up in the notion of a 'real truth'. Imam appeared to imply that the characterization, the picture of an event, a person, a situation, either accords with an existing understanding perceived to be 'true', or indeed creates a representation that articulates something that has been hitherto half-formed, dimly perceived and disparately represented. 'Ah, now I see!' is the response to the crystallization of a 'complete' image. Or again, and significantly, the articulation may mesh with other texts, other representations not built upon the listener's own experience but upon the oft-articulated perceptions of others – truth may be inherent in the degree of 'fit' with other representations. Truth as the product of the ability of art to change and create awareness is a well trodden path. As my erstwhile colleague, Angus Graham, Professor of Classical Chinese, once put it,

> To do more than amuse, the work will have to enlarge awareness of one's world and of oneself, which is to tell the truth in one or other of the specialized senses in which the word 'truth' is applied to the

arts. In the first place there is the truth to oneself, the sense specified by 'sincerity' and 'authenticity', words which commend self-awareness and warn against self-deception ... At the level of sensation, the arts break down the habit of noticing only the practically relevant, and restore the plenitude of the response when the senses are open to what normally eludes them. The value of the vivid and distinct image in poetry derives from the sharpening of awareness, not from its accuracy alone, which is why, however accurate it may be, becoming a cliché erodes the effect. As for 'truth to life', 'truth to nature', whether a novel or drama illuminates the constants of human nature or the detail of contemporary trends, it does so not by telling new facts, but by forcing us to imagine concretely situations we know only in the abstract, or to see all sides of an issue which involves us personally. (Graham 1985: 69)

The thrust of Graham's work is to explore the relation between awareness and the 'moral category' in the context of free will and responsibility, but the focus here is upon the processes involved in 'making aware' – the establishment and perception of notions of 'truth', since, as Imam is pointing out, making aware is as integral to the ethics of the text as it is to its aesthetics.

'Truth value' as manifest in 'making aware' would appear to have been an issue for Imam in making decisions about the publication of poetry in the newspaper he edited. The very boundedness and formal structuring provided by the surrounding 'technical' elements create an entity which can be assessed and measured in its capacity so to do. Yet the 'text in action' in this way, regardless of whether it is a highly formalized genre such as Hausa poetry or a much more fluid and hybrid activity such as jokes or advertising, brings together the moment of becoming aware with the evanescence of the speech event such that 'I realize, I understand, I agree (potentially)' merge into a single indivisible moment.

Setting aside the issue of the psychology of denial and how that may affect the perception of 'truth', it is usually the case that a recognition of 'truth' value leads to acceptance, agreement, concurrence. It was Abubakar Imam's acceptance of 'truth' that led him, by his own account, to publish; he was, at least to some degree, 'in agreement'. The branch of knowledge that has studied and taught the skills of persuasion, has been 'rhetoric' – and *persuasion* as a communicative process between actors in a speech event was achieved through *eloquence* – a quality inhering in language and its performance. The many devices, figures, oratorical techniques were described, named and taught in the schools of rhetoric of the ancient and medieval worlds. The rejection of the rhetoric of oral poets by Plato was a reaction to the overblown, convoluted, formulaic edifices produced by the sophists. Eloquence became in itself suspicious, the sweet-talking of liars and flatterers. As the Italian philosopher and critic Benedetto Croce eloquently put it:

> It will not be superfluous to observe that the meaning given in modern times to the word Rhetoric, namely, the doctrine of ornate form, differs from that which it had for the ancients. Rhetoric in the modern sense is above all a theory of elocution, while elocution ... was but one portion, and not the principal one, of ancient Rhetoric. Taken as a whole, it consisted strictly of a manual or *vade-mecum* for advocates and politicians; it concerned itself with the two or three 'styles' (judicial, deliberative, demonstrative), and gave advice or furnished models to those striving to produce certain effects by means of speech. No definition of the art is more accurate than that given by its inventors the earliest Sicilian rhetoricians, scholars of Empedocles (Corax, Tisias, Gorgias): Rhetoric is the creator of persuasion ... It devoted itself to showing the method of using language so as to create a certain belief, a certain state of mind, in the hearer; hence the phrase 'making the weaker case stronger' ...; the 'increase or diminution according to circumstances' ...; the advice of Gorgias to 'turn a thing to jest if the adversary takes it seriously, or to a serious matter if he takes it as a jest', and many similar well-known maxims. He who acts in this manner is not only aesthetically accomplished, as saying beautifully that which he wishes to say; he is also and especially a practical man with a practical end in view. As a practical man, however, he cannot evade moral responsibility for his actions; this point was fastened upon by Plato's polemic against Rhetoric, that is to say against fluent political charlatans and unscrupulous lawyers and journalists. Plato was quite right to condemn Rhetoric (when dissociated from a good purpose) as blameworthy and discreditable, directed to arouse the passions, a diet ruinous to health, a paint disastrous to beauty. (Croce 1953: 423)

Ideology in process: typification and evaluation

Time and again the process of persuasion marries two complementary dimensions of the text within the norms and expectations of the genre, requiring from the listener complementary dimensions of response: on the one hand the speaker sets out for the listener a characterization of the events, the people, the circumstances, that go together to make up the topic of the utterance. The audience is invited to recognize and acknowledge that picture and, in the process of 'becoming aware', recognize the 'truth' of that representation. The second dimension is the evaluative overlay bound up in the characterization and in the evaluatory language that accompanies each representation. Each genre will be embedded in a set of evaluatory expectations about how to interpret any particular characterization it contains. As soon as you recognize a particular form of verbal delivery as marking what in your society functions as eulogy you know the positive evaluative framework within which the characterization will be framed (you may also be aware that irony may reverse the evaluative charge); the satirical song will imply deceitful cowardice in the depiction of the heroic action; the romantic narrative will require a happy ending.

An evaluative framework can be overt, covert or apparently absent, and also stated in the words or bound up in the presuppositions. 'Apparently absent' is a way to grasp the contingent nature of much evaluative interpretation. When I say to you, 'the tide comes in about every twelve hours', you will perhaps first wonder why I said it 'out of the blue' (and even wonder about my sanity), and then conclude it must be some gnomic utterance which requires metaphorical interpretation to insert it into a frame of reference predicated upon notions of the good and the bad, the things that are right with the world and the things that are wrong. It is incomprehensible not because it clashes with our experience of the external world but because there is no moral category of discourse to which it seems to belong. On the other hand, if I say to you, 'a couple were killed by a falling tree in last night's storm' you can take it not only as a statement of fact but as a terrible tragedy also – a 'very bad thing' derived not from the loaded language I have used but from the perceived nature of the event. Finally, when we hear the radio tell us that 'three terrorists assassinated a leading politician last night' the overt evaluative charge is manifest in the ideological evaluative overtones that are carried in the word 'terrorist' as against 'freedom fighter' and 'assassinated' as against 'killed'. This ideological dimension of language use (Hodge and Kress 1993) is intertwined with those parts of the utterance which convey the characterization of the subject matter. 'Awareness' is intimately bound together with value. Persuasion is the end result of both 'awareness' and the acceptance of an evaluative framework within which that 'awareness' is situated. Part of the iteration and reiteration of narrative in society is the working out and exploration of the clashes, inconsistencies and ambiguities of values, and in this context one of the handy elements in such working through is the presence of a multitude of regular characters, stereotypes (the wicked stepmother, the dutiful son, the arrogant boss, the downtrodden servant, the staunch friend, the pesky neighbour, the recalcitrant child) where the focus can be upon the inexhaustible possibilities of interaction between these characters, whether in the ubiquitous soap operas of TV or the headline characterizations of the tabloid press, let alone the oral narrative traditions of societies all around the world.

In relation to the two dimensions under discussion in oral and written literary texts, then, there are primary questions from the point of view of the listener: what is its representational validity, is there verisimilitude in its representation of the topic? Do I react by saying, 'Yes, that is what she/he/it is like!'? And secondly, is it ethically acceptable? Are there value ascriptions present and do they accord with my views? There are, clearly, a series of consequential questions: Can I accept one but not the other? Can it be 'true' if the text passes the first test, but seems to have no judgements attached? Are there judgements already formed in the listener or does the text articulate and thereby form the views of the listener? Does agreement with the first induce acceptance of the second? To consider these kinds of questions is to view texts, and oral literary texts in particular, as central to the process of ideological articulation.

Evaluative/ethical discourses

Bakhtin draws a distinction between two aspects of language that go to make up the communicative capacity of any particular utterance. On the one hand, he assigns to grammatical form and to the sentence a 'finality' and a determinability which sets it apart from other elements that go to determine composition and style, namely that which he terms the 'expressive' aspect, 'the speaker's subjective emotional evaluation of the referentially semantic content of his utterance' (Bakhtin 1986: 84). In a significant passage Bakhtin discusses the locus of this 'expressive' aspect, making it clear that he rejects the notion that the expressive aspect is inherent in the 'words and sentences', that is to say within the systematic elements of a language. Rather, it is through the surrounding intonational and contextual elements that this 'expressive' dimension is conveyed,

> Can the expressive aspect of speech be regarded as a phenomenon of *language* as a system? Can one speak of the expressive aspect of

language units, that is, words and sentences? The answer to these questions must be a categorical 'no.' Language as a system has, of course, a rich arsenal of tools – lexical, morphological, and syntactic – for expressing the speaker's emotionally evaluative position, but all these tools as language tools are absolutely neutral with respect to any particular real evaluation. The word 'darling' – which is affectionate in both the meaning of its root and its suffix – is in itself, as a language unit, just as neutral as the word 'distance'. It is only a language tool for the possible expression of an emotionally evaluative attitude towards reality, but it is not applied to any particular reality, and this application, that is, the actual evaluation, can be accomplished only by the speaker in his concrete utterance. Words belong to nobody, and in themselves they evaluate nothing. But they can serve any speaker and can be used for the most varied and directly contradictory evaluations on the part of the speakers. (Bakhtin 1986: 84–5)

Yet, although his 'no' is emphatic in its rejection of any such allocation of expressive content to 'any particular real evaluation', Bakhtin does recognize the dimension of the meaning of words and sentences that contains the potential to carry that evaluative expressive 'charge' – in his illustration he acknowledges that his chosen word, 'darling', is 'affectionate in both the meaning of its root and its suffix'. His point is that in actual usage 'darling', may be sardonic, mischievous, masking aggression, and a myriad other expressive modes in addition to its apparent base meaning. Nevertheless, it could be argued that the word is, contrary to his view, never 'neutral' and never 'just as neutral as the word "distance".' To suggest that 'words belong to nobody and in themselves they evaluate nothing' is to draw attention to the addressivity of the utterance and the relations between the people involved in any particular instance of speech; however, I would argue, that does not mean that the 'expressive' dimension of utterances is separable from the linguistic elements as Bakhtin attempts to do. Within the equipment provided to the speaker inherent in the words and the grammar of the language is a dimension of meaning that is then available and manipulable by the speaker both in play and in straight talk. To make a satiric use of 'darling' is a derivative process involving an acknowledgement that the word carries a particular positive charge of affection and pleasure. The subsequent alteration of that charge in context, becoming one element in a text/utterance that 'is enveloped in the music of the intonational-evaluative context in which it is understood and evaluated' (Bakhtin 1986: 166), is a necessarily secondary activity in the knowledge of that original charge, rather than the production of an expressive charge out of words that are intrinsically expressively 'neutral'. Bakhtin is most graphic in insisting upon this separation of the expressive element within utterances from the neutrality of elements of language in the following passage,

> The sentence as a unit of language is also neutral and in itself has no expressive aspect. It acquires this expressive aspect (more precisely, joins itself to it) only in a concrete utterance. The same aberration is possible here. A sentence like 'He died' obviously embodies a certain expressiveness, and a sentence like 'What joy!' does so to an even greater degree. But in fact we perceive sentences of this kind as entire utterances, and in a typical situation, that is, as kinds of speech genres that embody typical expression. As sentences they lack this expressiveness and are neutral. Depending upon the context of the utterance, the sentence 'He died' can also reflect a positive, joyful, even a rejoicing expression. And the sentence 'What joy!' in the context of the particular utterance can assume an ironic or bitterly sarcastic tone. (Bakhtin 1986: 85)

Bakhtin's insistence upon assigning the expressive element to the utterance in particular context brings with it particular problems. On the one hand he acknowledges that a sentence such as 'He died' *obviously* carries a 'certain expressiveness' but has to ascribe that expressiveness not to the sentence or the words themselves but to the recognition of the sentence as being typical of a speech genre that typically carries certain kinds of expressiveness. The displacement of the expressive dimension away from the sentence to the speech genre removes the dimension of evaluative/expressive meaning from the text itself as a collection of words and sentences. Expressiveness is no longer inherent in the text but in the context of utterance. Yet, the basic building-blocks of discourse are surely not 'neutral' in their expressiveness, their intrinsic specification includes expressive charge, which can then be patterned and organized in texts, reversed in charge and rhetorically deployed in a myriad ways, as Bakhtin demonstrates in the passage above. The image of neutral, inert entities becoming alive and active and thereby charged in the deployment of a speaker is one which relies upon a minimal allocation of meaning at the level of the lexeme, while contextual usage makes up the bulk of the existing and potential elements of the meaning of a word or phrase. But to understand the nature of the reversals and games that people play with language it is necessary to assign a commonality of perception that involves an agreed understanding of the expressive dimension of words, not only at the level of the utterance but at the lexically specified point of departure – the word. For example, the following sequence of sentences relies upon the interplay between the contextual, expressive dimension of intentionality in the utterance and the lexically-specified, underlying, commonly understood expressive charge of certain key words and sentences:

> Good friends, sweet friends, let me not stir you up
> To such a sudden flood of mutiny.
> They that have done this deed are honourable; –
> What private griefs they have, alas! I know not
> That made them do it; – they are wise and honourable,
> And will, no doubt, with reasons answer you.
> I come not, friends, to steal away your hearts:
> I am no orator, as Brutus is;
> But, as you know me all, a plain blunt man,
> That love my friend; and that they know full well
> That gave me public leave to speak of him.
> For I have neither wit, nor words, nor worth,
> Action, nor utterance, nor the power of speech,
> To stir men's blood: I only speak right on;
> I tell you that which you yourselves do know;
> Show you sweet Caesar's wounds, poor, poor dumb mouths,
> And bid them speak for me: but were I Brutus,
> And Brutus Antony, there were an Antony
> Would ruffle up your spirits, and put a tongue
> In every wound of Caesar, that should move
> The stones of Rome to rise and mutiny. (*Julius Caesar*, Act 3, sc. ii)

Mark Antony's edifice is built upon the ambiguities inherent in questioning whether the apparent expressive, evaluative charge of the words he is using is to be taken 'at face value' or as the opposite. In each case, it is the 'usual' meaning that is in play in this context of utterance. 'Good friends, sweet friends' directed at us, complete with its usual positive evaluative charge, appears to mean what it says, to retain in the utterance the charge it comes with, Mark Antony appears to be genuinely addressing us in the crowd as 'friends' without implication that we are the enemy. 'Mutiny', having an intrinsically negative expressive charge, would appear on the surface to be something to be avoided, a negated negative being a positive benefit. Yet, we know that Mark

Antony is playing with the reversal of 'charge' (otherwise known as irony) in his speech. As a member of the crowd we can immediately explore the possibilities: if he wishes to stir us to 'mutiny' then the ideologically negative overtones of 'mutiny' can simply be reinterpreted as the positive elements of 'resistance to injustice', another negated negative, hence positive attribute. Hence 'to not do a bad thing' becomes 'to do a good thing (resist injustice = negated negative)'. The key element underlying the alternative interpretations is the ascription of mutiny against just rule on the one hand and resistance to unjust rule on the other, and the ascription of just/unjust to the topic of the speech, the conspirators who have murdered Caesar. The bald statement that follows, with its echo running through the whole speech, is of course the classic case of the reversal of expressive/evaluative charge. The positive charge that accompanies 'honourable' is not the product of the context or the relations surrounding this utterance, it is a primary lexical feature of the word itself, a more unneutral word it would be hard to find. The fact that Mark Antony means by it its opposite is a product of the utterance working with the specifications of the item not simply a charging of a neutral term.

Being wise and honourable accords with the justifiable reasons for action (on the grounds of previous unjust actions by Caesar) that, as a sequence of positive attributes, are ascribed to the conspirators. All the evaluative terms in this particular equation are, of course, reversed in the ironical interpretation – unwise, dishonourable, unjustified, and the implication of a lack of unjust action on Caesar's part. Inherent evaluative ambiguities come to the fore in the following lines where, rather than simply re-reading the text with a reversal of polarities, the ambiguity between the positive qualities of a convincing speaker and the negative attributes of a deceiving, eloquent rogue are the topic of the speech. On the one hand, Mark Antony talks of 'not stealing away' hearts – a phrase with negative implications of deceit and theft, juxtaposed against the positive qualities of the convincing eloquent orator. The juxtaposition of himself against Brutus, combined with the available ironical reinterpretation of intended meaning – himself as truthful convincer and Brutus as deceiving rogue, is then extended with ironical metacommentary upon his own speech. Saying he is devoid of eloquence is an element within his eloquence, and is combined with an eschewal of deceitful oratorical device that, as a negated negative, reinforces the simple positives of 'plain blunt man that love my friend'. The contextual knowledge we have in hearing Mark Antony tells us to reverse the polarities of self-deprecation and of laudable sentiments addressed to the conspirators, while taking at face [value state]ments addressed to us or about himself and Caes[ar ...] through the speech and through the play. That inte[rplay,] at the level of the context, intentions and address[ees,] allows us to navigate our way through the interpr[etation.] But that process works upon the intrinsic evaluati[ve charge] with the words themselves, supplied through co[mmon usage,] through the ethical and evaluative dimensions of language.

Not all elements of language are supplied with expressive charge, nor is expressive charge immutable or unambiguous. There is a fundamental difference between the primary characteristics of a word like 'honour', in any language, with its primary ascription of evaluative charge, and a word like 'table' where evaluative overtones are, if at all, ascribed through metaphorical extension in the interpretative process of secondary meaning in a particular context: when I place my cards upon the table, the positive implication of my honesty is spread across the elements that go to make up the image, the information provided and the meeting place for the exchange, a neutral and fair arena for display. The 'table' constitutes one part of the construct that carries the charge. Familiarly, of course, the idioms of everyday usage provide an armoury of conventionally ascribed expressive charge upon standard, rather than uniquely formulated, extensions. The intrinsically uncharged 'pillar' carries the oft-repeated charged extension, as 'pillar of the community' demonstrates. Thus, it is both through conventional extension and through contextual usage that expressive charge may additionally be ascribed. But 'honour' is always a positive, as 'dishonour' is its polar opposite, regardless of whether irony reverses the charge in context. Some words, however, are intrinsically ambiguous as to their polarity, not simply ambiguous as to whether they are charged or not. And again, the ideological process that calls an action 'brave' (and therefore positive) in one context, and 'foolhardy' (hence negative) is a separate question. The issue here is the range of words which are intrinsically ambiguous: in Hausa there is a single term, 'kunya' which in some contexts has negative connotations and implies 'shameful', while in others carries the positive charge as meaning 'modesty'. The English word 'simple' may carry in one context the negative connotations of 'naïve' or 'unsophisticated', or in another may imply the positive qualities associated with 'simplicity', or 'directness', or 'clarity'. The ambiguity may be part of the strategy of the utterance in terms of forcing a judgement by the listener of intentionality, or it may simply be that the speaker envisages a perception that is framed in such a way that a harmonisation between the word and surrounding words in context of usage directs a particular charge, as it is usual for there to be an expectation on the part of the listener and the speaker that the utterance, at the level of evaluative/expressive charge, will not be internally contradictory or inconsistent. It will be 'nonsense' if the utterance is interpreted to mean that Brutus is an honourable man and in equal measure not an honourable man. As the speech unfolds, the natural tendency is, as irony is detected, to continue to interpret through the ironic lens. This does not mean, however, that the good points and the bad points of an individual, circumstance or action cannot be delineated, of course not. Part of the ideological process is precisely to draw such discriminations within the same sequence. Nevertheless, as it is not usual to describe a person as tall and short at the same time, so also at the level of expressive charge, to say someone is kind and cruel is to require the listener to assume two separate dimensions to the subject – one cruel, the other kind. To make 'sense' at the level of expressive charge, there has to be seen to be consistency of value ascription, ambiguities detected and probable interpretation provided, separate references understood for contradictory elements of evaluative charge, and overall impression gained of the speaker's view from the overall pattern of the evaluations inherent in the language as used. 'Doesn't think much of him, does she?' comes the cross-check with another listener who has just experienced the same piece of communication. 'She'd have my vote!', comes the response from the listener whose feelings have just been convincingly articulated as evaluatively charged propositions.

Frequently, the expressively charged dimension of a sequence of utterances displays inherent patterning at the level of evaluative charge. Not only does Mark Antony exploit the reversal of charge through irony, the rhetoric of his language deploys expressive charge in oft-repeated patterns. The patterns are the parallelisms of rhetoric and the evaluative charges laid within them. In the passage quoted above, two key evaluative ambiguities are turned from negative charge to positive as the text unfolds. 'Mutiny' moves from negative charge as 'revolt against that which is right' ($-(+)$) to positive 'revolt against evil deed' ($-(-)$); while 'orator' slips from negatively charged 'deceiver' to the positive 'convincer' (of the truth). Those two movements are dependent upon the question and proposition that frame the whole speech: the implicit question concerning the value to be ascribed to 'this deed', namely the killing of Caesar, is it justifiable killing ($+$) or reprehensible murder ($-$)? The proposition contains the internal contradiction that requires resolution – Mark Antony loved Caesar, and Caesar has been killed: given the first proposition, the seemingly positive charge given, at the beginning of the speech, to the second is surely contradictory. The need to perceive consistency is the key upon which the ironical perception is built, and the evaluative reading harmonized. The transitions are framed within a parallel sequence of statements, following upon the apparent seal of approval given to the deed ('they that have done this deed are honourable'):

X	Will/could convince	Y	Of the valuation of 'this deed'
I (Mark Antony)		you	
Brutus		you	
I make Caesar's wounds		you	
Brutus make Caesar's wounds		you	

The patterning of the evaluative charge in sequences of negated negatives combined with a positive charge undergoes a change as the ambiguous orator changes from 'deceiver' to 'convincer of the truth' and the negative mutiny (against that which is right) changes to positive revolt (against evil action):

Let me not stir mutiny (against the good)−(+) − (−) private griefs/reasons → + I come not to steal away (deceive) − (−) I am no orator (deceiver) − (−) I have neither wit, words, worth, action, utterance, power of speech (the tools of persuasion) − (−)	they are honourable + this deed (justifiable killing) + I am a plain, blunt man (truth teller) + that love my friend + I speak right on (the truth) +

At this point persuasion becomes not the reprehensible action of deceit, but the positive attribute of truth-telling, as Mark Antony passes *la parole* first to Caesar's wounds and then those wounds in combination with Brutus's persuasive powers that will produce the alternative sense

110 *Orality*

of mutiny, 'justified revolt against an evil deed':

| Sweet Caesar's wounds (speak the truth)
+
Brutus speak (the truth)
+ | → | mutiny (against evil deed)
−(−) |

The juxtaposition of a negated negative with a positive element is one common feature of the rhetoric of value, encountered in many areas of discourse, whether literary or not. The context of value ascriptions provides the background against which ambiguity can be exploited as we see in this passage, and the harmonization of evaluative frame can require the reconsideration of evaluative intent, as ironic or satiric, in order to create sense out of apparent contradiction.

Contrary to Bakhtin, the contention of this discussion is that the patterning and ascription of particular value is indeed a process that depends upon perception within contexts of utterance, but that the determination of meaning in context is dependent upon the pre-existing conventions concerning expressive charge that accompany the words and phrases that are deployed by the speaker in any particular utterance. It is at the level of the word and its lexical specification that expressive charge is perceived. The fact that metaphor, irony, and many of the other processes of rhetoric exploit, extend, reverse and charge words in the interplay of discourse does not mean that the expressive dimension is absent from the primary specification of language.

Evaluative language

The notion of expressive charge, as used above, relies upon a broadly applicable distinction between words and phrases which are 'descriptive' and those which, in addition to their primary meaning, carry the evaluative charge referred to. There has, of course, been lengthy debate about the language of ethical discourse among moral philosophers, anthropologists, sociolinguists and others. One part of that debate has been the relationship between notions of fact, knowledge and evidence on the one hand, and the world of belief, principles, attitudes and convention, the relation between 'is' and 'ought'. In an article debating the arguments concerning the different kinds of descriptive statement, including those which encapsulate 'institutional facts' (i.e. those which relate to rules and conventions, the 'oughts' of everyday life), the philosopher John Searle summarizes a particular view of the nature of those two categories of word or phrase:

> The inclination to accept a rigid distinction between 'is' and 'ought', between descriptive and evaluative, rests on a certain picture of the way words relate to the world ... Briefly, the picture is constructed something like this: first we present examples of so-called descriptive statements ('my car goes eighty miles an hour', 'Jones is six feet tall', 'Smith has brown hair'), and we contrast them with so-called evaluative statements ('my car is a good car', 'Jones ought to pay Smith five dollars', 'Smith is a nasty man'). Anyone can see that they are different. We articulate the difference by pointing out that for the descriptive statements the question of truth or falsity is objectively decidable, because to know the meaning of the descriptive expressions is to know under what objectively ascertainable conditions the statements which contain them are true or false. But in the case of evaluative statements the situation is quite different. To know the meaning of the evaluative expressions is not by itself sufficient for knowing under what conditions the statements containing them are true or false, because the meanings of the expressions is such that the statements are not capable of objective or factual truth or falsity at all. Any justification a speaker can give of one of his evaluative statements essentially involves some appeal to attitudes he holds, to criteria of assessment he has adopted, or to moral principles by which he has chosen to live and judge other people. Descriptive statements are thus objective, evaluative statements subjective, and the difference is a consequence of the different sorts of terms employed.
>
> The underlying reason for these differences is that evaluative statements perform a completely different job from descriptive statements. Their job is not to describe features of the world but to express the speaker's emotions, to express his attitudes, to praise or condemn, to laud or insult, to commend, to recommend, to advise and so forth. Once we see the different jobs the two perform, we see that there must be a logical gulf between them. Evaluative statements must be different from descriptive statements in order to do their job, for if they were objective they could no longer function to evaluate. (Searle 1967: 109–10)

That which in this articulation constitutes a gulf between two different types of statements, has been represented here as an additional dimension of meaning, intimately bound up with the political process of persuasion, that is itself part of the armoury of patternable, and thus recognizable, speech deployed in articulating and evaluating the world.

Alternative discourses: the advertiser's armoury

In many contexts the language of moral evaluation has been supplanted by the imagery and symbolism of advertising, such that while the process may remain fundamentally similar, i.e. the selling of an event, a person or a situation, the language has been transformed. Where advertising in the 1940s and 1950s told us that Brand X was 'good' for us, now the simple juxtaposition of not only sand, sun and sex with the object, but even the absence of the object juxtaposed with a joke against itself has become the process whereby a minimalist presence of the product can be evoked. And that, for the advertising executive in this day and age, is enough. The changes within the 'discourse type' of advertising have been perceptively analysed by Guy Cook, reflecting a move away from the evaluatively loaded language of the good and the bad, through 'pseudo-scientific' representations of the advantageous, into the idyllic and idealized lifestyles associated with sex, sun and sand of the 1970s:

> Advertising ... has changed, becoming more subtle and more entertaining than the crude hard selling of the 1950s and 1960s ... What of the people in ads and the kind of personal or social relationships between them? They too change. The obedient housewife of the 1950s and 1960s becomes the sex object of the 1970s, the power-dressed executive of the 1980s the super-fit woman of the 1990s. The patriarch of the 1950s and 1960s becomes the vain Don Juan of the 1960s and 1970s, the selfish executive of the 1980s becomes the smug family man of the 1990s. (Cook 1992: 17, 222)

until advertising has, in the 1990s, minimalized the presence of the product in favour of anything that will arrest the attention, constantly reversing trends and searching for the unexpected, in humour, in shock, in wit and in visual and verbal association. Cook examines aspects of form in language and in the associated arenas of music, pictures and 'paralanguage' that contribute to the effectiveness of advertisements as a discourse type. In so doing he highlights both the interrelations between ads themselves and their ideological function as persuasive communication, showing how radically the process of persuasion has changed and continues to change.

In terms of the expressive charge that we have discussed earlier, Cook provides an analysis of an advertisement which deploys charged language not dissimilar to the language of morality to which we referred earlier, framed in a parallelistic pattern that links a product with health, goodness and motherhood, and what could be more charged than that:

> Text of advertisement:
> 'I FOUND A WAY TO BE A GOOD MOTHER AND STILL BE A GREAT MOM.'
> Every time you buy Sunny Delight, you win two ways. You're still a good mother because you're giving your kids something healthy. Plus, they'll think you're great because they're getting something delicious. Kids love the refreshing taste of orange, tangerine and lime. You'll love the vitamins they get in every glass.

In the opening line of the ad for Sunny Delight orange drink ..., for example, there is a graphological parallelism between the phrases 'Good Mother' and 'Great Mom' because both use the same word-initial capitals (a repetition which could be perceived even by someone who knew neither English nor the Latin alphabet). There is also phonological parallelism because, when spoken, both phrases repeat sounds in the same sequence: \g\\m\\g\\m\. There is lexical parallelism: 'great' is a synonym of 'good' and 'mother' of 'mom' ... Both in this opening line and in the remaining copy, there are grammatical parallels. The copy has five parallel constructions.

> 1. I   found   a way to be   a Good Mother
>   Ø Ø   Ø   a Great Mom
> 2. Everytime you   buy   Sunny Delight
>   you   win   two ways
> 3. You   're   still a good mother
>   you   're giving   your kids something healthy
> 4. Plus,   they'll think   you're great
>   because   they're getting something delicious
> 5. Kids   love   the refreshing taste of orange, tangerine and lime
>   You   'll love the vitamins they get in every glass.

These grammatical equivalences are reinforced by lexical repetitions, for the second of each pair of structures repeats, in the same grammatical slots, some of the words of the first: 'be' in 1, 'you' in 2, 'you' in 3, 'they' in 4, 'love' in 5. The effect, as in the *Ballad of Reading Gaol*, is to create equivalence of meaning between those units which are lexically different, but occur in the same grammatical positions:

To be a Good Mother	=	to be a Great Mom
Buy Sunny Delight	=	win two ways
Being a good mother	=	giving your kids something healthy
They think you're great	=	they're getting something delicious
The refreshing taste of Orange, tangerine and lime	=	the vitamins they get in every glass

(Cook 1992: 135–6)

The patterning described by Cook sets up intricate links between the three core elements: that which typifies the product: its name 'Sunny Delight', and descriptive elements, 'taste', 'orange, tangerine and lime', 'vitamins in every glass', along with words that assign charge to the product either in terms of pleasure or of value, 'refreshing', 'healthy', 'delicious' (and the words of the name itself 'Sunny', 'Delight'); the directness of the addressivity of the text singles out the 'mother' and associates her/you with the evaluatively charged words 'good', 'win', 'great'. But, it is in the third element of the text, the relationship between mother and child, that the core values are articulated: it is *they* who will say 'Great Mom', 'they think you're great' as you exchange the product for their approval. Winning in two ways heaps others' assessment of positive charge upon your own knowledge of your own goodness. This overt articulation of evaluatively charged language has tended to be replaced not only by iconic visual representations in recent years, but has tended to become less and less part of the articulation at all. Cook illustrates extensively, but one neat example is through his discussion of cigarette advertising, where even lifestyle associations have been effaced to be replaced by the attention-grabbing technique of offering, not the immediately understandable product, but a puzzle, a clue, a seeming piece of nonsense, which the observer/listener approaches on the assumption that there is a meaning in it somewhere. It is the undoing of the cryptic which is the engagement sought by the advertiser, and incidentally along the way comes an association with an identity, a name, hardly even a product any more:

Ads do not always refer to the advocated behaviour directly, though in the case of ads which encourage purchase the identity of the product must be clear. Naming is often oblique, and demands some induction on the part of the receiver; but, as in riddles and lateral thinking problems, addressees derive pleasure from their own successful inferencing strategies and ability to decipher unusual ways of encoding the product name. In Britain, some recent famous and popular campaigns, such as those for Silk Cut cigarettes, are widely believed not to name their product ... Nothing could be further from the truth, for these ads consist entirely of an elaborate and roundabout naming. In the wordless pictures, a piece of silk iconically signifies SILK, which is the signified of the signifier 'silk'; another object or action iconically signifies a CUT, which is the signified of the signifier 'cut'; the two signifiers then combine to form a composite signifier 'silk cut' which in turn names the cigarettes. (Cook 1992: 224)

The ad designer need go no further than to name – to display the object. The free play of associations is relied upon to do the rest, building upon the essential indeterminacy of the connotational process, happy in the knowledge that there is no such thing as bad publicity. The intimate connection between naming and praising is familiar in praising traditions all over the world.

As Cook has demonstrated, over time the idioms deployed in pursuit of the identification and typification of the 'product' (and he is at pains to point out that the 'typified' may be, for example, a charity, a political party, an individual as well as a commercial 'product') change quite radically, advertisements being more and more self-reflexive in their propensity to strike off in new directions in reaction to being typecast themselves. The idiom of the morally charged concepts, the good, the bad and the ugly, being less common, and living now alongside a wide variety of types of 'soft-sell' within a minimalist tendency, perhaps derived from a sensitivity among ad-makers to the allergic reactions of many people to what nowadays smacks of crude propaganda.

The tendency to move away from moralistic discourse, evident in the public world of advertising, is mirrored in the decline of many other forms of public certainty. Brave new worlds of ideological certainty, be they socialist or capitalist, have given way to the occasionally confused pragmatism of middle-ground politics, and the arbiters of daily morality, the television soaps, explore the intricate indeterminacy of all the 'grey areas' of human behaviour. The moral certainties of nineteenth-century Europe and the articulation of such certainties every Sunday from the pulpit, or in the tracts of church teaching, or in the standardizing education systems, or in the ethics of the workplace, have given way to a silencing of overtly moralistic public discourse, or at least an attenuation and a transformation of it, so that values are refracted and reinterpretable. Yet in the Islamic world, one of the dimensions to the scepticism displayed in relation to western societies has been the distaste, not just for the products of cultural imperialism, but for the apparent absence of ethical discourse at the heart of public culture. Islam places the public articulation of moral discourse at the heart of public culture in many non-western societies. The strongly charged language of personal behaviour, religious practice and belief holds a dominant position, whether within a liberal or authoritarian, pluralist or religiously homogeneous society, across the public idioms of discourse, be they sermon, newspaper comment, radio broadcast or public speech. Revolt, objection or criticism is framed in terms of the language of reform, reform as the recovery of the moral and religious values that are seen to be outlined within the Qur'an, and exemplified in 'model' societies that embody such values. Resistance to the influence of 'the West' is not only to the introduction of Coca Cola, McDonalds and CNN as consumable commodities but also to the dominance of public culture and public communication by the discourses that accompany such commodities. The ideological battle is for space – the space within which public communication takes place, and for the nature of the language which occupies such space. As a Nigerian colleague of mine once commented, 'in Europe I walk into a newsagent and the shelves are full of pornography, the newspapers full of trivia; I go home and the television is full of horror stories and violence; at work we only talk of the matter in hand and how to do it faster, cheaper, more; where is the contemplation and discussion of what is right and what is wrong? I go back to Nigeria and it is becoming the same, and yet we struggle to keep the discussion of what is right and what is wrong at the forefront of public discussion.' My response was to suggest that he was seeing not the absence of moral discourse but the refraction of it away from directly expressed Victorian values into the indirect and allusive language of fictional narratives, of the 'soft-sell' in all aspects of public culture. Unimpressed, his reaction was to point to the power of moral renewal movements across the Islamic world, disparagingly referred to in the West as 'fundamentalism'.

Direct or refracted, overtly moralistic or allusive and indeterminate, the ideological process marries the characterization of the subject matter with the surrounding evaluative discourse that sets it within a context of discriminations, some ambiguous, some clear, that go to make up the 'text'. The poetics of the ideological process entail the establishment of structures and patterns within the complex of language, music, and visual images that constitute the utterance. The artistry and playfulness of the human mind is manifest in this patterning, patterning that directs meaning and which is perceived in and for itself as part of what constitutes the 'text' in performance. Our discovery of the 'awareness' of the subject, and the assessment of it embedded in the charged language or images that surround it, is a consequence of our engagement with the text.

From ideological process to ideology

So what in the end do I take from Abubakar Imam and his comment? Perhaps that beyond the issue of the genre and its conventions and expectations, beyond the social context of any relationship between the poet and himself the listener, beyond the style of the text itself, there has to lie something else. A poem worthy of publication is so because it has conveyed to him an awareness, a 'typification', and a 'moral category' without which the whole exercise would have been baseless; without an acknowledgement of 'truth value' the poem is for him but 'a rhetoric blameworthy and discreditable ... a diet ruinous to health, a paint disastrous to beauty'.

From where, then, does this typification derive? Is it traceable no further back than the words I use in the manifestation of my utterance? Does it only come into being at the moment of my articulation? It is observable only when manifest, clearly, in that you cannot see what is going on in my head, my ideas are only objects of your contemplation when given objective form in text or talk. Yet, there is in my mind a continuity of presence through memory which allows the repeated articulation of the same idea. As memory fails, and time passes, the variability of the articulation may increase, yet I know that each articulation takes as its point of departure the memory of the same event, person or experience. My eviction by my erstwhile landlord was a singular event that lives in my memory. In the pub, over dinner, and on other occasions I have retailed the events of that afternoon time and time again. The embroidery has grown, the slant has changed, and no doubt the landlord's rendering of the events has always been very different, but each manifestation harks back to a single source in memory. That single source is the sequence of actions and utterances the memory retains: the landlord gathering my belongings and placing them on the pavement; his statement that I owed him many months of rent; my insistence that I had paid his agent; his refusal to believe it; his pushing of me along the hallway; my trip and tumble down the front stairs; my negotiation of a temporary stay with a friend. The sequence of events and words is fixed in memory, as is the general sense of each utterance. But I have told the anecdote in a myriad different ways: as knockabout farce based upon a sequence of misunderstandings; as an illustration of my worst days of hardship as a student; as an illustration of the rapacious power of the propertied classes; as an illustration of the good samaritanship of my friend; and as an illustration of the encumbrance of accumulated personal possessions. Each rendering wraps the same sequence of events in a different interpretative and ideological framework, but all of them based upon an idea, a memory retained in the mind and available for rearticulation in words. Of course, the idea in the mind can inform other modes of expression that do not rely upon words: if I were an artist I could paint a picture, so clearly does the scene live in my mind.

In the passage from my head in a new and original rendering the same anecdote makes the transfer into perceivable form, perceivable by me and by you. But, most importantly, that manifestation has the potential to be shared by more than us two. When the manifestation is a shared perception among a group of people, then we are beginning to see the move from ideological process to ideology. Shared ideas, shared beliefs, shared memories, known to be so shared because they are re-articulated by numerous individuals separately or in common activity together, constitute the building-blocks of ideology. When we share a view that landlords constitute an identifiable group who are oppressive (as manifest, and justified, by my example which, I claim, is typical), then at the broader level of generalization, built upon that example, we have one element in an ideological position which is ready to expand the range of manifestations which are, by analogy, part of a pattern of unjust behaviour by this group of people. And so our search is on for further support of our general position on landlords.

Stereotypes and the kaleidoscope of human speech and action

The process of typification and evaluation discussed earlier in this chapter is rarely, if ever, one which occurs *tabula rasa*. Each utterance is set against a context of previous utterances, not only in the immediate context of performance, but also in the broader context of familiar, oft-repeated representations that constitute the building-blocks of so much cultural discourse. It is not possible to present a picture of your curmudgeonly neighbour to me without raising in me the half-remembered representations from television shows, the parts of my own personal experience, and the typical view of what the expected reactions and views of such a person would be. Nor would you wish me to ignore that background knowledge. You would most likely wish to evoke in me a variety of correspondences, 'you know what that kind of person is like ...; you've seen it before of course ...; just like Grumpy in that cartoon, you remember ...!' A deal of your effort may well go into evoking in me a wide variety of parallels as a way of fixing and clarifying the representation you are seeking to make. You propose, and I confirm, that we share an understanding of the salient features of a particular typical combination of characteristics. Once certain features have been acknowledged there is an expectation that the rest will fit round. 'You mean he sweeps only his side of the path and leaves a line of sweepings on your side? Unbelievable, but what would you expect!' That action summarizes a whole series of available others: the complaints about windblown leaves, the demand to cut the hedge, the sign about 'no parking', all of which are seen to be consistent manifestations of a personality, each reinforcing the consistency of the pattern. The interpretative process both creates the parts of the picture that go together to establish the item, but at the same time allocates it to a category which is already established within the world of cultural stereotypes. At the moment of such allocation I may sense the finality of that categorization by responding, 'Ah, but we musn't jump to conclusions, maybe he's not all that bad, perhaps there is a reason for his behaviour!' The finality of consignment to a stereotypical category was a little too final for me, I hanker after a modicum of flexibility to interpret on the basis of individual circumstance and individual action rather than the impersonal frame of type. Rather in the way that the private and the public intersect to create alternative frames of interpretation and consequential significance, so also the individual and the type become frames of reference that have very differing implications for the flexibility of speaker and listener. As you and I discuss our neighbour, we veer backwards and forwards between that which is typical of his kind of person and what were the particular actions of this individual and how we should interpret them. Perhaps his picking up the child's piece of paper was not the action of an unreasonably angry individual making a point about other people littering his garden (another example to support the 'curmudgeonly' thesis), but was simply a kind-hearted action intended to ensure that the child did not lose an important piece of homework (a counterexample requiring a reassessment of the individual and perhaps even a reassessment of the allocation of the type). 'Perhaps he's not so bad after all!' you say. More usually, perhaps, we would not be discussing such a silent individual but would be making our interpretations on the basis of oral interchanges. Nevertheless, the interpretative process is no less subtle even if the person tells you what is in their mind, because the perception still involves the classification of the action and the words in terms of their degree of 'fit' with experienced patterns of 'typical' motives and behaviour.

My concern here is not with the psychology of the process but the manner of the deployment of stereotypes in the discourse that takes place. Time and again, the creativity of oral literary forms turns upon the manipulation of cultural stereotypes in the typification of people in society and the forces they are prey to. Anecdotes, jokes, tales, narratives of many kinds deploy recognizable characters both with the economy of the caricaturist and with the creativity of the kaleidoscope. Interest, in the Hausa oral narrative, centres around the verbal interactions between characters, not in the detailed, lengthy exposition of personality and nature; where the shorthand of 'types' can assume a broad degree of common knowledge, not of specific information about a particular character but of the expected ways in which a person 'would act' in any particular circumstance, then two factors have come simultaneously into the communicative context: on the one hand, an assumed solidarity among the audience and between them and the speaker, a solidarity which, unspoken, sets as a priori the notion that there is shared knowledge. It is precisely so disconcerting for an outsider to begin to realize that such an assumption has been made, when he or she begins to feel that much is going 'over my head', and that there is in fact far less shared than seems to be assumed. In fact, of course, there will be a wide array of degrees of 'assumable knowledge' within any assembled company, young and old, men and women, insiders and outsiders, etc., and the degree of actual shared knowledge may be limited. Nevertheless, an important effect of the use of types is to imply a level of common knowledge. On the other hand, the shorthand of 'types' induces a dynamism into the narrative. Rather than having the speaker explain each action and its consequences, the reversion to 'type' allows the audience to anticipate future outcomes and consequences from the moment of the initial action or dialogue. This anticipatory dynamism is both the key to humour (who hasn't seen the comic encounter coming from the moment that the curmudgeonly neighbour is joined in the story by the do-it-yourself enthusiast) and indeed to the tragedy of anticipated clash between immovable object and inexorable force. Knowing the characters, you can see the outcome from a long way off, and of course the twist at the end plays with all those available dimensions of expectation. The anticipatory dynamism is manifest in dialogue and action rather than in character. It is the switch to the narrative of character development, of psychological drama and of the development of personality which moves away from the shorthand of stereotypes, the focus then being upon the effect of speech and action upon the personalities involved, a different kind of dynamism in the construction of a text.

The deployment of stereotyped characters in narrative has the advantage not only of allowing a concentration upon the action and the dialogue but of enabling a variable degree of telescoping, from the most sketchy and brief evocation to a more extended rehearsal of the salient features of the 'typical' character. One of the most telescoped of all usages is that which occurs in jokes where the minimal nominal reference to the type is all that often occurs, 'Do you know the one about the X?' It was sufficient to name the type to bring forward the sometimes many and varied characteristics that are connotations of that name. Those connotations inhabit the cultural world of the joke itself; the many manifestations of the 'stupid, ignorant X person' that are part of the assumed shared knowledge of speaker and listener, who have heard perhaps hundreds of such jokes, are part of the cultural frame of reference of joke-making. Neither you nor I would be seen dead implying that an 'X person' was any of those things outside of that joking context. A narrative, on the other hand, may rehearse the characteristics of the stereotypes, in extenso, in order to remind the knowledgeable listener of the various sides to the character. Trickster stories will often exemplify such associated elements of the trickster, such as avarice, laziness, physical weakness, licentiousness, cowardice, quickwittedness, eloquence, etc., in addition to an ability to outwit. Each culture will have its own set of associations that go with particular characters, and it is a commonplace that equivalent types recur, not only the tricksters of the oral narratives of Africa and the New World, but also in the heroes, villains, helpers and guides that people peoples' imaginations, be they Odysseus, Athena, Asterix, Superman, Sunjata or Sunjata's sister. Nevertheless, the more extensive presentation of the stereotype still allows the focus to be on the interactions between that representative of the stereotype and the other characters who people the story. In so doing, the narrator may bring into play the contradictions between that type and others, providing clues as to how to apprehend and appreciate other parallel encounters that form part of daily experience. When the disobedient child suffers for his or her temerity, the fact that the narrative evoked the stereotype of that kind of child allows the identification of a real child with that category. Stereotypes set up categories for characters in narrative but crucially also for a way of looking at real life. As prisms through which to classify and group people and actions in real life therefore, the type is necessary and central.

The stereotype so often carries with it not merely a name and a set of physical and and behavioural characteristics, but also a flag, a label, of an evaluative nature. The harridan, the clod, the thief, the shrew, the bully, the jolly postman, the barber, the dutiful son, the errant daughter, the unfaithful wife, the cuckold, the wise old woman, the good samaritan, and on and on; each of these comes with an evaluative charge alongside the type characteristics of behaviour and speech that are appropriate to each one. It would be an odd narrative which assumed in its listeners the expectation that the good samaritan was by nature always evil, or the thief always good. There is usually required some reworking of the underlying charge in the context of the narrative, so Robin Hood was good because he stole (bad) from those who were bad $-(-)$ and gave it to those who were good ($+$). Part of the shorthand provided by the array of connotations surrounding the stereotype is the ability to assume knowledge quickly in the listener of the 'moral categories' which underlie the working out of the text so that villains get their comeuppance and the virtuous are rewarded. The point of some narratives, trickster stories are a case in point, is to play with the moral categories themselves, such that that lazy, cowardly trickster offloads the retribution for his villainy onto an innocent party. Is this the revenge of the weak over the mighty? Is it a real reversal of moral codes, perhaps not? The power of stereotypes is their evocation of moral category, predictable outlook and expected actions in whatever new circumstance is being outlined. The evocation of the known is a primary requisite of any revision, revolution or reworking. To laboriously outline the known as if it were being described for the first time, is counterproductive when the focus is on the statement about the known or the elements of the new.

Of course, the mapping of real people onto the stereotypes of our imaginations goes on around us all the time. One has only to read the newspaper to be gripped by the machinations of political ogres, rapacious entrepreneurs, femmes fatales, saintly aid workers, lost children, overweening bosses, unsung heroes and tellers of great stories. Time and again one may wonder whether the evoked stereotype really did fit the reality, was the person really such a villain, maybe reality was not quite so clear, and of course we all know that indeed reality is not quite like that. Nevertheless, these stereotypes remain the necessary shorthand vocabulary of our hurried attempts to make sense of the world around us, and we both map reality on to these stereotypes and use these stereotypes to understand what we see. To understand is to be able to say, 'Ah now I see where to fit that person or that event!' and such understanding is the first step to being able to remember it and to be able to forget it, for now.

So far I have used the term stereotype with reference to characters, personalities, people. But these people interact in situations that are equally likely to have been encountered before. Stereotype characters interact when faced with the ever-repeated contradictions of life: the love triangle, the power struggles of the generations over time, the contradictions of desire and obligation, alienation and reconciliation, growth and decay, love and hate, the individual and the group, the self and the other, wealth and poverty, oppression and liberty, etc. The television soaps all around the world play out permutations of action and reaction around these issues carried by characters we recognize as composites built anew out of the stereotypes that we are everywhere familiar with. The narrative focus upon dialogue and action is facilitated both by the use of stereotyped *personae* and by the insertion of the *dramatis personae* into situations that must occur in reality and in imagination over and over again all over the world. These familiar situations provide the contradictions and questions that the dialogue and action then work through in an infinite number of available ways. Like the grains of sand on the chessboard, permutations grow exponentially because interaction and language are indeterminate. With the anticipatory potential of the stereotypes, the kinetic energy of the contradictions of the situations, and the infinite variability of human response and action it is not surprising that oral narrative is inexhaustible. The final chapter will return to some of these issues in discussing the significance of speech-act theory.

In relation to oral literature the nexus of content, form and context brings us back to the cardinal central relationship between speaker/performer and listener/audience in the moment of communication; as Gramsci put it, 'spoken communication is a means of ideological diffusion which has a rapidity, a field of action, and an emotional simultaneity far greater than written communication' (Gramsci 1985: 382). Within the memory of the speaker lies knowledge relating to content, genre and event. The genre provides a further framework of expectations for the articulation of ideas and events. The creativity of the speaker mediates between memory and the speech event, the experience of which is the one shared item between the speaker and the listener. Where the listener perceives the characterization as 'true' and the moral framework as appropriate, the retention of the experience may depend not only upon these two elements of the experience but also upon the aesthetic judgement and the emotional experience that went with it. That memory may then constitute the basis of a repeated process in which the listener becomes the speaker in turn. But the relevant experience is not for the listener alone. It is also an experience shared by the original speaker, who themselves may, from the experience of articulating a characterization and a moral framework (with all the emotion that may accompany that process), rework in memory the articulation in order to provide an alternative slant or progression. As an iterative process, then, it is the evanescent, immediate shared experience of the moment of communication that stands at the centre of the cultural creativity and political potential under discussion here.

In the remainder of this chapter I will illustrate the link between shared experience of the articulation of a particular typification and its simultaneous embedding within an evaluative framework which led directly to action in its immediate audience. The illustration draws upon an event, a moment of moral articulation, which is held to have had profound political and ethical repercussions. Luckily, it is also a moment where we have descriptions of the event beyond the content of the speech itself, descriptions by people who were present and who have described their feelings and reactions, and also the actions that they took in the moment of the event, actions that they indicate were directly a consequence of what was being articulated in the speech itself. It is thus both the tracing of the path of an ideological process as we have discussed it in this chapter and the articulation of an ideological position.

Hubert Humphrey and the 1948 Democratic National Convention

In July 1948 the Democratic Party of the United States held its national convention in Philadelphia during a heatwave (Caro 2002: 439–50). Hubert Humphrey, the 37-year-old Mayor of Minneapolis, was one of the 108-member Platform Committee involved in lengthy discussion of policies and positions that the Democratic Party should take on a range of issues. Party leaders were concerned not to split the party between southern Democrats decidedly lukewarm on civil rights and those northern liberals putting forward a radical agenda on the issue. Caro describes how, for two days and nights, Humphrey struggled and argued, resisting the efforts of the majority leaders on the committee to formulate a conservative plank on civil rights as the favoured position that they would ask the convention to endorse. While some were impressed with Humphrey's persistence, others reacted like Senator Scott Lucas of Illinois who was heard to say, 'Who does this pipsqueak think he is?' Eventually, when the liberals were soundly defeated in the committee, Humphrey vowed to bring a minority resolution to the convention when the matter came up for discussion and to ask the convention to endorse an alternative liberal position. In the time between the meeting and the debate in the convention, Humphrey came under further strong pressure to withdraw. He was warned that the southern Democrats might walk out, the issue could split the party and so assist the Republicans, and his own career would be ruined.

The night before the issue was due to be debated, Humphrey sat up for hours with colleagues debating what to do. At five o'clock in the morning he finally decided to go ahead. 'Get the hell out of here and let me write a speech and get some sleep', he said to them as they departed. The following afternoon the hall was stiflingly hot, not helped by the fact that the Secret Service had closed all the doors in anticipation of President Truman's arrival. The room was packed with hot, bored delegates eager to see the president when the virtually unknown Hubert Humphrey stepped up to the microphone. Robert Caro describes the moment as follows:

> For once he paused for a long moment before beginning to speak, as if he was gathering himself, a very thin figure perspiring so heavily under the glare of the lights that sweat made his black hair glisten and ran down his high forehead; and his face, as David McCullough puts it, was 'shining', with sweat and sincerity. 'No braver David ever faced a more powerful Goliath', Paul Douglas, who was sitting in the throng below him, was to say twenty years later ... And as he began to speak, his words slashing across the murmur of the restless throng, 'the audience' as one writer put it, 'grew quiet, suddenly aware that someone they wanted to listen to was talking'.

I have included the full text of what Hubert Humphrey said in Appendix 2. The speech lasted only eight minutes, only 37 sentences. The speech as I discuss it here is as published by Wilson (1996: 3–6). The early parts of the speech are focused around the problem of the dissension in the Democratic Party on the issue of civil rights. He congratulates his opponents on their sincerity and commitment and frames his position in terms of respectful dissent. But he sets his flag upon the greater good, the larger issue, and the founding principles of the Democratic Party. He quotes from Senator Barkley of Kentucky speaking of Thomas Jefferson,

> He did not proclaim that all the white, or the black, or the red, or the yellow men are equal: that all Christian or Jewish men are equal: that

all protestant and catholic men are equal: that all rich and poor men are equal: that all good and bad men are equal. What he declared was that all men are equal; and that equality which he proclaimed was the equality in the right to enjoy the blessings of free government in which they may participate and to which they have given their support.

Humphrey then talks of progress made, and the importance of Truman's new 'emancipation proclamation'. He affirms the pledges (contained in the minority report) upon which all Americans need to be able to rely, and raises the issue beyond the competing parties to the world at large,

> Every citizen has a stake in the emergence of the United States as a leader of the free world. That world is being challenged by the world of slavery. For us to play our part effectively we must be in a morally sound position. We can't use a double standard. There's no room for double standards in American politics for measuring our own and other people's policies. Our demands for democratic practices in other lands will be no more effective than the guarantee of those practices in our own country.

There then follows his challenge to the floor of the convention, 'Friends, delegates, I do not believe that there can be any compromise on the

Photograph 3 Hubert Humphrey (courtesy of the Lyndon Baines Johnson Library)

guarantees of the civil rights which we have mentioned in the minority report'. At this point, Humphrey reaches toward the heart of his moral position through the rhetoric of the counterpoint and the summative symbolism, with religious overtones, of hope and freedom wrapped up in the idea of America:

> To those who say that we are rushing this issue of civil rights, I say to them we are a hundred and seventy-two years late. To those who say that this civil rights program is an infringement on state's rights, I say this, the time has arrived in America for the Democratic Party to get out of the shadows of state's rights to walk forthrightly into the bright sunshine of human rights. People – people – human beings – this is the issue of the 20th century. People of all kinds, all sorts of people – and these people are looking to America for leadership and they are looking to America for precept and example.
>
> My good friends, my fellow Democrats, I ask you for a calm consideration of our historic opportunity. Let us forget the evil passions and the blindness of the past. In these times of world, political, spiritual – above all spiritual – crisis, we cannot and we must not turn from the path so plainly before us. That path has already led us through many valleys of the shadow of death. And now is the time to recall all those who were left on that path to American freedom. For all of us here, for the millions who have sent us, for the whole two billion members of the human family, our land is now more than ever before, the last best hope on earth. And I know that we can, and I know that we shall begin here the fuller and richer realization of that hope. That promise of a land where all men are truly free and equal, and each man uses his freedom and equality wisely and well.

The rhetorical patterning, the typification of his subject matter and the powerfully charged evaluative language of his 'moral categories' are plain to see in the above extract. Caro reports that by the time that Humphrey was halfway through his sentences the audience was cheering every one of them. The demand that the principles of equality be given effect through a civil rights programme lay at the moral heart of his challenge to the party.

To date this discussion has presented something of the background to a public speech event, something of the text itself, and something of the reported reaction of the audience in general terms. There have been many rousing speeches and many such pieces of rhetoric and so why have I chosen to present this one? Commentators have remarked on the significance of the speech at the Democratic Convention. Wilson (1996: 7) comments that, 'The 1948 convention speech was so powerful that it left in its wake several repercussions both for the civil rights cause and for Humphrey himself. First and foremost, this speech was said to have "ushered in the second era of redressing racial injustice in America". This occasion marked the starting point for civil rights progress in the legislature.' And Caro (2002: 445) writes about it in these terms,

> At the time, there were not a few comparisons between Humphrey's speech and what has been described as 'the only convention speech that ever had a greater impact upon the deliberation of the delegates' – William Jennings Bryan's 'Cross of Gold' oration of half a century before – but later events were to blur the memory of Humphrey's speech so that today it is all but lost to history. Nothing, though, could ever dim the memory of that speech for those who were there to hear it. 'It was the greatest speech I ever heard.' Paul Douglas would say a quarter of a century later. 'He was on fire just like the Bible speaks of Moses.' Recalling the 'magnificent' line about moving out 'into the bright sunshine of human rights', Douglas would say, 'To me, he will always be the orator of the dawn.'

In the case of this example can we delve a little further to ask what exactly was the immediate impact of the speech, how did that manifest itself in action or words other than in general applause? We do know that when the vote was taken, the majority group view was defeated by Humphrey's minority plank by a vote of 651.5 to 582.5, and when the result was announced a huge roar of triumph filled the hall, and commentators assign significance to it in leading to other moments, other debates, other pieces of legislation. A post-mortem on the result would analyse the political forces that lined up on one side or the other. Our interest here is in examining the 'oral communicative moment', and whether it is possible to go beyond the text and the speaker to understand the dynamic of that moment between Hubert Humphrey and his audience.

Robert Caro, with his masterly command of both substance and detail, provides a fascinating insight into what actually happened in the convention hall as Humphrey was speaking and immediately after he had turned away from the podium. Action taken by members of the audience led to a manifestation of agreement that was in itself a spur to further action by others, a tide that turned. Caro comes close to describing not only the flow of the tide one way and then the other but also the usually imperceptible between-time when the tide is actually turning. He quotes (Caro 2002: 443–4) from the recollections of the Democratic senator, Paul Douglas and his interactions with the then Mayor of Chicago, Ed Kelly, in this discussion of the moment the speech ended and the delegations from each of the states began to respond, with Minnesota being Humphrey's own state:

> The Minnesota delegation's seats were surrounded by those of Georgia to their left, Louisiana to their right, Virginia behind them, and Kentucky in front of them, so that when the Minnesotans jumped up, the first delegation to do so, coming shouting to their feet as Humphrey shuffled his papers together and turned away from the podium, their banners were surrounded by the seated, glaring delegates from the South. But their banners were not alone for long. While Humphrey had been speaking, there had been something else that Paul Douglas would never forget: 'hard-boiled politicians dabbing their eyes with their handkerchiefs.' Turning to Ed Kelly, Mayor of Chicago, who was seated beside him, Douglas said, 'Mr Mayor, that was a great speech. Mr Mayor', he said, 'we can win now. If Illinois will lead a parade, we can win. We will fall in behind you.' Kelly had been adamantly opposed to the stronger civil rights plank because he thought it had no chance of passage and would only divide the party. 'Paul', Kelly said now, 'we ought to have a parade, and Illinois ought to lead it. I would like to do so. But I am getting old, my legs are tired, and I couldn't hold up under this terrible heat.'

'He paused for a moment,' Douglas was to recall, 'and then he said, "But Paul, I want you to lead the parade".' Lifting the Illinois standard from its socket, Kelly handed it to Douglas, and then turned to the delegation, pointed at Douglas, and motioned for them to follow him. The towering, white-thatched figure moved down the aisle. A forty-piece band that had been organized by James Caesar Petrillo, president of the American Federation of Musicians, had been kept hidden under the podium because it was not supposed to begin playing until President Truman appeared in the hall later that evening to give his acceptance speech. But Petrillo had been staring up at Humphrey as Humphrey spoke, and suddenly now, Petrillo motioned the band to begin playing. As Douglas led Illinois forward, the big California delegation fell in behind it. 'Then New York, overcoming the caution of its Tammany leaders ... Delegation after delegation joined us ... Here and there groups of sullen Southerners and conservative Northerners remained stubbornly in their seats, but the main mass of Democrats was moving with jubilant feet toward a better and more equal America.'

In this example, then, we are able to get close to seeing one particular set of interactions between the speaker and an audience, in this case on a large stage, where the characterization of the issue and the moral framework into which it is woven are one component in a process of persuasion and change, a speech that did move mountains (a vote of 651.5 to 582.5) and one which, through Robert Caro's narrative, allowed us to see some elements of the outcome of the reception of the speech event in addition to what went into it, an ideological process in action.

Concluding remarks

The study of oral literature has the peculiar advantage of being able to start from the particularities of the communicative moment – the process of creativity, performance and retention – while focusing upon the textual elements most directly connected with the communicative process – its purpose as a speech act, the characterization of its topic and the ideological framework within which the topic is embedded. The speech act and the text itself are in constant interaction with the culturally specific genre expectations that surround them.

The dynamics of cultural production, and an understanding of how such matters operate in different contexts, lies at the heart of understanding how shared perceptions are created and spread, how alternative perceptions are forged and propagated, how fashions rise and fall. These lie at the heart of power relations between people, the power to renew, reverse, revise and retain perceptions and understandings that underpin relations between individuals, generations, genders, groups and classes. Consent is all, consent to a new vision, consent to a revision. The ideological process of creating a new characterization 'enveloped in the music of the intonational-evaluative context in which it is understood and evaluated' (Bakhtin 1986: 166) is always absorbing, absorbing to watch as we all do, and absorbing to undertake, as some of us do, for good or ill.

5
Academic Approaches to Orality

Orality versus literacy: the Great Divide debate

The Great Divide has been viewed as a set of characteristics that, in generalizing about societies, distinguishes between 'oral societies' and 'literate societies'. While acknowledging the very broad-brush nature of such a typology, proponents have seen a grouping of repeated characteristics around these two poles, and have generally concentrated their attention upon the significant changes and 'advances' that are made with the introduction of literacy. Along with the polar typology go a wide variety of seemingly natural correlates. Not only are 'oral societies' small-scale, community-based, face-to-face societies, but they are, according to Ong, typified by particular ways of thinking – 'aggregative' rather than 'analytical' thought processes, situational rather than abstract thinking, 'empathetic' rather than 'objective' relations between thinker and object thought about, and many others (Ong 1982: 36–57). The notion that societies move from such characteristic ways of thinking to another more advanced mode is summed up by Ong as follows:

> It will be seen that most of the characteristics of orally based thought and expression discussed earlier in this chapter relate intimately to the unifying, centralizing, interiorizing economy of sound as perceived by human beings. A sound-dominated verbal economy is consonant with aggregative (harmonizing) tendencies rather than with analytic, dissecting tendencies (which would come with the inscribed, visualized word: vision is a dissecting sense). It is consonant also with the conservative holism (the homeostatic present that must be kept intact, the formulary expressions that must be kept intact), with situational thinking (again holistic, with human action

at the center) rather than abstract thinking ... The denominators used here to describe the primary oral world will be useful again later to describe what happened to human consciousness when writing and print reduced the oral–aural world to a world of visualized pages. (Ong 1982: 73–4)

Constructed upon the edifice of supposed inevitable differences in ways of thinking typical of 'orality' and 'literacy' are then a series of further correlates that reinforce the paradigms. Finnegan summarizes these paradigms in the following manner:

Orality – and hence oral transmission – has been seen as characteristically and essentially found in cultures without writing and also, going back in history, without modern commerce or transport systems, resting on traditional and communal norms. Correspondingly, literacy has been associated with cultures characterized by the development of urban and bureaucratic systems and the rise of secular and scientific enquiry, patterns arguably further intensified with the advent of printing ... This dichotomizing framework may sound extreme, but it has been extremely influential in comparative study. It is less popular nowadays than in the past – certainly in an explicit form – but the assumptions underlying it are still persistent. They surface from time to time in both general discussions and specific treatments of orality and literacy ... The one (is) the characteristic setting for oral tradition, typified as small-scale and face to face, rural and non-industrial, communal and conformist rather than individualist, and dominated by ascribed kinship, religion and revered traditions; the other – the locale for written transmission – typically industrial, urban and bureaucratic, characterized by a respect for rationality, individual achievement and impersonal norms, heterogeneous and secular. (Finnegan 1988: 140)

Finnegan's own discussion and that of many other scholars who have worked on the functioning of oral communication in 'non-literate' cultures, and on cultures in which literacy is a socially restricted phenomenon, points to complex relations between the modes of oral and written communication that have to be seen embedded in their own social and historical contexts, and that the supposed typical 'ways of thinking' just do not hold water when examined in particular ethnographic contexts. Furthermore, not only are the overall dichotomies unhelpful, they obscure a clear understanding of the significance of oral communication in both the so-called 'oral societies' and 'literate societies'. Finnegan (1988: 155) quotes Steven Feld on his conclusions after examining the poetic culture of a non-literate culture, that of the Kaluli of Papua New Guinea:

> These confounding typologies of society, social organization, techno-economic complexity, and symbolic focus do little to explain the dynamics of oral and literate processes, but rather, simply blur or push aside social detail, historical accuracy, and the complexities of oral-literate interactions for the sake of sweeping generalizations that do not provide real evidence for the assertion that oral/literate are fundamentally different states of mind. (Feld 1986: 20)

In a preliminary chapter to an extended discussion of the historical and social contexts of a number of examples from oral literary genres in southern Africa – 'maps of experience', Leroy Vail and Landeg White demonstrate the way in which the notion of oral versus literate societies is a direct descendant of the primitive versus civilized dichotomy of so much post-Darwinian thought – Levy-Bruhl, Tylor, Frazer all thought in terms of that pair of terms. Where McLuhan and Ong maintained much of the primitive versus civilized overtones of earlier writing, for others such as Milman Parry it was the sophistication rather than primitivism of oral poetics that expressed the Rousseau-like thrust of a romantic recreation of 'oral society'. For Vail and White the dichotomy has had the deleterious effect of estranging oral forms from a proper consideration of the link between performance and history:

> By insisting on the determinacy of 'form: the one part of literature is oral, the other written' Parry effectively broke the link between performance and history ... it is essential to restore that link ... (Vail and White 1991: 32)

The work of many scholars of oral literature has reinforced the view that there are other ways of looking at the world of oral communication that do not deal in the paradigm of the western and the non-western world but rather focus upon general issues that arise time and again in considering both the process and the product of oral verbal creativity, in whatever culture it occurs. These issues are of composition, of performance and of transmission over time.

There are fundamental differences (or are there?) between composition in circumstances of oral performance and composition in writing.

Finnegan again summarizes common conceptions about the nature of oral composition:

1. The text of oral literature is variable and dependent on the occasion of performance, unlike the fixed text of a written book.
2. The form of composition characteristic of oral literature is composition-in-performance, i.e. not prior composition divorced from the act of performance.
3. Composition and transmission of oral literature is through the process mentioned above and not (as we once thought) through word-for-word memorization.
4. In oral literature, there is no concept of a 'correct' or 'authentic' version. (Finnegan 1988: 89)

The core issue in relation to the first of the above propositions is the notion of a canonical text, an authoritative version that encompasses the 'essence', the 'essential elements', the 'core' of a narrative or any other kind of 'text'. The oral : literate divide opposes an absence on the one hand and a presence on the other. The presence is illustrated not only by the existence of the great authoritative written texts that lie at the heart of the continuation and spread of world religions, but by the simple durability and fixity of anything written. The fixation upon the literal word on the page belies a series of complex issues about the nature of the written word. On the one hand, the text may well be perceived (and does it really exist anywhere other than in the mind of the reader; in what sense does it exist if it has not been read for hundreds of years?) differently by different readers. As an influence upon people can it really be said to be 'fixed'? Further, what is it that is being fixed through writing? It cannot be said to be the narrative itself, if the narrative is reworked again and again both in writing and in other media: The Romeo and Juliet story was not fixed by Shakespeare, nor earlier by Arthur Broke, nor Matteo Bandello, nor by Franco Zeffirelli, nor Sergei Prokofiev, nor Leonard Bernstein, nor by others who have retold the 'Romeo and Juliet' story in countless ways. It is perhaps as equally true of the 'Romeo and Juliet' story that it 'exists' as an idea that is separate from any particular instantiation of it. And that is not so far removed from the notions of variability that obtain in the discussion of oral narrative.

In relation to the process of composition, however, there are clear and obvious differences between oral and literate processes. The existence of an object on paper which can be adjusted, rewritten until a 'final' version is sent on its temporary way is clearly distinct from the oral 'text' for which 'revision' constitutes another performance and in which reworking constitutes a weaving of another element into the flow of the text. There has been little work published upon the indigenous aesthetics of the oral performance which might lead to an assessment of various perceptions of the 'polished' product as against the 'unfinished symphony'. The dominant view has been that oral composition has typically involved 'composition in performance', a process of improvization that requires particular skills and leads to great variability as between one rendering of a text and another. The scholarly literature on this form of composition is large and derives much of its impetus from the work of Parry and Lord and their oral-formulaic theory (Foley 1985, 1988, 1990). Finnegan (1988: 88) describes how the work of Parry and Lord has been followed by similar work on, for example, Tamil heroic poetry, English and Scottish ballads, Hebrew poetry and biblical studies, Greek folk poetry, West Sumatran sung narrative poetry, the Nibelungenlied, the Song of Roland, and Hittite epic. The focus upon the effects of 'composition in performance' and therefore the variability which obviates the notion of 'correct' version sets up processes of composition in which, instead of verbatim memorization, verbal formulae, core images and clichés (using Harold Scheub's terms) are repeatedly deployed by the performer in setting out a narrative. These formulae are detectable in the resultant text and are the marks that typify oral as against written composition. While the scholars who have pursued the study of such processes do not claim exclusivity for the oral-formulaic theory, as Finnegan puts it of the four characteristic propositions set out above, 'these four characteristics have been widely accepted as *the* typical form of oral literature (not just oral epic) to be found widely and predictably in "oral cultures", and one which it is reasonable, furthermore, to predicate of oral culture in historical periods of which we can no longer obtain the full contextual evidence' (Finnegan 1988: 89).

The general applicability of this as a model has been contested by other scholars who have pointed to the existence of genres of oral literature in which careful prior composition to produce a fixed text has been the norm in societies where nothing is committed to writing. Finnegan goes on to survey extensive work on oral genres in Pacific cultures and reaches the following conclusion:

> First the fact of prior composition in many cases is indisputable; the pattern is composition *followed* by a series of rehearsals – sometimes over many months – *followed* by performance. Unlike what would be

expected on the currently accepted view there is a clearly observable and locally recognized split between composition and performance. Second, there *is* memorization by the listeners and the performers for the words to be recorded, as it were, in the first place and then later performed by the group ... It is clear ... that, contrary to what we might predict, there is definitely a local concept of the 'correct' and 'authentic' version of the kind we normally expect only of written literature. (Finnegan 1988: 101–2)

Not only does the evidence of certain genres in Pacific cultures go against the 'typical' paradigm, verbatim memorizers of poetry in Somali culture are well attested and maintain both canonical versions and individual authorship as recorded within an 'oral culture'. Finnegan points out also the complexities not only of the data concerning these oral processes but also the current reality in which oral performance so often occurs in cultures in which writing is also known. Somali culture is one in which there is a long tradition of Arabic scholarship based upon the study and reading of Islamic texts, often canonical texts par excellence. The notion of authoritative version is not a concept unfamiliar to the average Somali man or woman. Finnegan alludes also to the variations in the circumstances in which composition takes place. Processes for single performers may be very different from those which obtain in the case of group performances. In the Hausa song tradition with which I am familiar, a famous singer, Mamman Shata, has always proclaimed his ability to compose in performance, a mark of his skill and pre-eminence. That feature, if it is indeed the case, is linked to the pattern of his performances in which he trains his chorus to repeat the same lines without variation throughout a song and his voice sings the lead through all the main verses. A rhythm set up by drummers allows the chorus to know when to come in without their having to know in advance what Mamman Shata will sing. Minimal rehearsal is required. On the other hand, the group working under the praise-singer Dankwairo require a great deal more rehearsal and preparation precisely because they co-operate more intricately and closely in performance. The lead role passes from one person to another and the chorus voices come in on the last lines of main verses as well as singing the chorus lines themselves. Memorization is much more a part of their process precisely because of the nature of the group performance.

Fixity and variability are not necessary correlates of literacy and orality, they are two ends of a continuum where technology (writing, print, audio recording, film, etc.) allows the fixing and repeatability of a verbal 'product' but the social circumstances of the creation of that 'product' situate it at a point along that continuum. As the oral rendering of the 'same' story by a man and then a woman in Hausa society (Ahmad 1997) can show variability which correlates with their different ideological positions, so also the 'same' narrative in a variety of written forms can display the effects of different ideological reworkings. At the same time fixity in oral genres may be part of widespread cultural expectations. When Bob Dylan played some of his well-known songs (known from the canonical version on one particular album) in an entirely different style that the audience did not expect and were unfamiliar with, he was greeted with catcalls and a call of 'Judas'.

The process of transmission over time can involve the verbatim memorization of oral text, as the Somali example shows, but may equally involve a flexible ongoing process as described by Goody of the versions of the Bagre myth:

> Since there is not one original that could be studied as a text, nor a single keeper of the oral tradition, the Bagre expands, develops and contracts with each telling, in a 'generative', 'creative' way that characterizes much oral activity of a 'literary' kind. (Goody 1987: 189)

Goody examines the complex relationships between literacy and the processes of recording, the associated social construction of knowledge and power, and a notion of oral culture which is closely similar to the oral-formulaic school as outlined above, and subscribes to the Great Divide, summarizing his position in the following terms:

> The material we have examined on the differences between written and oral languages or registers ... , displays some striking similarities to another difference which has been talked about in vague cultural terms. This is the difference between what Lévi-Strauss refers to as the domesticated and the savage, what others refer to as primitive and advanced, or as simple and complex, hot and cold. Some major differences touched upon in this discussion can reasonably be attributed to the advent of writing and the subsequent developments – the formalization of discourse, the extension of some forms of abstraction, of logic (i.e. the syllogism) and of rationality, not in the sense that common usage usually espouses but in a more restricted fashion that refers to the analysis of formal propositions in ways that seem to depend upon visual inspection and material manipulation. (Goody 1987: 290–1)

138 *Orality*

Cognitive skills that have been seen to be associated with writing have been the subject of lengthy and intensive investigation, working from the notion that orality has constituted a lack, an incapacity, a background and an historical condition. The seeming dominance of writing in 'modern' societies and in the personal lives of individuals living within them are aptly illustrated by the self-portrait presented by Jack Goody at the very end of his book on the interface between the oral and the written:

> Today, not an unusual day, I have spent the time typing on a typewriter, dictating responses to my mail, reading newspapers, books, papers and a dissertation, drafting memoranda. Virtually the only oral communication I have had has been on the telephone, voice-to-voice but not face-to-face. Not all these activities depend upon an ability to read and write, but most do. They involve a type of interaction that is markedly different from oral discourse. Most of them require other actors, as authors or readers, but indirectly and in ways that are more reflective than speaking. I may consider a letter before writing it, alter phrases, even tear it up. The process and context of creation (and of reception) is very different. Indeed I may simply write for myself, trying to put down on paper the kind of commentary of the inner voice that accompanies all my acts, a self-commentary. But once again the process of writing down is more deliberate, like dictating an utterance and turning it into a text. It is at once more reflective and at the same time permits me to reorganize the order of things, to work out the meaning of things, to explicate more formally. And while formal operations may lead to copying, to stagnation, they may also help to break through the crust of customary thinking by bringing out 'contradictions', 'illogicalities', 'non-sequiturs', categorical ambiguities and so on, which are more likely to be glossed over in speech. Cognitively as well as sociologically, writing underpins 'civilization', the culture of cities. (Goody 1987: 299–300)

Perhaps a picture of the daily life of a very small proportion of people in present-day western society, but one which is, in my view, less and less true for the vast majority of people whose daily lives are filled with speech, radio, television, telephones, recorded music, and who, after school, rarely, if ever, need to read anything other than a newspaper or an application form, and still less often write. The implicit negative side to this graphic illustration of the underlying correlations that go with writing, is plain from the above: oral discourse is a small part of daily working life, oral discourse limits reflection and care in composition, it reduces the possibility of puzzling out meaning and, above all, it is the locus of 'customary thinking' replete with contradictions, illogicalities and non-sequiturs. And, most sweeping of all, oral discourse = lack of civilization = rural world = lack of certain cognitive skills.

Goody investigates, however, the differing ethnographic contexts in which forms of literate and oral communication interact and the role and use of writing and speech in particular social environments. The complexities of such interactions lead to a wide variety of patterns in terms of the three factors discussed by Finnegan – namely composition, performance and transmission both of texts and of the skills of creating such texts. A 'text' may be oral in performance and composed in writing and that composition stored or passed on in writing; an oral composition may be performed and then be transferred to oral recording or transcribed as a written text – both processes involving the 'fixing' of a text; a narrative may be composed in writing, performed orally and repeated by the hearers to others in a chain of oral transmission, varying as it goes; a variety of oral testimonies may be gathered and woven together into a single composite written narrative, a history or a 'myth'. Faced with a written text we may need to know its track record: how did it get to be in this written form and what is its status? Finnegan again illustrates:

> A piece of text on the page, once it has been recorded and published, may represent a number of differing starting-points: a fixed and memorized text, a unique and perhaps one-off performance never repeated in a similar form, a version by an experienced specialist who, despite minor verbal variations, has gone through many similar performances often in his career, an experiment by a young poet still in his apprenticeship, or a gallant try by a willing but inexperienced non-specialist in response to a foreign researcher's proddings. We would do well not to assume from the similar-looking transcriptions on a published page that the kind of transmission that lies behind it was always of an already frozen text. (Finnegan 1988: 169–70)

The differing intervention of writing and orality in parallel artistic genres is neatly illustrated in Finnegan's examination of three forms of performance in Milton Keynes (Finnegan 1989). Classical music-making relied upon a canonical, fixed, written score with a very separate existence from the orchestral performance, with prior composition and later performance. Jazz music in Milton Keynes, likened to oral-formulaic composition, relied upon phrases, motifs and 'formulae' that were commonly known among the musicians, but the performance itself constituted the locus in which the particular composition took place, reflected in the orally improvised end-result. A third, entirely oral mode of music-making was to be seen in rock bands where intensive rehearsal provided the locus for the group interaction in which the composition took place. Only when the band had practised the songs so that they could perform them consistently to their satisfaction, in a fixed form that relied upon memory built out of repeated oral practice, would the band actually perform in front of an audience. In each of these modes of music-making, composition and transmission involved different elements of oral and written intervention in the construction of a performance.

Within the field of oral composition and transmission there is clearly a continuum varying from highly stable fixed and memorized forms to the most flexible and creatively malleable processes of re-rendering, with the oral-formulaic theory having established a common pattern, but one which is not necessarily exclusive or typical. Oral composition, performance and transmission display often complex interrelations with the written word, the written word as source, as destination and as parallel manifestation for 'texts' ranging right along the fixed : flexible continuum. If we focus upon the interactions between the oral and the written in everyday discourse and in the composition, performance, and transmission of crafted language, 'texts' in the broadest sense, then we do not require the framework which sees writing as a necessary step on the path from the primitive to the civilized and as a mark of difference between 'us' and 'them'. Since 'we' live in an equally oral world of discourse as any of 'them', it is the 'uses of orality', to rephrase Hoggart, that can allow us to begin to dismantle the hegemonic binary Great Divide which seems to dog our every footstep. We can examine the struggles to control the terms of verbal trade as between literary communication and oral communication (see, for example, Hofmeyr (1995)). We can examine the problems of literate representation of the oral communication and the relative cultural nexuses of oral and literate forms (see, for example, Brown 1998). We can focus upon the communicative moment and its cognitive, social, political and interpersonal characteristics, and situate that communication in its generic, rhetorical, and historical context in such a way that avoids treating orality as all the opposites to the string of features associated with literacy – a condition that Finnegan (1988: 147) characterized as '(having) been held responsible for just about everything that is supposed to be characteristic of western civilization', this comment coming after a quote from Harvey Graff (1982) on the supposed effects of literacy:

A truly daunting number of cognitive, affective, behavioral, and attitudinal effects. These characteristics usually include attitudes ranging from empathy, innovativeness, achievement-orientation, 'cosmopoliteness', information-and-media-awareness, national identification, technological acceptance, rationality, and commitment to democracy, to opportunism, linearity of thought and behavior, or urban residence. Literacy is sometimes conceived of as a skill, but more often as symbolic or representative of attitudes and mentalities. On other levels, literacy 'thresholds' are seen as requirements for economic development, 'take-offs', 'modernization', political development and stability, standards of living, fertility control, and so on. (Graff 1982: 13–14)

In the contemporary world of increasingly global oral communication the relegation of the 'oral' to the tendentious and unhelpful paradigm of the Ongian binary classification of types of society is no longer appropriate. The oral is a set of communicative conditions apparent in *all* societies and it is the implications of those conditions which have been obscured by the focus on the so-called 'advances' purportedly engendered by 'writing' and by the relegation of the oral as a feature of western antiquity or, apparently, non-western 'oral societies'. The features of these communicative conditions for the constitution of human societies – the power of the spoken word – are evident wherever we turn.

In considering, then, the particularities of orality and their implications for cultural production, it is necessary to start from the characteristics which the simulacrum of orality so assiduously attempts to imitate: the moment of communication between speaker and listener. Its simultaneity of articulation and perception is central to our considerations.

Poetics

In considering the nature of orality and the academic fields of enquiry which most directly impinge upon the issues under discussion here, poetics is perhaps the most pertinent. Poetics is variously conceived, and consequently varied in practice. In its very broadest sense it has been used to encompass all and any aspect of the theory of literature, ranging from a consideration of artistry in language use, whatever the form or nature of the communication (and which consequently does not attempt to draw a distinction between the 'literary' and the 'non-literary'), through to the study of those elements of 'textuality' which are viewed as providing the basis for a distinction between the literary and the non-literary. With this latter focus, there is the basis for judgements that distinguish between literature and ephemera, and indeed for the assessment of 'great' literature as compared to minor literature.

Alternatively, there is a perception of the meaning of poetics which narrows in upon the notion of a theory of 'poetry' as opposed to prose. Deriving from Aristotle, this notion perceives of 'poetry' as being an immanent quality of insight and of imagination that transcends the boundaries of expressive form. Following this notion of poetry, there can be 'poetry' that is in prose or indeed in any other expressive medium so long as it is viewed as capturing such qualities. At the same time there can be texts which display all the formal characteristics of 'poetic' form in the sense of versification or other genre-related features of language use, but which are viewed as being 'prosaic' in the derogatory sense, mere verse rather than poetry.

Formalist perspectives, focusing upon that which makes literature different from everyday speech, nevertheless returned not to the notion of an immanent quality invested in the text, but to the notion of the distinctiveness of the 'literary' as being a product of the self-referentiality of the text. In this respect, a presumption is that 'everyday' or 'non-literary' language does not draw attention to itself, that language is a hollow vessel through which the contemplation of meaning and intention takes place. In contrast with that perspective, the language that shouts about itself, that trips up the listener and says 'notice and enjoy these patterns, these sounds, these intricacies, these puzzles', is the outcome of play and artifice on the part of the speaker. That intention and effect, to draw attention to the medium, thus constitutes a primary characteristic of the 'poetic' or the literary, according to this view. Such patterning may draw attention to the text itself, but not to the detriment of interpretation. The markedness of the text is equally a pointer to the meanings deployed within it as to the nature of the form itself. That which is special is so because its meanings are particularly significant, or at least that is the assumption of the listener about the intentions of the speaker. This link between the self-referentiality of the text and its meanings leads to a joint focus upon the nature of the work itself and the nature of the relationship between the text and that which it seeks to represent about the world. The construction of a representation of people, of social relations, of history and of the world around us, and both the partiality and contested nature of such representations has always been at the centre of the examination of texts. The issue has long been, in western poetics, how reliable this verbal representation of the external world is. To what extent is the reader/listener able to grasp or rely upon any interpretation of a text? On what authority is the text to be given credence? Does it matter anyway? And all of these issues start from a presumption that a text is an attempt to portray an aspect of 'reality', a mimetic construct of variable reliability, that has its own characteristics as a text that must be comprehended in the attempt to assess its reliability as a mimetic project. The notion that a text is an objective entity that has determinable patterns and organization requiring some form of fixed interpretation built upon the significance of those objectively present structures has been thoroughly demolished by more recent positions which deny any objectively assessable transition from the text to its interpretation. Such views maintain the primacy of the reader/listener in defining the process of interpretation, having no authority other than their own imagination in the move from text to meaning. Where an assumption had been that certain 'universal truths' were available within the particulars of a text, now there were no such termini available to be sought.

Consonant with a move away from the notion of authority in text, speaker or listener, or indeed in any notion of the 'vraisemblable', has been an interest not in authority but in the dynamics of human expression and the affectivity of communication. Taking a position that starts not with assumptions about the objective nature of the 'text' but with the experiential nature of art, and the arts of language use in particular, this focus has either placed the speaker/author at the centre in the sense that it has been concerned with the process of the constitution of the subject position in communication and the expressive mechanisms available to that subject, or it has focused upon the listener and the affective nature of the communication. From this perspective, the text, and particularly the crafted text, is viewed as one component within a process of interpersonal transaction, rather than as an objective entity separable from the transaction itself. This pragmatics of poetic discourse chimes with the perspective taken in this discussion where the very nature of orality is such that the transaction is all, even if the text may survive in recognizably reminiscent forms. The varying degrees to which poetics has focused upon the poet, the world as a reality represented through the text, the characteristics of the text, or the audience itself, has led to different schools and trends in the development of the field of poetics. Nevertheless, it is perhaps poetics more than any other field in which we see a combination of a sensitivity to textual form and the playfulness, creativity and artistry of language use along with the consideration of the theoretical problems of meaning and communication. Orality and the process of entextualization (see the discussion below about 'political language') with all its correlates of form, of genre, of event and of interpretation, is necessarily embedded within interpersonal transactions that relate to ways of knowing and ways of communicating that knowledge, and in that sense relate most directly to the social dimensions of such transactions – creation and reception of knowledge within the nexus of gender, nation, race, history, ideology and culture. Orality is the transaction that runs from speaker through message to audience, from poet through text to listener. Those transactions have been the object of study over many centuries and in many cultures. And a particular emphasis has often been put on instruction in the terms of such trade – treatises on effective speaking, guidance on persuasion, prescriptive discussion of what to say and how to say it.

Rhetoric

Effectiveness in speaking is a subject of debate and interest with a long pedigree. In the Africa of ancient Egypt, canons for effective speaking were outlined in the maxims of Ptahhotep (Fox 1983) ... Summarized by Fox as:

> Keeping *silent*; waiting for the *right moment* to speak; *restraining* passionate words; speaking *fluently* but with great deliberation; and keeping your tongue at one with your heart so that you speak the *truth*. (Kennedy 1998: 130; my emphasis)

Kennedy (1998) presents an overview of Chinese rhetorical traditions in which similar maxims are articulated in the Shu Ching 'Book of History', a text by a number of anonymous authors or editors, summarized by Oliver (1971) as follows:

> to rule well meant to communicate honestly, intelligently, and effectively ... Ministers must be courageous in speaking with utmost frankness to their monarchs; and kings must be unmistakably clear what responsibilities and duties they expect their ministers, generals and officials to exercise. Social harmony and individual dignity ... could not be attained by evasive speaking, by false flattery, or by curbing honest criticism. The kind of speech repeatedly recommended was

that which aimed to achieve the speaker's goal through means that would enhance rather than undermine communal contentment. Disruptive personal attack or appeal to self-interest in persuasive appeals was always to be condemned ... The best speaking was that which showed that the good of each one inhered within what was good for all. (Oliver 1971: 102)

Not only have there been guidelines for the effectiveness of speaking such as the above. Models of 'standardized' speeches for particular circumstances have been part of the rhetorical apparatus not only of ancient Greece and Rome but also of, for example, the Aztec Empire of Central America. In the 'General History of the Things of New Spain', the Franciscan friar, Bernardino Sahagún, compiled between 1547 and 1562 an encyclopedia of Aztec society, which included 89 orations (*huehuetlatolli*) (Kennedy 1998: 100–2) which were memorized for verbatim delivery on appropriate occasions: prayers to the gods; speeches given by and to a king at the time of his election; speeches of parents to children; speeches to a merchant on departure and return from a trading expedition, among many others (Abbott 1987). These examples of formal language were replete with repetition and metaphor, and marked by the self-deprecation in royal speeches of the unwilling candidate who has fame thrust upon them. And, as with our previous examples, injunctions on how to speak are made by father to son:

> Thou art to speak very slowly, very deliberately: thou art not to speak hurriedly, not to pant, not to squeak, lest it be said of thee that thou art a groaner, a growler, a squeaker. Also thou art not to cry out, lest thou be known as an imbecile, a shameless one, a rustic, very much a rustic. Moderately, middlingly art thou to carry, to emit thy spirit, thy words. And thou art to improve, to soften thy words, thy voice. (Anderson and Dibble VII: 122; quoted in Kennedy 1998: 105)

The art of preparing public speeches is perhaps best known from the ancient world of Greece and Rome, where professional speechwriters, such as Demosthenes and Antiphon, could, for example, be hired to write a judicial speech for reproduction in the presence of a jury. Handbooks on oratory defined the conventional parts of a speech: the proemium (introduction aimed at getting the attention and sympathy of the audience), narration (background and necessary facts), proof (stating the question at issue, the thesis and the supporting arguments), and epilogue (recapitulation of main points and attempt to stir the emotions of the audience) (Kennedy 1998: 7). The process of designing a speech was similarly defined and taught:

> Greek and Roman writers on rhetoric taught that there was a series of steps in the composition of a speech, which by the Hellenistic period became the 'parts' or as they are sometimes now called 'canons' of rhetoric: invention, or the planning of the thought and arguments; arrangement of the contents into a systematic structure; and casting of the contents into an appropriate style of words and sentences, artistically adorned; then the memorization of the speech, and finally its delivery with good control of the voice and effective gestures. These five steps originated as a pedagogical device for novices.
> (Kennedy 1998: 219)

Each of these five steps had its own subjects of study: 'invention' included those elements that conveyed the credibility of the speaker (ethos), the argumentation deployed in the speech (logos: argument by syllogism, by example and analogy), the topics commonly deployed in favour of a particular position (topoi); 'arrangement' included the conventional parts of a speech outlined above; 'style' referred to the many and varied elements of word choice, figures of speech and register, and other distinctive features of language use; 'memorization' referred to mnemonics and formulae that assisted with transmission; and finally 'delivery' related to different ways of using voice and gesture in the execution of the speech itself.

Aristotle distinguished three types of rhetoric determined on the basis of what was expected of the audience: judicial, deliberative and epideictic:

> An audience is either called on to make some decision or take some action or it is not. If asked to make a decision about the justice or legality of an action in the past, the species is judicial. If asked to make a decision about the advantage of some future action the species is deliberative. If no decision is required other than whether or not a good speech has been given, the species is epideictic.
> (Kennedy 1998: 220)

The character of the speech of the effective speaker, in this case a king, is described in Hesiod:

> Whomsoever the daughters of great Zeus honor
> And mark at his birth as a god-nurtured prince.

On his tongue they pour sweet distillation,
And words from his mouth flow honeyed: the people
All look toward him discerning precedents
With straight justice, and with unfaltering address.
He quickly and skilfully settles even a great dispute;
Thus are there sagacious princes, for when the people
Are misguided in assembly, these end the wheeling recriminations
Easily, persuading with gentle words. (Walker 1996: 244)

One of the most notable discussions of the art of persuasion and man-management through speech and writing comes from an adviser to kings writing around 300BC in India, cited in Kennedy (1998: 183–5):

> Portions of Kautilya's *Arthashastra* of special rhetorical interest are those in which he lists topoi that are useful in a variety of situations and those in which he reveals the existence of a technical terminology to describe features of rhetoric. Chapter 14 of book 1, for example, deals with how to win over factions for or against an enemy's cause in a foreign state. Thirty-four different categories of people who might be disaffected are listed: those deluded by false promises, those prevented in the exercise of their rights, criminals, the oppressed, and so forth. Then suggestions are offered as to what the foreign king's spies might say to win them over ... Chapter 10 of book two describes the contents and style of royal writs. It provides a list of topoi ... and reveals the remarkable extent to which features of rhetoric were conceptualized and named in ancient India:

Kennedy cites the following passage from Shamasastry's translation of Kautilya, book 2, ch. 10:

> As to a writ addressed to a lord, it shall contain polite mention of his country, his possessions, his family and his name ... Having paid sufficient attention to the caste, family, social rank, age, learning, occupation, property, character, and blood-relationship of the addressee, as well as to the place and time, the writer shall form a writ befitting the position of the person addressed.
>
> Arrangement of subject-matter, relevancy, completeness, sweetness, dignity, and lucidity are the necessary qualities of a writ. The act of mentioning facts in the order of their importance is *arrangement*. When subsequent facts are not contradictory to facts just or previously mentioned, and so on till the completion of the letter, it is

termed *relevancy*. Avoidance of redundancy or deficiency in words or letters; impressive description of subject-matter by citing reasons, examples and illustrations; and the use of appropriate and suitably strong words is *completeness*. The description in exquisite style of a good purport with a pleasing effect is *sweetness*. The use of words other than colloquial is *dignity*. The use of well-known words is *lucidity*. (Shamasastry 1923: 78–9)

Insofar as such injunctions derive from an observation of the practice of persuasion, moving from, presumably, Kautilya's 'ethnographic' understanding to a normative set of principles, they can highlight the issue of subjective notions of skill and effectiveness, both normatively expressed and through comment upon the observation of the actual practice of human communication. The scope of the injunctions of Kautilya are interesting in that they are framed within a broader context that relates the use of language to the exercise of force:

Negotiation, bribery, causing dissension, and open attack are forms of stratagem (upāya):

Negotiation is of five kinds:

Praising the qualities (of an enemy), narrating the mutual relationship, pointing out mutual benefit, showing vast future prospects, and identity of interests.

When the family, person, occupation, conduct, learning, properties, etc. (of an enemy), are commended with due attention to their worth, it is termed praising the qualities (gunsankīrthana).

When the fact of having agnates, blood-relations, teachers (maukha), priestly hierarchy (srauva), family, and friends in common is pointed out, it is known as narration of mutual relationship (sambandhōpākhyāna).

When both parties, the party of a king and that of his enemy, are shown to be helpful to each other, it is known as pointing out mutual benefit (parasparōpakārasamadarsanam).

Inducement, such as 'This being done thus, such result will accrue to both of us', is showing future prospects (āyātipradarsanam).

To say, 'What I am, that thou art; thou mayest utilize in they works whatever is mine', is identity of interests (ātmōpanidhānam).

Offering money is bribery (upapradāna).

Causing fears and suspicion as well as threatening is known as sowing dissension.

Killing, harassing, and plundering is attack (danda).

Clumsiness, contradiction, repetition, bad grammar, and misarrangement are the faults of a writ.
Black and ugly leaf (kālapatrakamachāru) and uneven and uncoloured (virāga) writing cause clumsiness.
Subsequent portion disagreeing with previous portion of a letter causes contradiction (vyāghātha).
Stating for a second time what has already been said above is repetition.
Wrong use of words in gender, number, time and case is bad grammar (apasabda).
Division of paragraphs (varga) in unsuitable places, omission of necessary divisions of paragraphs, and violation of any other necessary qualities of a writ constitute misarrangement (samplava).
(Shamasastry 1923: 81-2)

The concerns of classical rhetoric and the injunctions of the likes of Kautilya reflect a preoccupation with felicitous and effective communication, the avoidance of misunderstanding or a lack of understanding and the attendant frustration and conflict that may arise. Where such rhetoricians are occupied with the formal speeches of kings and courtiers, the issues remain nevertheless the same in relation to the everyday speech of us mere mortals.

Pragmatics

In recent years the academic discipline of linguistics has embraced the study of both the innate linguistic structures of the human mind and the features of everyday conversation and verbal interaction between people. This latter field, pragmatics and more broadly sociolinguistics, has taken up some of those same issues adumbrated in the earlier discussions of the students of rhetoric.

A premise introduced by Grice (1975), one of the founders of the modern field of pragmatics, was that in human conversation people adopt certain conventions in order to facilitate effective two-way communication, and that these conventions operate in circumstances where people wish to co-operate with each other in communication. Clearly, if I cover my ears, or shout continuously at you without listening, then I am avoiding any such conventions, but usually, I hope, we do in fact share an aim in allowing communication between us. Grice termed his shared aim the 'co-operative principle' and within it posited a series of conventions or 'maxims' that were put into effect in a variety of

150 *Orality*

different ways. Where Kautilya talked of 'completeness', Grice talked of the 'quantity maxim', giving the right amount of information, not too little and not too much, for the purpose of the communication; where Ptahhotep talked of 'keeping your tongue at one with your heart so that you speak the truth' Grice talks of the 'quality maxim', saying that which you believe to be true and for which you have evidence; where Kautilya talked of 'relevancy' so also does Grice talk of the 'maxim of relation'; where Kautilya talked of 'arrangement', 'lucidity' and 'sweetness' so Grice talked of the 'maxim of manner', avoiding ambiguity and obscurity, being brief and being orderly. The development of the field of pragmatics in linguistics has built upon the conversational analysis of Grice and others and the speech-act theory of Austin and Searle to analyse in detail the manifestations in everyday conversation of these broader principles and maxims. In so doing other principles have been outlined that operate in face-to-face communication, all of which relate to the choices people arrive at in making appropriate statements and responses. Leech (1983), for example, outlines the dynamics in speech of the way in which aspects of 'politeness' operate. Maxims of tact, generosity, approbation and modesty relate to the interpersonal relations between speaker and hearer. Leech analyses the operation of the politeness principle in relation, for example, to the following alternatives:

> Answer the phone!
> I want you to answer the phone.
> Will you answer the phone?
> Won't you answer the phone?
> Can you answer the phone?
> Would you mind answering the phone?
> Could you possibly answer the phone?
> (adapted from Leech 1983: 108)

Leech demonstrates the various ways in which imperatives, question forms, negatives, can contribute to differing degrees of indirectness and tactfulness, and analyses in great detail the use of language and implications of these general maxims. Choices between one or other of the above phrases are determined by differential application of particular maxims, but illustrate points on scales that have relevance for many issues in the consideration of orality, entailing as they do the necessary presence of speaker and hearer:

> 1. The COST–BENEFIT SCALE ... on which is estimated the cost or benefit of the proposed action to speaker or hearer.

2. The OPTIONALITY SCALE on which illocutions are ordered according to the amount of choice which the speaker allows to the hearer.
3. The INDIRECTNESS SCALE on which, from the speaker's point of view, illocutions are ordered with respect to the length of the path (in terms of means–ends analysis) connecting the illocutionary act to its illocutionary goal. (adapted from Leech 1983: 123)

In further discussion of alternative interpersonal relationships, Leech goes on to consider deliberate breaches of maxims in the practice of irony and of banter. A statement that conforms to the 'politeness principle', such as 'Do help yourself!', when uttered with sarcastic irony, means in reality 'Don't take so much food!'; or the command of 'Come here, you bastard!' can, in circumstances of banter, be affectionate. These are second-order reversals of first-order maxims in the play of language. Leech demonstrates the different degrees to which social intercourse is governed by such maxims in different societies by illustrating the Japanese conventions on modesty in speech in comparison with British English. An illustration of a conventional but seemingly extreme self-deprecation in politeness is provided by the Aztec standard speeches referred to earlier. Kennedy discusses the speeches made by and to the king on his installation and makes the following comment:

> The rhetorical technique of protesting selection was carried to an extreme in the Aztec ritual of a newly chosen king. In his first speech the new king utterly debases himself as 'filth' and 'excrement' and totally unqualified for the position to which the god has called him. Perhaps a mistake has been made? Perhaps he is dreaming? What is he to do? Gradually, however, he begins to show some acceptance of the situation: 'Howsoever thou wilt require of me, that I shall do, that I shall perform. Whichsoever road thou wilt show me, that one I shall follow; whatsoever thou wilt reveal unto me, that I shall say, that shall I pronounce' (Anderson and Dibble VII: 44). (Kennedy 1998: 103)

Returning to modern-day pragmatics, much of the development of the field derives from the work of Austin and Searle, who worked with a primary distinction between locutionary acts (saying something), illocutionary acts (performing an act in saying something, e.g. in saying X, the speaker *asserts* something), and perlocutionary acts (performing an act by saying something, e.g. by saying X, the speaker *convinces* the hearer of something) (adapted from Leech 1983: 199). Both Austin and

Searle focused upon different categories of illocutionary act, with Searle proposing a revision of Austin's categories into the following:

1. *Assertives*: committing the speaker to something's being the case, to the truth of the expressed proposition, assessable in terms of true or false; the use of verbs such as 'deduce', 'conclude', 'insist'.
2. *Directives*: attempts by the speaker to get the hearer to do something; the use of such verbs as 'request', 'order', 'invite'.
3. *Commissives*: committing the speaker to some future course of action; the use of such verbs as 'promise', 'offer', 'volunteer'.
4. *Expressives*: expressing the psychological state of the speaker; the use of verbs such as 'thank', 'congratulate', 'condole'.
5. *Declarations*: utterances which, through their performance, bring about an alteration in the status or condition of the referred to object; examples such as 'I hereby declare you man and wife', 'I name this ship "Titanic", "I resign".' (adapted from Searle 1979: 12–17)

Searle went on to consider second-order problems in the discussion of illocutionary acts, the use of metaphor, the approach to indirect speech, the interpretation of fictional discourse, among others (Searle 1979), in the same way that Leech, much later, considered second-order manipulation of conversational principles like irony and banter. As ever, usage is such that the above categories, as they are applied either to verbs or to broader utterances, are neither exclusive nor all-encompassing. As Searle points out (1979: 28), a verb such as 'warn' can, in one usage, be an assertive 'I warn you that the bull is about to charge', and in another a directive 'I warn you to stay away from my wife!'

Nevertheless, speech-act theory and its development in pragmatics has provided the tools for a detailed analysis of the language of interaction, of strategies of discourse and their guiding principles, which focuses upon language use in a variety of situations, viewing language not as a formal system of grammar, but as a set of alternative ways in which a person can solve problems in communicating with others:

> A speaker, qua communicator, has to solve the problem: 'Given that I want to bring about such-and-such a result in the hearer's consciousness, what is the best way to accomplish this aim by using language?' For the hearer, there is another kind of problem to solve: 'Given that the speaker said such-and-such, what did the speaker mean me to understand by that?' This conception of communication leads to a

rhetorical approach to pragmatics, whereby the speaker is seen as trying to achieve his aims within constraints imposed by principles and maxims of 'good communicative behaviour'. (Leech 1983: x–xi)

The resolution of the problems so graphically described by Leech gives rise to a myriad different ways of speaking. Both choices between available alternatives – to say 'answer the phone!' rather than 'Could you possibly answer the phone?' – are ways of speaking that are available and understood within the speech community to which I belong. The investigation of ways of speaking within the myriad speech communities of human society leads us onto the work of those scholars who have developed the broad field of the 'ethnography of speaking' within sociolinguistics and linguistic anthropology.

The connection between the concerns of students of rhetoric and those of sociolinguists is well illustrated in the preface to a foundational volume edited by Gumperz and Hymes (1972: vii):

> The theoretical goal of the type of sociolinguistic investigation represented here is best illustrated by the notion of communicative competence: What a speaker needs to know to communicate effectively in culturally significant settings. Like Chomsky's term on which it is patterned, communicative competence refers to the ability to perform. An attempt is made to distinguish between what the speaker knows – what his inherent capacities are – and how he behaves in particular instances. However, whereas students of linguistic competence seek to explain those aspects of grammar believed to be common to all humans independent of social determinants, students of communicative competence deal with speakers as members of communities, as incumbents of social roles, and seek to explain their use of language to achieve self-identification and to conduct their activities. While for linguistic theory in the former sense the ability to formalize sentences as grammatically acceptable is the central notion, for sociolinguistics as represented in [this] book, the central notion is the appropriateness of verbal messages in context or their acceptability in the broader sense.

The ethnography of speaking

In the 1972 volume *Directions in Sociolinguistics: the Ethnography of Communication* the coiner of the phrase 'ethnography of communication', Dell Hymes (1962) focused upon 'communicative competence' by highlighting the social context of communicative events, and went on to outline key notions for the development of this field (Hymes 1972: 53–8). 'Speech community', following work by Bloomfield (1933), constituted those people, participating in a network of interaction, who 'share knowledge and ability (competence) for the production and interpretation of socially appropriate speech' (Bauman and Sherzer 1989: 6). Difficult to determine in practice, such a community is not necessarily coterminous with 'speakers of the same language' or territorial units, and may in fact cover speakers of more than one language: 'members of the same speech community need not all speak the same language nor use the same linguistic forms on similar occasions. All that is required is that there be at least one language in common and that rules governing basic communicative strategies be shared so that speakers can decode the social meanings carried by alternative modes of communication' (Gumperz and Hymes 1972: 16). One of the cardinal issues for the pursuit of this field of study has been the heterogeneity of speech communities; not only are human societies sometimes very different from each other in their cultures of communication, and many detailed ethnographic studies have documented these differences (see, for example, the studies in Bauman and Sherzer 1982, 1989; Brenneis and Macaulay 1996; Gumperz and Hymes 1972), but in the many different manifestations of speech form, each of which has its own set of expectations and interpretations associated with it,

> The speech community is viewed as inherently heterogeneous; the structure of the heterogeneity must be described. Language use does not occur in isolated sentences, but in natural units of speaking; stated abstractly: speech acts, events, and situations; stated more concretely: greetings, leave-takings, narratives, conversations, jokes, curing techniques, or periods of silence. (Bauman and Sherzer 1989: 9)

A second term outlined by Hymes was 'speech situation', repeated occasions where certain ways of speaking were appropriate, 'ceremonies, fights, hunts, meals, lovemaking, and the like'. Within such situations, certain 'speech events' would take place, a sequence often of 'speech acts' appropriate to that situation. For Hymes these constituted a hierarchy of embedded components in which

> the same type of speech act may recur in different types of speech event, and the same type of speech event in different contexts of

situation. Thus a joke (speech act) may be embedded in a private conversation, a lecture, a formal introduction. A private conversation may occur in the context of a party, a memorial service, a pause in changing sides in a tennis match. (Hymes 1972: 56)

The hierarchy of 'act', 'event', 'situation' and 'community' are delimiting frameworks for the identification and description of moments of communication. There are at least two other frameworks within which the act of communication is embedded, the one epistemological, the other hermeneutic.

The first framework that systematizes the nature of knowledge within communication is, as Habermas has described it, built upon four basic premises. These premises are that I seek to speak the truth in communicating a proposition to you and that you can share in that knowledge; secondly, that I have chosen to speak in a comprehensible manner in order that you may understand what I have to say; thirdly, that I speak according to my best understanding and therefore as truthfully as possible in order that you can trust me; fourthly, that what I say is right and therefore you are in a position, having heard and understood me, to agree with me. Habermas termed such premises 'validity claims' applicable to communicative action in general:

> I shall develop the thesis that anyone acting communicatively must, in performing any speech action, raise universal validity claims and suppose that they can be vindicated [or redeemed: *einlosen*]. Insofar as he wants to participate in a process of reaching understanding, he cannot avoid raising the following – and indeed precisely the following – validity claims. He claims to be:
> a. *Uttering* something understandably;
> b. Giving [the hearer] *something* to understand;
> c. Making *himself* thereby understandable; and
> d. Coming to an understanding *with another person*. (Habermas 1979: 2)

Constructed upon these premises are the secondary contradictions, alternative strategies and oppositional genres that reverse the premise. We are all very well aware of the fact that a great deal of communication is focused upon not telling the truth, and there are ways of speaking that build upon a conventional acceptance that an ironical interpretation is available, that the veil of imagery is there to obscure a direct unmistakable truth, or that satire challenges the good faith of a precursor in the chain of communication. Similarly, an act of communication may be embedded in a consciously fashioned exclusion of a hearer from comprehension, a switch to a language, or an idiom, or a subject matter requiring prior knowledge, that the speaker knows will exclude part of his or her audience; rare, however, is the 'communicative' act that seeks not to communicate something, requiring perhaps a distinction between the use of language and communication – there are many occasions, and not only expression of incomprehensible and inarticulate rage, where the use of the iconic elements of language has other functions than the communication of lexical meaning – the Latin mass used where no church attender understands the words, or the use of Soninke in courtly praise where no one present understands the 'lexical meaning' although the symbolic importance of the narration is well understood by all present (Farias 1995: 234). The desire of the speaker to be seen to be speaking truthfully, whether the audience accepts that profession of good faith or not, is perhaps an unmediated part of the equation insofar as a wish to be seen to be lying is unusual in circumstances other than the expression of statements that could only be seen to be so if they had been extracted under duress. I may switch from one statement in public to its opposite in private and others may assume that I do; nevertheless, the framework within which the public statement is embedded is that it is an expression of my intention to speak truthfully. Finally, the proposition that what I say is right, and that on that basis you should agree with me is perhaps also rarely deliberately reversed. Self-denigration can be a part of the formal rhetoric of modesty, but the epistemological status of 'I say that which is wrong and therefore you must disagree with me' is questionable, and in that sense, Habermas's notion that the premises outlined constitute the necessary premises for the person wishing to participate in a 'process of understanding' is most apparent here. In looking at how agreement is arrived at, Habermas acknowledges the significance of the opposite:

> The goal of coming to an understanding [*Verständigung*] is to bring about an agreement [*Einverständnis*] that terminates in the intersubjective mutuality of reciprocal understanding, shared knowledge, mutual trust, and accord with one another. Agreement is based on recognition of the corresponding validity claims of comprehensibility, truth, truthfulness, and rightness. We can see that the word *understanding* is ambiguous. In its minimal meaning it indicates that two subjects understand a linguistic expression in the same way; its maximal meaning is that between the two there exists an accord

concerning the rightness of an utterance in relation to a mutually recognized normative background. In addition, two participants in communication can come to an understanding about something in the world, and they can make their intentions understandable to one another.

If full agreement, embracing all four of these components, were a normal state of linguistic communication, it would not be necessary to analyze the process of understanding from the dynamic perspective of *bringing about* an agreement. The typical states are in the gray areas in between: on the one hand, incomprehension and misunderstanding, intentional and involuntary untruthfulness, concealed and open discord; and, on the other hand, pre-existing or achieved consensus. Coming to an understanding is the process of bringing about an agreement on the presupposed basis of validity claims that can be mutually recognized. (Habermas 1979: 3)

The second framework within which speech acts are embedded is one which relates to the domains within which a speech act works in the process of establishing effective communication, hermeneutic in Habermas's sense ('Hermeneutics watches language at work, so to speak, language as it is used by participants to reach a common *understanding* or a shared *view*' (Habermas 1990: 25)). This framework sets the speech act within domains of relation between it and the actors and references entailed with it. In this respect, a set of correlations are established between the premises of the speech act as adumbrated above and four essential domains of relations. The speech act can be considered in its relation to the external world – in the search for ways to represent the world of 'facts', the sign and its referent are repeatedly assessed in terms of truth and objectification, when I say a hawk is a handsaw it is the contravention of the perceived relation of sign to referent that demands of you that you cast around in your mind for a way of interpreting this 'falsehood', a metaphor or a madness. That same speech act is viewable from within another domain, one which takes as its direction of interest the interpersonal relations between you and me, the social world within which we interact and the rightness of my utterance judged within the shared norms and conventions we believe we hold in common. The third domain within which that same speech act can be considered is that of my own subjective condition. Was it a cry for help? Was it a sign of madness? Was I simply full of the joys of spring? And what does the assumed truthfulness of the act in relation to the mental and emotional process of my mind signify? The fourth domain assesses the speech act as it participates in the linguistic processes which create comprehensibility in the utterance (Habermas 1979: 66ff).

In considering the speech acts performed within these contexts, there then come into play the many and various ways of speaking, the styles and genres that each culture deploys in communication. And it is here that the wheel returns to text and to rhetoric; one direction that the pursuit of the ethnography of speaking has taken has been the nature of verbal art in different societies – the genres of speaking may be crafted, conventional, designed and appreciated as manifestations of skill. In this, the field of sociolinguistics merges with that of poetics, of oral art, and of literary studies. The pursuit of contexts in which such language is deployed has led into the area of political language and the dynamics of power relations in society. The history of the interlinking between different fields of enquiry – linguistics, anthropology, folklore and sociology – in the development of the 'ethnography of speaking', and particularly the range of issues that have emerged from a growing number of case studies, is outlined in the preface to the second edition of *Explorations in the Ethnography of Speaking*, edited by Bauman and Sherzer (1989). And they conclude, portentously, that they 'envisage the ethnography of speaking in the next phase of its development as assuming a place ever more clearly as an integrative, discourse-centred perspective on language, literature, society, culture and history that transcends disciplinary divisions of intellectual labor' (Bauman and Sherzer 1989: xxii).

Performance and political language

Orality is performance and, unless it is mime or instrumental music, performance involves orality. The spoken word requires (at least usually) a relationship between a speaker and a listener. The politics of language use in performance is a well-researched field. In addition to the wide range of material and depth of ethnographic study that is available in the 'ethnography of speaking' school, a number of studies within political anthropology have examined similar issues from a variety of perspectives. Bloch (1975) focused upon the way in which formalized oratory served the interests of ruling elites in reinforcing traditional authority, while the papers edited by Paine (1981) laid more emphasis upon the negotiation of power relations through language. The overview by Parkin (1984) reinforces the interest in the processes of cultural debate:

> In conclusion, there is a dimension of discourse in which the speaker is assumed to control knowledge. There is a second in which the

discourse is scrutinized and its assumptions criticized and even negotiated between speaker and audience. But there is also a third in which ... unintended and accidental events have somehow to be accommodated in the discourse. Whether these are really accidents of history rather than its logical unfolding does not matter. They should add up to a widening of historical perspectives, or to put it another way, to an increasing awareness of social inequalities. (Parkin 1984: 363)

The concern that Parkin expresses is to situate the communicative moment in historical processes, thereby linking the communicative event to broader analyses of society. Intensive examination of the local negotiation of meaning has been undertaken in many studies. Bauman and Briggs (1990), like Parkin, see one of the tasks facing those studying the politics of language use as being to find ways to bridge the gap between intensive local ethnographic study and the broader consideration of social organization and ideology:

> Recently, however, critics and practitioners alike have identified certain limitations engendered by a mode of analysis that hews too closely to the speech or performance event as the primary frame of reference and unit of analysis. The difficulties are several. First, there is the problem of history, the need to link series of speech events into historical systems of interrelationship in discourse-centred terms. Second, there is the perennial micro–macro problem of how to relate the situated use of language to larger social structures, particularly the structures of power and value that constitute the political economy of a society. Again, the problem is to identify discursive practices that mediate between the situated use of language within speech events and those larger structures. And finally, there is the problem of linking the artful speaking of performance to other modes of language use so that performance analysis does not fall into the trap of segregating poetics from other ways of speaking. (Bauman and Briggs 1990: 79)

Their direction was to suggest the individual instance is best set within a historical frame of broader issues by examining trajectories of 'entextualization', 'decontextualization' and 'recontextualization' – how a piece of discourse becomes a 'text' and is then transferred and re-used. Such trajectories would transcend the local instance and relate to broader issues:

> Building upon the accumulated insights of past performance analysis, the investigation of the interrelated processes of entextualization,

de-contextualization (decentering), and recontextualization (recentering) opens a way towards constructing histories of performance; toward illuminating the larger systemic structures in which performances play a constitutive role; and toward linking performances with other modes of language use as performances are decentered and recentered both within and across speech events – referred to, cited, evaluated, reported, looked back upon, replayed, and otherwise transformed in the production and reproduction of social life. (Bauman and Briggs 1990: 80)

As Bauman and Briggs point out, the text, along with all its associated performance correlates, may thus be adapted – shifting its audience, its potential field of interpretation and meaning, as it does so. This process of recycling naturally involves adaptation to new contexts, and the ideological process of reshaping the moral and cognitive dimensions of the text is part of the broader political process that is manifest in the situating of the 'new version' into the new political dynamic of a new performance and a new audience. However, it is not necessarily the 'entextualized' object as 'the text' that is decontextualized but rather the significance of the content which is renegotiable – the entextualization is part of the embedding of meaning within genre, event and social context along with all their expectations, correlations and evaluations that go to make up a 'tradition'. For example, the meaning 'the disadvantaged shall become great and the privileged shall lose out' that is entextualized in the Cinderella story (along with a number of other meanings) becomes deployed as a political use of language, and thus enters into the social negotiation of significance, when it is deployed in circumstances where 'I' am telling 'you' in front of 'them' that what I view as your arrogance in present circumstances will lead to your demise. I may not use the Cinderella story, no matter, the Cinderella story has its own appropriate moment for its recitation, its own genre and event category – but the meaning is recontextualized and in being so is reset into another historical, political and discourse context. The entextualization of the meaning through its insertion into the Cinderella story provides a continuity of potential presence; usually the Cinderella story would be deployed to convey this meaning rather than the obverse, namely that the privileged shall ride high and the disadvantaged suffer – nevertheless, as we saw in earlier chapters, artistic creativity and the use of irony may change or indeed reverse the significance in a new context. In this sense, then, the political process of recontextualization may be significant only for certain elements of 'the text' – in the Cinderella example above, any other narrative conveying the same 'moral' could have substituted. The key consideration is the necessity to convey the criticism of 'arrogance' and to restrict, as far as possible, the available interpretations to those conveying criticism and the negative value 'arrogance'. Whether the story was Cinderella or King Lear is in this respect perhaps not directly material to the politics of the occasion. However, the effectiveness of the political use of such meanings draws in many other issues relating to genre and the cultural architecture of the society in question. The inappropriate use of a genre may obviate the effectiveness of the communication. To tell a fairy story in response to a question about the chemical make-up of the ozone layer is to fail to pass stage one in the effective use of language. You risk getting zero on that question, except of course when the zany, the comic, the absurd and the incoherent is part of the point of the speech genre itself, in which case you may get ten out of ten.

Concluding remarks

Any consideration of effectiveness has to take into account the nature of the speech act itself and the expectations that surround it derived from its position within speech and event categories. All such speech and event categories – genres, performance occasions – have correlates concerning who is entitled to speak and who is not, who is being spoken to and who is not, who can be present and listen and who can not. Each and every one of these issues is a political issue for local negotiation, or may be the subject of statements or assumptions that there can be *no* negotiation, and for the expression of 'global' rather than 'local' conventions – it is not just you who cannot speak directly to the king, it is everyone; it is not just this wife who is restricted to a particular genre of song, it is all women; such narratives are for the aristocracy only, not for the ordinary farmer.

The pursuit of the dynamics of cultural articulation leads us into the world not only of the articulation of perceptions of reality and values, a reality of conscious, rational understanding and humanist values but also of the articulation of prejudice, viciousness, bigotry and the reification of the other in such a way that sentient humans may, without qualm or second thought, commit individual murder and communal genocide. It is the chains of thought and feeling that lead from the individual desire to protect and favour nearest and dearest to the institutionalized racism of social systems that require elucidation as they are manifest in discourse, just as much as the articulation of 'ideals', 'community values' and the manifestations of the great and the good.

At the heart of the current discussion therefore is a concern with the articulation of views of good and evil and a central ambivalence between a philosophical concern with values and truth and the investigation of the articulation of what is presented as values and truth. One person's lies and propaganda are another person's truth and values. My concern here is to consider the importance of oral discourse in relation to the process of persuasion, whether it be persuasion to what I personally may hold to be 'good' or 'evil'. Absolute values I leave to the philosophers.

One of the central questions that arises in relation to the dynamics of cultural production is: why does one symbolic manifestation become over time a dominant 'tradition/belief/world view/set of ideas', while another fades away as quickly as it is articulated. Is it simply that those who are already powerful are able to impose their views on others? Hardly, since the treasured history of so many traditions, from Jesus to the Sandinistas, relates the precarious struggle of the 'early church' in its attempt to survive and recruit, as a weak and vulnerable group, in the face of implacable and powerful enemies. One view will, of course, claim the overwhelming power of 'truth' or 'God's will' in the success and survival of the message and its carriers. Another view, based upon an acknowledgement of the unpredictability of human response (manifest in the unpredictability of popularity and fashion, for example), formulates the post hoc justification in terms of the suitedness of the message to the moment. That one particular individual, and his or her articulation of views and beliefs, captured the communal 'mood of the moment', put into words what so many individuals had been vaguely feeling, stirring the blood into communal effort and identification, be they Mao, Lenin, Churchill or the local village firebrand. The lesson of new intellectual movements such as the reformist Jihad in early nineteenth-century northern Nigeria is, of course, that it is rarely one individual alone who articulates a particularity and the articulations themselves are moments in an ongoing dialogue with other individuals and with other intellectual sources. Jihadist literature was a co-operative, continuing production line, translating into other languages, providing commentaries and recensions that quickly became absorbed into 'the text'. A group of scholars passed their manuscripts around and on to others. The emergence of 'the texts' was a continuing process, much as the new testament of the Christian church is a compilation of later memoirs and reconstructed narratives. The ascription of a central text to a single individual is part of the construction of authority and power manifest in the later keepers of the 'tradition'. Nevertheless, it is individuals articulating in 'real time' contemporary visions which make such dominant discourses 'real'; who knows what revolutionary upheavals lie latent between the covers of dust-covered books, and lost in long dead memories! Is it that conscious manipulation in planned campaigns for the 'hearts and minds' of people necessarily produces compliant acceptance of a new, or rediscovered, agenda? Do the spin doctors have it all their own way? Or is it that, like a law of physics, one action produces an equal counter-action? That empires must rise and fall, and that repression must be followed by liberation, even if only eventually, and that if it was your turn before, it must be my turn now. A quick look around our world would tend to suggest that no such free pendulum is at work. That there is no predictability in progress, or indeed in how, why or when new articulations will emerge to grab the fevered imaginations of the people and turn the old order upside down. Who would have predicted the sudden collapse of the old Soviet Union, or that cracks would appear in the fabric of apartheid South Africa such that the prophets of apocalypse seeing nothing but blood and more blood would be confounded by a miraculous peaceful transition? Of course, the issues are of economic forces and of geopolitical processes, but the question before us here concerns the perceptions that are articulated about what is happening and what must happen, and the processes that take place as one set of views spreads and grows among ordinary people until a new dispensation of political and economic forces is seen to be acceptable, nay even desired. Creating a vision of a new society is no mean feat. Creating one which a majority of people buy into is the hardest part. It is the power of the spoken word, carrying with it the simultaneous perception of a speaker and a reaction to his or her words, which lies at the heart of the latter process.

6
Concluding: On the Centrality of the Evanescent

The issue of analysing and understanding the dynamics and significance of the oral communicative moment is not a new one. The previous chapter has outlined some of the approaches that have been taken in a number of fields of academic investigation. In 1895 one of the founding fathers of sociology and social anthropology, Emile Durkheim, pointed to the significance of a whole range of phenomena (which he was seeking to establish as 'social facts') that required their own method of investigation and an acknowledgement of their own disciplinary demands, some of which lay outside the 'crystallized form' of established beliefs and practices that were visible in 'legal and moral regulations, religious faiths, financial systems'. These were no less social facts for Durkheim even though they were more fluid 'social currents' rather than social institutions. While his focus was upon establishing 'rules of sociological method' at the birth of the modern discipline of sociology, his description of 'social facts' that fall outside of the framework of social institutions chimes closely with the concerns that this book has pursued:

> Since the examples we have just cited (legal and moral regulations, religious faiths, financial systems, etc.) all consist of established beliefs and practices, one might be led to believe that social facts exist only where there is some social organization. But there are other facts without such crystallized form which have the same objectivity and the same ascendancy over the individual. These are called 'social currents'. Thus the great movements of enthusiasm, indignation, and pity in a crowd do not originate in any one of the particular individual consciousnesses. They come to each one of us from without and can carry us away in spite of ourselves. Of course, it may happen that,

in abandoning myself to them unreservedly, I do not feel the pressure they exert upon me. But it is revealed as soon as I try to resist them. Let an individual attempt to oppose one of these collective manifestations, and the emotions that he denies will turn against him. Now, if this power of external coercion asserts itself so clearly in cases of resistance, it must exist also in the first-mentioned cases, although we are unconscious of it. We are then victims of the illusion of having ourselves created that which actually forced itself from without. If the complacency with which we permit ourselves to be carried along conceals the pressure undergone, nevertheless it does not abolish it. Thus, air is no less heavy because we do not detect its weight. So, even if we ourselves have spontaneously contributed to the production of the common emotion, the impression we have received differs markedly from that which we would have experienced if we had been alone. Also, once the crowd has dispersed, that is, once these social influences have ceased to act upon us and we are alone again, the emotions which have passed through the mind appear strange to us, and we no longer recognize them as ours. We realize that these feelings have been impressed upon us to a much greater extent than they were created by us. It may even happen that they horrify us, so much were they contrary to our nature. Thus, a group of individuals, most of whom are perfectly inoffensive, may, when gathered in a crowd, be drawn to acts of atrocity. And what we say of these transitory outbursts applies similarly to those more permanent currents of opinion on religious, political, literary, or artistic matters which are constantly being formed around us, whether in society as a whole or in more limited circles. (Durkheim 1938 [1895]: 4–5)

Durkheim's representation of the variable visibility of 'collective manifestations' according to the degree to which they are internalized by the thinking subject, and his focus upon the dynamics by which 'collective representations' are formulated and circulated, combined with the power to stir to action, for good or, as he points out, for ill, lie at the heart of many of the issues explored here. While Durkheim focuses upon how 'collective representations' come upon us 'from without', we have here explored both the reception by the thinking subject and also the creative process that initiates and reworks such articulations. And again, Durkheim consciously distinguishes between two categories of 'social fact', the widely studied world of social institutions, the well 'crystallized forms' of legal and moral regulations, religious faiths and financial systems, as he puts it, and the more intangible, more diffuse world of 'social currents' but which have the same 'objectivity and the same ascendancy over the individual' as manifestations of the former class of phenomena. He points to the importance of understanding the dynamics of what goes on in relation to this world of 'social currents'. In the present discussion the central element has been the oral communicative moment in which the world of 'social currents' are first articulated, then shared, and then ignored or adopted or rejected on the basis of a complex web of criteria relating to the speech event and the context in which it occurs.

The oral communicative moments that have been the subject of this discussion have been sometimes individually recorded and commented upon, thus identifiable and referred to as specific events, as in the case of the intervention by Chief Standing Bear discussed in the introductory chapter, the resignation speech by Sir Geoffrey Howe discussed in Chapter 1, or the address by Hubert Humphrey to the US Democratic National Convention in 1948 presented in Chapter 4. In other cases they are not only the moments that surround us all as individuals in our daily lives, but are the sequence of moments that underlie historically significant periods in collective history – the sequence of unrecorded (but perhaps remembered) discussions, meetings, speeches, individual positions articulated, and thus shared, in the shipyards in Gdansk that saw the emergence of the Solidarity Movement in Poland and the first steps in the collapse of the Soviet system; or the shared experiences and motivations that brought people onto the streets of Bucharest and brought down Ceausescu, or Serbia and produced the fall of Milosevic, or onto the streets of Tbilisi, or Soweto, or Paris. One of the questions addressed in this discussion has been how do we experience the reality of commonality that is embedded in these oral communicative moments? – moments that are also repeatedly simulated, evoked and variably represented. A core problem relates to the issue of intention and effect. As discussed earlier, even if we can read off something of the speaker's intention through interpretation of the content and implications of the message, how can we be sure that the intention was translated into effect? If you were to observe me haranguing an assembled company, urging them to immediately attack an adjacent police station, and then subsequently you observe that same group of people doing precisely that action following the end of my speech, can you be sure that my intention was the cause of the subsequent action? Were you to interview each of the people who took part in the storming of the police station, it is perfectly possible that not one of them acted through having ingested and adopted the views that I had articulated. Maybe I had indicated that the attack on the police station was necessary and appropriate because the police were oppressive and unjust and the police station was a symbol of a corrupt and hated government. Yet the first person you subsequently interview perhaps indicates that he has a brother in the cells and he participated in the attack in order to liberate him; the second person says he is a builder and a destroyed police station will need rebuilding – a profitable contract if he can get it; the third person is a practised pyromaniac and saw a wonderful opportunity; and so it might go on. And then finally, you find a person who rearticulates as his or her own motivation the sentiments that I originally set out. Are you now beginning to observe the smallest detail of the emergence, the dynamic, of Durkheim's 'social currents'? And why does that one emerge to sweep away a civilization while millions of others wax and wane without trace? The 'problematique' at issue here is in some ways the same as that articulated by Durkheim, namely one of method, understanding what happens, how and why, in the oral communicative moment.

The approach adopted in this book has been to set the oral communicative moment at the heart of the matter. That event is fleeting, powerful and evanescent. It is predicated upon the relation between speaker and listener, it involves the experience of the speaker and the experience of the listener in the event, and it is that ungraspable, unrecordable experiential moment that is gone as soon as it ended. It is, however, intimately linked to its residue – the traces it leaves behind – and it is only subsequently visible through the traces it leaves behind – those traces are representations of it that may, or may not, survive over time. They are memories, they are texts, they are recordings – memories of the event that can be evoked and articulated, texts of the words that were said, recordings that may capture what was said, the sound that accompanied the event, the visual images of who was there. These immediate traces are, of course, malleable, reworkable, adaptable into further representations. The intricate relationships between performance and literature, the move from script or story to play, film, or other form of performance, and back again, these issues are well beyond the orbit of this book, being well-trodden paths of literary and cultural studies and the writing of history. Here, I have focused less upon the subsequent artefacts, the 'traces' left behind, than upon the range of issues that surround the moment itself in terms of frames and occasions that articulate with it. Let me represent the model in terms of concentric circles. At the centre lies the 'oral communicative moment' which is itself a combination of the evanescent fleeting experience rolling ever forward

168 *Orality*

in time and the 'residue' that remains as artefacts of memory and text (see Figure 6.1). As indicated above, these 'residues' themselves generate further experiential moments through the reworking of a text into performance and the reworking of text into text.

Surrounding the event itself lie the frames within which it is formulated and perceived. As they were discussed in Chapter 2, these frames relate to expectations and norms (and, indeed, violations and variations to them) about ways of speaking (see Figure 6.2).

Effectiveness and aesthetics are bound up with the styles and genres of speech that are appropriate to the third circle of issues surrounding the event, namely the occasions, the social contexts within which the event

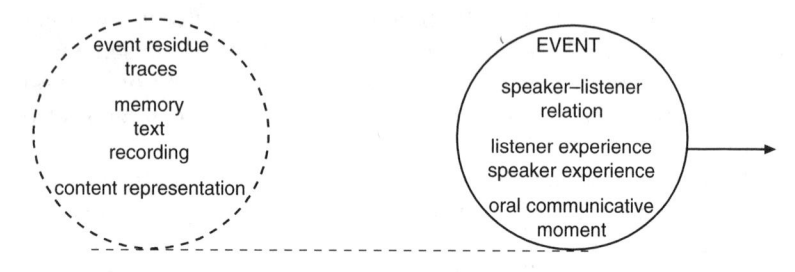

Figure 6.1 The oral communicative moment

Figure 6.2 Frames and the speech event

takes place. The outer circle within the graphic representation in Figure 6.3 encompasses the range of social relations within which the experience of the event occurs, and the cultural frames within which it is embedded. The event, and its accompanying frame, occurs on particular occasions that fall into a variety of categories linked to religious practices, political processes, economic activities and a range of other social practices. The relations between the participants will impact also upon the event – kinship relations, status distinctions, gender relations, class positions, group identity affiliations and so on. In Chapter 3 we explored some of the issues concerning the social nexus of the event – contestation, notions of the private and the public, and other issues of social and political embeddedness of the oral communicative moment. Chapter 4 presented the set of concentric circles as elements that interact in the business of articulating ideological positions for individuals and for society more generally (Figure 6.3).

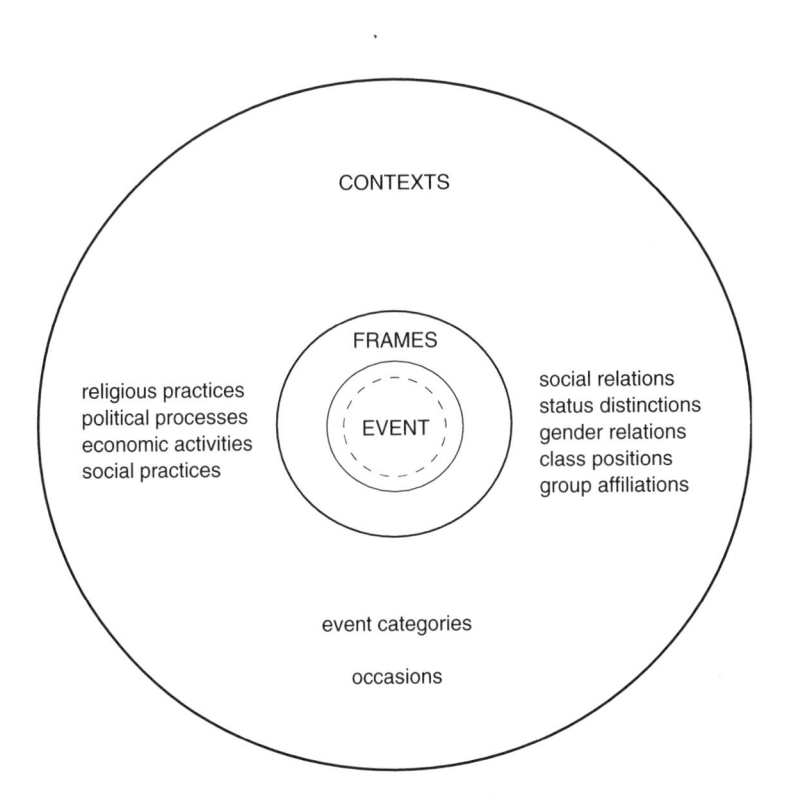

Figure 6.3 Contexts for the speech event and its frames

In the immediacy and ubiquity of the oral communicative moment, intentionality and effect combine to focus the direction of individual and shared thought and action. Culturally bounded expectations of ways of speaking and individual creativity provide the spark that can ignite revolution or calm the soul. This book has explored, from a cross-cultural perspective, the centrality of orality in the ideological processes that dominate public discourse, providing a counterbalance to the debates that foreground literacy and the power of written communication.

Appendix A: Sir Geoffrey Howe's Resignation Statement to the House of Commons, 13 November 1990

Set out below is an amalgam of the full broadcast speech and various additional excerpts carried in national newspapers but not actually included in the broadcast. The text has been edited to more closely represent the wording of the original speech thereby allowing for pauses, the use of the terms 'right honourable Friend' which newspaper journalists replace in print with the person referred to. Those parts of the speech in italic were not broadcast on television and are derived from printed sources. Those parts in plain text and bold represent the words carried on national television. Paragraphing in the parts sourced from print represents the divisions made either by the print journalists or by the written text provided to them. Paragraphing in those sections checked against the video source marks the turning of the page in Sir Geoffrey Howe's hand as he spoke from his notes. Italic text is not on the video tape and therefore has not been marked up to indicate pauses, stress or audience response. In the broadcast of the speech, the BBC political correspondent, Nicholas Jones, summarized in a 'voice over' the main points of those sections which were edited out of the video version. Dotted underlining represents emphatic movements of the head and body, continuous underlining marks hand movements made to emphasize a point.

1. *I find to my astonishment that a quarter of a century has passed since I last spoke from one of these back benches. Fortunately, however, it has been my privilege to serve for the last twelve months of that time as Leader of this House of Commons. So I have been reminded quite recently of the traditional generosity and tolerance of this place. I hope that I may count on that today, as I offer to the House a statement about my resignation from the Government.*
2. **It has been suggest**ed, / even in**deed** by **some** of my **right** honourable **Friends,** / that I deci**d**ed to re**sign** / **solely** because of **questions** of **style,** / and **not** on matters of **sub**stance at all. / *Indeed,* / if **some** of my / former **colleagues** are to be believed, / I must be the **first min**ister in **his**tory / to have resi**gn**ed because he was / in **full** agree**ment** with **Gov**ern**ment** policy. / [LONG LAUGHTER ON ALL SIDES]
3. The **truth** is, / Mr **Speak**er, / that in many as**pects** of **pol**itics, / **style** and **sub**stance / complement each other. / Very o**ften** they're / **two sides** of the same **coin**. /

4. My right honourable Friend, the Prime Minister and I have shared together something like 700 meetings of Cabinet or Shadow Cabinet over the last 18 years, some 400 hours alongside each other, at more than 30 international summit meetings. For both of us, I suspect, that is a pretty daunting record.
5. The House might well feel that something more than simple matters of style would be necessary to rupture such a well-tried relationship.
6. It was indeed a privilege to serve as the Prime Minister's first Chancellor of the Exchequer, to share in the transformation of our industrial relations scene, to help launch our free market programme, commencing with the abolition of exchange controls, and, above all, to achieve such substantial success against inflation, getting it down within four years from 22 per cent to four per cent upon the basis of the strict monetary discipline involved in the medium-term financial strategy.
7. Not one of our economic achievements would have been possible without the courage and the leadership of the Prime Minister. And, if I may say so, they possibly derived some little benefit from the presence of a Chancellor who wasn't exactly a wet himself.
8. It was, too, a great honour to serve for six years as Foreign and Commonwealth Secretary and to share with the Prime Minister in some notable achievements in the European Community from Fontainebleau to the Single European Act.
9. But it was as we / moved on to consider the / crucial monetary issues / in a European context / that I have come to feel increasing concern. / Some of the reasons / for this anxiety / were made very clear / by my right honourable Friend / the Member for Blaby / in his resignation speech just over twelve months ago./ [LAWSON IS NODDING]
10. For like him, / I concluded at least five years back / that the conduct of our policy against inflation / could no longer rest solely / on attempts to measure and control / the domestic money supply. / We had / no doubt / that we should be helped in that battle / and indeed in other respects / by joining the Exchange Rate Mechanism / of the European Monetary System. /
11. There was, or should have been, nothing novel about joining the ERM. It has been a long-standing commitment. And we found, for a quarter of a century after the Second World War, that the very similar Bretton Woods regime did serve as a useful discipline.
12. And now, as the Prime Minister has acknowledged two weeks ago, our entry into the Exchange Rate Mechanism can indeed be seen as an 'extra discipline for keeping down inflation'.
13. But it must be said that this important practical conclusion has only been achieved at the cost of substantial damage to her own administration, and, more serious still, to its inflation achievement.
14. For, as my right honourable Friend the Member for Blaby / has explained, / the real tragedy is / that we did not join the Exchange Rate Mechanism / at least five years ago. / [MURMURED CALLS OF HEAR! HEAR!] That was, as he also made clear, / not for want of trying. /
15. Indeed, the so-called Madrid conditions came into existence / only after the then Chancellor of the Exchequer and myself as Foreign Secretary / made it clear that we could not continue in office / unless a specific commitment / to join the Exchange Rate Mechanism / was made. / As the House will no doubt have observed, / neither member of that particular partnership / now remains in office. /

16. Our successor as Chancellor of the Exchequer / **has**, during the last **year**, / had to devote a good **deal** of his considerable **tal**ent / to **dem**onstrating exactly how those Ma**drid** con**dit**ions / have been at**tain**ed / so as to make it ... / so as to make it **pos**sible to ful**fil** ... [LAUGHTER FROM THE OPPOSITION, SLIGHT SMILES FROM MAJOR AND THATCHER] / to ful**fil** a com**mit**ment / whose a**chiev**ement / has long been in the **nat**ional **in**terest. /
17. It is now, alas, / im**pos**sible to re**sist** the con**clu**sion / that to**day**'s **high**er rates of in**fla**tion / **could** well have **been** a**void**ed, / had the **ques**tion of ERM mem**ber**ship / been **prop**erly con**sid**ered and re**solv**ed / at a **much ear**lier **stage**. / [LAWSON NODS; CRIES OF HEAR! HEAR!]
18. There are, I fear, developing grounds for similar anxiety over the handling, not just at and after the Rome Summit, of the wider, much more open question of Economic and Monetary Union.
19. Let me first make clear certain important points on which I have no disagreement with my right honourable Friends. I do not regard the Delors Report as some kind of sacred text that has to be accepted, or even rejected, on the nod. But it is an important working document. As I have often made plain, it is seriously deficient in significant respects.
20. I do not regard the Italian Presidency's management of the Rome Summit as a model of its kind – far from it. It was much the same as my right honourable Friend will recall in Milan some five years ago.
21. I do not regard it as in any sense wrong for Britain to make criticisms of that kind, plainly and courteously, nor in any sense wrong for us to do so if necessary alone. As I have already made clear, I have, like the Prime Minister and other right honourable Friends, fought too many European battles in a minority of one to have any illusions on that score.
22. But it **is cru**cially im**port**ant / that we should con**duct** those **ar**guments / upon the basis of a **clear** under**stan**ding / of the **true** relationship between this country, / the Com**mun**ity / and our Com**mun**ity **part**ners. / And it is here, I fear, / that my right honourable **Friend** / in**creas**ingly risks **lead**ing her**self** and **oth**ers a**stray** / in **mat**ters of sub**stance** / as **well** as of **style**. /
23. It was the / **late** Lord **Stock**ton, / formerly **Har**old Mac**mill**an, / who **first** put the **cen**tral **point clear**ly. / As **long** ago as **nine**teen sixty-**two**, / he **ar**gued that we had to place and keep ourselves / within the European Com**mun**ity. / He saw it / as essential then, / as it is today, / **not** / to cut ourselves **off** / from the realities of **pow**er, / **not** / to re**treat** / into a **ghet**to of senti**ment**ality / about our **past** / and so di**min**ish our **own** con**trol** / over our own destiny / in the **fu**ture. /
24. The pity is / that the Mac**mill**an **view** / had **not** been per**ceiv**ed more **clear**ly / a decade before, / in the **nine**teen **fif**ties. [CRIES OF HEAR! HEAR!; NODS FROM OTHERS] / It would have spared us so many of the **strug**gles of the last **twen**ty years / had we been in the Com**mun**ity / from the **out**set, / had we been ready, / in the / much too simple phrase, / to '**sur**ren**der** some sovereignty' / at a much **ear**lier **stage**. /
25. If we had been in / from the **start**, / as **al**most **ev**erybody now ack**now**ledges, / we should have had more, / not less influence / over the Eu**rope** in which we **live** to**day**. / We should **nev**er for**get** the **les**son of that iso**la**tion, /

26. Of being on the outside looking in, / for the conduct of today's affairs. / We have done best / when we have seen the Community, / not as a / static entity, / to be resisted / and contained, / but as an active process / which we can shape, / often decisively, / provided we allow ourselves to be fully engaged in it, / with confidence, / with enthusiasm / and in good faith. /
27. We must at all costs / avoid presenting ourselves yet again / with an oversimplified choice, / a false antithesis, / a bogus dilemma / between one alternative / starkly labelled / 'co-operation between independent sovereign states' / and a second / equally crudely labelled alternative / 'centralised federal super state', / as if there were / no / middle way / in between. /
28. We commit a serious error / if we think always in terms of / 'surrendering' sovereignty / and seek to stand pat for all time on a given deal / by proclaiming as my right honourable Friend, the Prime Minister, did two weeks ago, / that we have / 'surrendered / enough'. / The European enterprise / is not, / and should not be seen, / like that, / as some kind of / zero sum game. /
29. Sir Winston Churchill put it much more positively / forty years ago, when he said, / 'Is it not possible, / and not less agreeable, / to regard this / "sacrifice or merger" of national sovereignty / as the gradual assumption by all the nations concerned / of that larger sovereignty, / which can alone protect their diverse and distinctive customs and characteristics, / and their national traditions'. /
30. I have to say, Mr Speaker, that I find / Winston Churchill's perception / a good deal more convincing, / and more encouraging for the interests of our nation, / than the / nightmare image sometimes conjured up by my right honourable Friend, / who seems ... [SOUNDS OF SHOCK OR DISAPPROVAL FROM SOME, FOLLOWED BY OTHERS SHUSHING THEM; HOWE CONTINUES BUT WITH BACKGROUND TALKING CONTINUING] / who seems sometimes to look out / upon a continent / that is positively teeming with ill-intentioned people / scheming, in her words, 'to extinguish democracy', / 'to dissolve our national identities', / to lead us 'through the back door into a federal Europe'. /
31. What / kind / of vision / is that, / Mr Speaker, / for our business people, / who trade there each day, / for our financiers who seek to make London the money capital of Europe / or for all the young people of today? / [BACKGROUND TALKING CEASES] / These concerns are especially important / as we approach the crucial topic / of Economic and Monetary Union. / We must be positively / and centrally involved in this debate / and *not* fearfully / and negatively detached. / The costs of disengagement here / could be very serious indeed. /
32. There is talk of course, / of the emergence / of a single currency for Europe. / I agree that there are many difficulties about the concept, / both economic / and political. / And of course, / as I said in my own letter of resignation, / none of us wants the imposition / of a single currency. / But that / isn't / the real risk. /
33. The eleven others / cannot / impose their solution on the twelfth country / against its will. / But they can / go ahead without us. / The risk is not / imposition / but isolation. / The real threat / is of leaving ourselves with no say / in the monetary arrangements / that the rest of Europe

chooses for itself / with Britain once again scrambling to join the club later, / after the rules have been set, / and after the power has been distributed by others to our disadvantage. / That would be / the worst possible outcome./
34. It is to avoid just that outcome, to find a compromise both acceptable in the government and sellable in Europe that the Chancellor has put forward his hard Ecu proposal. This lays careful emphasis on the possibility that the hard Ecu, as a common currency, could, given time, evolve into a single currency.
35. I have of course supported the hard Ecu plan. But after Rome, and after the Prime Minister's comments two weeks ago, there is grave danger that the hard Ecu is becoming untenable. Two things have happened.
36. The first was that my right honourable Friend has appeared / to rule out from the start / any compromise at any stage / on any of the basic components / which all the eleven other countries / believe to be part / of EMU, / a single currency or a permanently fixed exchange rate, / a central bank / or common monetary policy. /
37. Asked if we would veto / any arrangement / which jeopardised the pound sterling, / my right honourable Friend replied simply, / 'Yes'. / That statement means / not / that we can block EMU, / but that they can go ahead / without us. / Is that a position that is likely to ensure, / as I put it in my resignation letter, / that we hold and retain / a position of influence in this vital debate? / I fear not. /
38. Rather to do so, we must, as I said, / take care / not to / rule in / or rule out / any one solution / absolutely. / We must be seen to be part / of the same negotiation. / The second thing that happened was, I fear, / even more disturbing. / Reporting to this House my right honourable Friend / almost casually remarked / that she didn't think many people would want to use the hard Ecu anyway, / even as a common currency, / let alone as a single one. /
39. It was remarkable, / indeed it was tragic, / to hear my right honourable Friend dismissing, / with such personalised incredulity, / the very idea / that the hard Ecu proposal / might find growing favour among the peoples of Europe, / just as it was extraordinary to hear her assert / that the whole idea of EMU / might be open for consideration / only by future generations. / Mr Speaker, / those future generations / are with us / today. /
40. How on earth / are the Chancellor and the Governor of the Bank of England, / commending the hard Ecu as they strive to do, / to be taken as serious participants in the debate / against that kind of background noise? / Mr Speaker ... [AUDIBLE EXPRESSIONS OF SHOCK AND DISAPPROVAL FROM TORY BENCHES, LAUGHTER FROM OPPOSITION] / Mr Speaker I believe that both the Chancellor and the Governor / are cricketing enthusiasts. [SLIGHT LAUGHTER] / So I hope there is no monopoly on cricketing metaphors. / It is rather like sending your opening batsmen to the crease / only for them to find, / the moment the first balls are bowled, / that their bats have been broken before the game, / by the team captain. / [VISIBLE MOVEMENT EXPRESSING DISQUIET AND DISCOMFORT ON TORY BENCHES; LAUGHTER FROM THE OPPOSITION]

(Order!)
41. The **point**, / Mr **Spea**ker, / was perhaps more **sharp**ly put by a British **bu**sinessman, / **tra**ding in **Bru**ssels and **else**where who **wrote** to me last week. / 'People throughout Europe' he **said**, / 'see our **Prime Min**ister's finger **wag**ging / and hear her **pas**sionate / "No! / No! / No!", / much **more** clearly / than the **con**tent of the **care**fully **wor**ded **for**mal **texts**.' / 'It is too easy', he **went** on, / 'for **them** to **be**lieve / that we **all share her att**itudes. / For **why else**', / he **asks**, / 'has she been our **Prime Min**ister for so **long**?' /
42. 'This **is**' my **cor**respondent **con**cluded, / 'a **des**perately **ser**ious sit**ua**tion for our **coun**try'. / And **sad**ly, Mr **Spea**ker, / I **have** to **a**gree. / The **tra**gedy **is**, / and it is for **me per**sonally, / for **my par**ty, / and for our **whole peo**ple, / and for my **right hon**ourable **Friend** herself, / a very **real tra**gedy, / that the **Prime Min**ister's per**ceived at**titude towards **Eu**rope / is **run**ning in**crea**singly **ser**ious **risks** / for the **fu**ture of our **na**tion. [CRY OF NO! FROM TORY SIDE; AITKEN VISIBLE BEHIND HOWE SHAKES HIS HEAD IN DISAGREEMENT] / It **risks min**imising our **in**fluence / and **max**imising **our chan**ces / of being **once** again **shut out**. / We have **paid hea**vily in the **past** / for **late starts** / and **squan**dered op**por**tunities in **Eu**rope. /
43. We **dare not let** that **hap**pen again. / If we de**tach** ourselves com**plete**ly, / as a **par**ty or as a **na**tion, / from the **middle ground** of **Eu**rope, / the **ef**fects will be in**cal**culable / and **very hard e**ver to **cor**rect. / Mr **Spea**ker, in my **let**ter of **re**signation, / which I **ten**dered with the **ut**most **sad**ness and **dis**may, / I **said** / that **Ca**binet **gov**ernment / is **all** about **tr**ying to per**suade** one another / from with**in**. / That was **my com**mitment / to **gov**ernment / by per**sua**sion, / per**sua**ding **col**leagues and the **na**tion. /
44. I have **tried** / to **do** that / as **For**eign **Sec**retary / and **since**. / But I **rea**lise **now** that the **task** has be**come fu**tile, / of **try**ing to **stretch** the **mea**ning of **words** / be**yond** what was **cre**dible, / of **try**ing to pre**tend** there **was** a **com**mon **po**licy, / when every **step forward risk**ed being sub**ver**ted / by some **cas**ual **com**ment or im**pul**sive **an**swer. [AUDIBLE EXPRESSIONS OF DISMAY AND DISAPPROVAL FROM TORY SIDE. AITKEN SHAKES HIS HEAD IN DISAGREEMENT] / The **con**flict of **loy**alty, / of **loy**alty to my **right hon**ourable **Friend**, the **Prime Min**ister, / and after **more** than **two de**cades to**ge**ther / that in**stinc**tive **loy**alty is **still** very **real**, / and of **loy**alty to what I per**ceive** / to be the **true in**terests of this **na**tion. /
45. That **con**flict of **loy**alty / has be**come** / **all too great**. / I no **lon**ger be**lieve** it **pos**sible / to re**solve** that **con**flict / from with**in** this **Gov**ernment. / That is **why** I have re**signed**. / In **do**ing so, I have **done** what I be**lieve** to be **right** / for my **par**ty and my **coun**try. / The **time** has **come** for **o**thers to con**si**der / their **own res**ponse / to the **tra**gic **con**flict of **loy**alties / with **which** I have my**self wrest**led / for per**haps** too **long**. [HOWE SITS DOWN]

Appendix B: Speech by Hubert H. Humphrey to the Democratic National Convention, July 14, 1948

From Wilson (1996) pp. 3–5

Mr. Chairman, fellow Democrats, fellow Americans, I realize that in speaking in behalf of the minority report on civil rights as presented by Congressman Biemiller of Wisconsin, that I am dealing with a charged issue, with an issue which has been confused by emotionalism on all sides of the fence. I realize that there are those here – friends and colleagues of mine, many of them who feel just as deeply and keenly as I do about this issue, and who are yet in complete disagreement with me. My respect and admiration for these men and their views was great when I came to this convention. It is now far greater because of the sincerity, the courtesy, and the forthrightness with which many of them have argued in our prolonged discussions in the platform committee. Because of this very great respect, and because of my profound belief that we have a challenging task to do here, because good conscience demands it, decent morality demands it, I feel I must rise at this time to support a report, the minority report, a report that spells out our democracy. A report that the people of this county can and will understand and a report that they will enthusiastically acclaim on the great issue of civil rights.

Now let me say this at the outset, that this proposal is made for no single region, our proposal is made for no single class, for no single racial or religious group in mind. All of the regions of this country, all of the states have shared in our precious heritage of American freedom. All the states and all the regions have seen at least some of the infringements of that freedom. All people, get this, all people, white and black, all groups, all racial groups have been the victims at times in this nation of, let me say, vicious discrimination.

The masterly statement of our keynote speaker, the distinguished United States Senator from Kentucky, Alben Barkley, made that point with great force. Speaking of the founder of our party, Thomas Jefferson, he said this, and I quote;

> He did not proclaim that all the white, or the black, or the red, or the yellow men are equal: that all Christian or Jewish men are equal: that all protestant and catholic men are equal: that all rich and poor men are equal: that all good and bad men are equal. What he declared was that all men are equal; and the equality which he proclaimed was the equality in the right to enjoy the

blessings of free government in which they may participate and to which they have given their support.

Now these words of Senator Barkley are appropriate to this convention, appropriate to this convention of the oldest, the most truly progressive political party in America. From the time of Thomas Jefferson, the time when that immortal American doctrine of individual rights, under just and fairly administered laws, the Democratic Party has tried hard to secure expanding freedom for all citizens. Oh yes, I know other political parties may have talked more about civil rights, but the Democratic Party has surely done more about civil rights.

We have made progress, we have made great progress in every part of this country. We have made great progress in the South, we've made it in the West, the North and in the East, but we must now focus the direction of that progress towards the realization of a full program of civil rights for all.

This convention must set out more specifically the direction in which our party efforts are to go. We can be proud that we can be guided by the courageous trail blazing of two great Democratic Presidents. We can be proud of the fact that our great and beloved immortal leader, Franklin Roosevelt gave us guidance. And we can be proud of the fact, we can be proud of the fact that Harry Truman has had the courage to give to the people of America the new emancipation proclamation.

It seems to me, it seems to me that the Democratic Party needs to make definite pledges of the kind suggested in the minority report to maintain the trust and the confidence placed in it by the people of all races and all sections of this country. Sure we are here as Democrats, but my good friends, we're here as Americans. We are here as the believers and the principle and ideology of democracy. And I firmly believe that as men concerned with our country's future, we must specify in our platform the guarantees which we have mentioned in the minority report.

Yes this is far more than a party matter. Every citizen in this country has a stake in the emergence of the United States as a leader of the free world. That world is being challenged by the world of slavery. For us to play our part effectively we must be in a morally sound position. We can't use a double standard. There's no room for double standards in American politics for measuring our own and other people's policies. Our demands for democratic practices in other lands will be no more effective than the guarantee of those practices in our own country.

Friends, delegates, I do not believe that there can be any compromise on the guarantees of the civil rights which we have mentioned in the minority report. In spite of my desire for unanimous agreement on the entire platform, in spite of my desire to see everybody here in honest and unanimous agreement, there are some matters which I think must be stated clearly and without qualification.

There can be no hedging. The newspaper headlines are wrong, there will be no hedging and there will be no watering down if you please of the instruments and the principles of the civil rights program. To those who say that we are rushing this issue of civil rights, I say to them we are 172 years late. To those who say that this civil rights program is an infringement on state's rights, I say this, the time has arrived in America for the Democratic Party to get out of the shadows of state's rights to walk forthrightly into the bright sunshine of human rights. People – people – human beings, this is the issue of the 20th century. People of all kinds, all sorts of people – and these people are looking to America for leadership and they are looking to America for precept and example.

My good friends, my fellow Democrats, I ask you for a calm consideration of our historic opportunity. Let us do forget the evil passions and the blindness of the past. In these times of world, political and spiritual, above all spiritual crisis, we cannot and we must not turn from the path so plainly before us. That path has already led us through many valleys of the shadow of death. And now is the time to recall those who were left on that path of American freedom. For all of us here, for the millions who have sent us, for the whole two billion members of the human family, our land is now more than ever before, the last best hope on earth. And I know that we can, and I know that we shall begin here the fuller and richer realization of that hope. That promise of a land where all men are truly free and equal, and each man uses his freedom and equality wisely and well.

My good friends, I ask my party, I ask the Democratic party to march down the high road of progressive democracy. I ask this convention, I ask this convention to say in unmistakable terms that we proudly hail and we courageously support our President and leader, Harry Truman and his great fight for civil rights in America.

References

Abbott, Don Paul. 1987. The ancient word: rhetoric in Aztec culture. *Rhetorica* 5(3): 251–64.
Ahmad, Said Babura. 1997. *Narrator as Interpreter: Stability and Variation in Hausa Tales*. Köln: Rüdiger Köppe Verlag.
Arnold, David. 2001. *Gandhi*. London: Longman.
Bailey, F. G. 1977. *Morality and Expediency*. Oxford: Blackwell.
Bailey, F. G. 1983. *The Tactical Uses of Passion*. New York: Cornell University Press.
Bailey, F. G. 1991. *The Prevalence of Deceit*. New York: Cornell University Press.
Bakhtin, M. M. 1986. *Speech Genres and Other Late Essays*. Translated by V. W. McGee. Edited by M. Holquist, University of Texas Press Slavic Series, No. 8. Austin: University of Texas Press.
Barber, Karin. 1991. *I Could Speak until Tomorrow: Oriki, Women and the Past in a Yoruba Town*. Edinburgh: Edinburgh University Press for the International African Institute.
Barber, Karin, ed. 1997. *Readings in African Popular Culture*. London: James Currey.
Bauman, Richard, and Charles L. Briggs. 1990. Poetics and performance as critical perspectives on language and social life. *Annual Review of Anthropology* 19: 59–88.
Bauman, Richard, and Joel Sherzer. 1989. Introduction to the second edition. In *Explorations in the Ethnography of Speaking*, edited by R. Bauman and J. Sherzer. Cambridge: Cambridge University Press.
Bauman, Richard, and Joel Sherzer, eds. 1982. *Case Studies in the Ethnography of Speaking*. Austin: University of Texas Press.
Bauman, Richard, and Joel Sherzer, eds. 1989. *Explorations in the Ethnography of Speaking*. 2nd edn. Cambridge: Cambridge University Press.
Beck, Charles D. 1957. *Urban Holiness Service*. Washington: Smithsonian Folkways Recordings.
Beetham, David. 1991. *The Legitimation of Power*. In *Issues in Political Theory* series, edited by P. Jones and A. Weale. London: Macmillan.
Bloch, M. 1975. Introduction. In *Political Language and Oratory in Traditional Society*, edited by M. Bloch. London: Academic Press.
Bloomfield, Leonard. 1933. *Language*. New York: Holt, Rinehart and Winston.
Brenneis, Donald, and Ronald K. S. Macaulay, eds. 1996. *The Matrix of Language: Contemporary Linguistic Anthropology*. Boulder: Westview Press.
Brown, Dee. 1991 [1970]. *Bury My Heart at Wounded Knee: an Indian History of the American West*. London: Vintage.
Brown, Duncan. 1998. *Voicing the Text: South African Oral Poetry and Performance*. Cape Town: Oxford University Press.
Caro, Robert A. 2002. *The Years of Lyndon Johnson: Master of the Senate (Vol. 3)*. New York: Alfred A. Knopf.
Cook, Guy. 1992. *The Discourse of Advertising*. London: Routledge.
Croce, Benedetto. 1953. *Aesthetic as Science of Expression and General Linguistic*. Translated by D. Ainslie. London: Peter Owen.

Czekelius, Annette. 1999. Artistry and effectiveness in language use: the evaluation of ways of speaking among the Berba of Benin. PhD, University of London.
Durkheim, Emile. 1938 [1895]. *The Rules of Sociological Method*. Translated by S. A. Solovay and J. H. Mueller. New York: The Free Press of Glencoe.
Fabian, Johannes. 1990. *Power and Performance: Ethnographic Explorations through Proverbial Wisdom and Theater in Shaba, Zaire*. Madison: University of Wisconsin Press.
Farias, Paulo Fernando de Moraes. 1995. Praise splits the subject of speech. In *Power, Marginality and African Oral Literature*, edited by G. Furniss and L. Gunnes. Cambridge: Cambridge University Press.
Feld, Steven. 1986. Orality and consciousness. In *The Oral and Literate in Music*, edited by Y. Tokumaru and O. Yamaguti. Tokyo: Academia Music.
Finnegan, Ruth. 1988. *Literacy and Orality: Studies in the Technology of Communication*. Oxford: Blackwell.
Finnegan, Ruth. 1989. *The Hidden Musicians: Music-Making in an English Town*. Cambridge: Cambridge University Press.
Foley, J. Miles. 1985. *Oral-Formulaic Theory and Research: an Introduction and Annotated Bibliography, Garland Folklore Bibliographies 6*. New York: Garland.
Foley, J. Miles. 1988. *The Theory of Oral Composition: History and Methodology*. Bloomington: Indiana University Press.
Foley, J. Miles, ed. 1990. *Oral-Formulaic Theory: a Folklore Casebook*. New York: Garland.
Fox, Michael V. 1983. Ancient Egyptian rhetoric. *Rhetorica: a Journal of the History of Rhetoric* 1: 9–22.
Furniss, Graham. 1996. *Poetry, Prose and Popular Culture in Hausa*. Edinburgh: Edinburgh University Press.
Furniss, Graham. 2001. Meaning and performance gradations in the expression of disapproval in Hausa. In *Von Ägypten Zum Tschadsee: Eine Linguistiche Reise Durch Afrika*, edited by D. Ibriszimow, R. Leger and U. Seibert (Würzburg: Ergon Verlag for the Deutsche Morgenlandische Gesellschaft).
Gandhi, M. K. 1982 [1927]. *An Autobiography or The Story of My Experiments with Truth*. London: Penguin Books.
Goody, Jack. 1987. *The Interface between the Written and the Oral*. Cambridge: Cambridge University Press.
Graff, Harvey. 1982. The legacies of literacy. *Journal of Communication* 32: 12–26.
Graham, Angus C. 1985. *Reason and Spontaneity*. London: Curzon Press.
Gramsci, Antonio. 1985. *Antonio Gramsci: Selections from Cultural Writings*. Translated by W. Boelhower. Edited by D. F. and G. Nowell-Smith. London: Lawrence and Wishart.
Grice, H. P. 1975. Logic and conversation. In *Syntax and Semantics*, edited by P. Cole and J. L. Morgan. New York: Academic Press.
Gumperz, John J., and Dell Hymes, eds. 1972. *Directions in Sociolinguistics: the Ethnography of Communication*. New York: Holt, Rinehart and Winston.
Habermas, Jürgen. 1979. *Communication and the Evolution of Society*. Translated by T. McCarthy. London: Heinemann.
Habermas, Jürgen. 1990. *Moral Consciousness and Communicative Action*. Translated by C. L. S. W. Nicholsen. Cambridge: Polity Press.
Hanks, William F. 1999. *Intertexts: Writings on Language, Utterance, and Context*. Lanham: Rowman & Littlefield.

Hodge, Robert, and Gunther Kress. 1993. *Language as Ideology*. 2nd edn. London: Routledge.
Hofmeyr, Isabel. 1995. The letter and the law: the politics of orality and literacy in the chiefdoms of the northern Transvaal. In *Power, Marginality and African Oral Literature*, edited by G. Furniss and L. Gunner. Cambridge: Cambridge University Press.
Hymes, Dell. 1962. The ethnography of speaking. In *Anthropology and Human Behaviour*, edited by T. Gladwin and W. C. Sturtevant. Washington, DC: Anthropological Society of Washington.
Hymes, Dell. 1972. Models of the interaction of language and social life. In *Directions in Sociolinguistics: the Ethnography of Communication*, edited by J. J. Gumperz and D. Hymes. New York: Holt, Rinehart and Winston.
Kennedy, George A. 1998. *Comparative Rhetoric: an Historical and Cross-Cultural Introduction*. Oxford: Oxford University Press.
Leech, Geoffrey. 1983. *Principles of Pragmatics*. London: Longman.
Oliver, Robert T. 1971. *Communication and Culture in India and China*. Syracuse: Syracuse University Press.
Ong, Walter J. 1982. *Orality and Literacy: the Technologizing of the Word*. London: Methuen.
Paine, R., ed. 1981. *Politically Speaking: Cross-Cultural Studies of Rhetoric*. Philadelphia: Institute for the Study of Human Issues.
Parkin, David. 1984. Political language. *Annual Review of Anthropology* 13: 345–65.
Perelman, C., and L. Olbrechts-Tyteca. 1969. *The New Rhetoric*. Translated by J. W. P. Weaver. Notre Dame: University of Notre Dame Press.
Searle, John R. 1967. How to derive 'ought' from 'is'. In *Theories of Ethics*, edited by P. Foot. Oxford: Oxford University Press.
Searle, John R. 1979. *Expression and Meaning: Studies in the Theory of Speech Acts*. Cambridge: Cambridge University Press.
Shamasastry, R. 1923. *Kautilya's Arthasastra*. 2nd edn. Mysore: Wesleyan Mission Press.
Sherzer, Joel. 2002. *Speech Play and Verbal Art*. Austin: University of Texas Press.
Shirer, William L. 1981. *Gandhi: a Memoir*. London: Abacus Books.
Street, Brian V. 1984. *Literacy in Theory and Practice*, Cambridge Studies in Oral and Literate Culture 9. Cambridge: Cambridge University Press.
Theisz, R. D. 2002. Standing Bear (Machunazha) (Ponca) (1829–1908). In *The Heath Anthology of American Literature*, edited by P. Lauter. Boston: Houghton Mifflin.
Tibbles, Thomas Henry. 1957 [1905]. *Buckskin and Blanket Days*. New York: Doubleday.
Tibbles, Thomas Henry. 1972 [1880]. *Standing Bear and the Ponca Chiefs*. Lincoln: University of Nebraska Press.
Vail, Leroy, and Landeg White. 1991. *Power and the Praise Poem: Southern African Voices in History*. London: James Currey.
Van Dijk, Teun A. 1998. *Ideology: a Multidisciplinary Approach*. London: Sage.
Walker, Jeffrey. 1996. Before the beginnings of 'poetry' and 'rhetoric': Hesiod on eloquence. *Rhetorica* 14(3): 243–64.
Wilson, Paula. 1996. *The Civil Rights Rhetoric of Hubert H. Humphrey 1948–1964*. New York: University Press of America.

Index

abuse, in Hausa 59
advertising 112–17
aesthetics of speech 3, 64–5, 168
  Berba 67–70
  Yoruba 65–7, 70
  see also speech
affectivity, and text 143–4
agreement 99–100, 156–7
  see also understanding
Akan society, public speaker
  (*okyeame*) 78
allusion 60, 66–7
  see also indirectness; innuendo
ambiguity 59–61, 105–8
appellation 70
appropriate language 57–8, 71, 73–4
  see also language
Arabic scholarship, Somalia 136
Aristotle, and rhetoric 146
Arthashastra 147–8
articulation
  critical discourse 65
  and memory 117–18
  values 19
  views of good and evil 161–2
Ashana, Malam (Mr Matches), Hausa
  speech performer 63
Ashanti society, power of silence 18
audience 72–3, 75–6, 78, 84–7, 146
  see also listener expectations
audience cultures 87–90, 98, 99, 117
awareness 98, 99, 101, 117
Aztec society, 'standardized' speeches
  145, 151

Bagre myth 137
beliefs 19, 94–5
Benin *see* Berba
Berba, aesthetics of speech 67–70
bureaucracy, and texts 55–6

categorization 73–4, 119–20
  see also event category

charge *see* evaluative charge;
  expressive charge
Chief Standing Bear trial 4–6, 7,
  8–11, 87
China, rhetorical traditions 144
choice
  genre 48–54, 59, 61
  ways of speaking 48–54, 70, 152–3
Cinderella 160–1
clarity 59–61, 67, 69–70
cliché 50
co-operative principle 69–70, 149–50
co-presence 15, 42
cohesion 69–70
collective manifestations 165
commonality 18–19, 22–3, 166
communication 144–9, 149–50, 155
  control of means 54
  delaying 13–15, 42
  knowledge within 155
  and meaning 154
communicative competence 152–3,
  153–4
communicative moment *see* oral
  communicative moment
complaining 48–54, 74
composition 133–6, 146
content, and form 61–4, 71
context 26, 72–3, 104, 118, 158, 169
  see also social contexts
contradiction 108–9, 110
control
  genre 76
  means of communication 54
convincing *see* persuasion
critical discourse 65
  see also discourse
criticism, and genre 59
cultural production 2, 45–6, 47, 130
  and power 92, 162, 163
cultural style, and performance
  87–90
  see also styles of speech

183

cultural values 43–6, 70–1
  see also values
culture 2, 3, 43–6, 70–1
  see also audience cultures; public culture

Dankwairo, Hausa praise singer 136
deception 4
decontextualization 159–60
Democratic National Convention Address 1948 124–30, 177–9
descriptive statements 110–12
discourse 65, 102–10, 115–17
Douglas, Paul, at Democratic Convention 1948 128–9
Dundy, Judge Elmer S., and Chief Standing Bear trial 4, 5, 8
Dylan, Bob, change of style 137

economy, financial 18–19
economy of speech 69–70
  see also speech
effectiveness 144–5, 161, 168
  in Sir Geoffrey Howe speech 33–4
  and intentionality 142, 166–7, 170
Egypt, rhetorical tradition 144
eloquence 99–100
Eminem (Marshal Mathers), rap artist 23–5
emphasis, in Sir Geoffrey Howe speech 31, 32, 33–4, 35
entextualization 144, 159–60
ethical discourse 102–10
  see also discourse
ethnography of speaking 153–8
evaluation 100–2, 118–20
evaluative charge 101, 108–10, 114, 122
evaluative discourse 102–10
  see also discourse
evaluative language 110–12, 127
  see also language
evaluative statements 110–12
event category 73, 74, 90
  see also categorization
expectations 46–7, 61, 64, 71, 161
  in Sir Geoffrey Howe speech 36–7
  of greetings 14–15

of listener and speaker 48–54
and stereotypes 120–2
expressive aspect of speech 10–11, 102–10
expressive charge 103–8, 113

fixity 15, 134, 135, 136–7, 139
form, and content 61–4, 71
formality 70–1
frames of reference 73, 79

Gandhi, Mahatma, speaking style 88–90
gender, and language 75–6, 137
generalization 81, 83, 118
genre 26–7, 46–7, 62, 90, 168
  boundaries 61–4
  choice 48–54, 59, 161
  control 76
  criticism 59
  disruption 63
  and event category 74
  in Hausa 59, 60–1, 62
  and power 76
  recognition 101
  transitions 62
good and evil, articulation of views 161–2
Great Divide debate *see* orality vs literacy
greetings, and expectations 14–15
groups, and ideology 92–3, 118
  see also speech community

Hausa
  abuse (*zagi*) 59
  ambiguity 107
  genres 59, 60–1, 62
  innuendo (*habaici*) 59–60
  poetry 61–2, 95, 97
  praising (*kirari*) 57, 61, 70, 136
  proverbs (*karin magana*) 60–1, 80–1
  Qur'anic exegesis (*tafsir*) 63–4
  riddles 82
  secrecy 28
  song (*waka*) 95, 117
  song tradition 136
stereotypes/typification 120
translation 43–4

hegemony
  of cultural production 45–6
  of English language 44
hermeneutics 157–8
Hesiod, on speaking 146–7
Howe, Sir Geoffrey 28, 30
  resignation speech 28–42, 171–6
    emphasis 31, 32, 33–4, 35
    expectation 36–7
    intentionality 40–1
    patterns 32, 33–4
    and persuasion 39–40
    power within 31–2, 39–40, 41
    responses 31, 34, 36–8,
      39–40, 40–1
Humphrey, Hubert 126
  Democratic National Convention
    Address 124–30, 177–9

ideological process 93, 118
ideology 4, 92–5, 101, 116–17, 118
illocutionary acts 151–2
Imam, Abubakar, Hausa writer
  95–7, 117
India, public speaking 147–9
indirectness 70
  see also allusion; innuendo
innuendo 59–60
  see also allusion; indirectness
intentionality 24, 25–7, 152–3
  in complaining 52
  and effectiveness 142,
    166–7, 170
  in Sir Geoffrey Howe speech
    40–1
  interest 97–8
interpretation 25–6, 59–61, 143
  Mark Antony speech 105–7
irony 106–7, 109, 151
is and ought 110–12
Islam
  and Hausa poetry 97
  Jihadist literature 162–3
  and public discourse 116
  and Somali texts 136

Jihadist literature (Nigeria)
  162–3
jokes 36, 121

Kautilya, and rhetoric 147–9
King, Martin Luther, speaking style
  88, 90
knowledge
  shared 120
  within communication 155

language 142
  appropriate 17, 57–8, 73–4
  and cultural values 43–6
  as currency of exchange 45
  evaluative 110–12, 127
  and gender 75–6, 137
  and ideology 101
  political 39–40, 158–61
  and roles 76
  social purposes 25
  standard 44
  and translation 43–5
listener expectations 48–54
  see also audience; expectations
literacy 15–17, 141
  vs orality 1–2, 54–6, 131–41
literate societies 16–17, 132
literature, patterns within 108–9,
  142
locutionary acts 151–2

Mamman Shata, Hausa singer 136
Mande society, power of silence 18
manipulation 27–8
Mark Antony speech 105–10
Mathers, Marshal (Eminem), rap artist
  23–5
Mayan texts 56
meaning 103–4, 142–3, 154
memories 27, 167, 168
  and articulation 117–18
  and speech event 123–4
memorization 145
metaphor 40, 101
the moment see oral communicative
  moment
moment of communication 20, 21,
  123–4, 155, 158–9
  see also oral communicative
    moment; performance,
    moment of
moral position 101, 127

moral responsibility 97, 100
morality
  and public discourse 115–17
  and stereotypes 122
  Mr Matches (Malam Ashana), Hausa speech performer 63
  musical performance 23–5, 136, 137, 139–40

naming 114–15
Native Americans
  oral tradition 10
  Ponca Indians 8–10
  see also Chief Standing Bear trial
Nigeria
  Jihadist literature 162–3
  professional speakers (*dan gambara*) 74–6
  and public discourse 116
  see also Hausa

oral communicative moment 3, 4, 130, 166, 167
  characteristics 20
  in Chief Standing Bear speech 5
  and commonality 166
  and cultural values 43–6, 70
  in rap 23–5
  and 'residues' 167–8
  see also moment of communication
oral societies 16–17, 131–2
oral traditions
  Native American 10
  Pacific cultures 135–6
orality 12–13, 15–17
  vs literacy 1–2, 54–6, 131–41

Pacific cultures, oral tradition 135–6
parallelism 113
parody 63–4, 71
patterns 117
  in Sir Geoffrey Howe speech 32, 33–4
  in Hubert Humphrey address 127
  within literature 142
  in Mark Antony speech 108–9
  and rhythm 33
  in Sunny Delight advertisement 113–14

perception, commonality of 18–19, 22–3
performance
  and audience 74–6
  and cultural style 87–90
  moment of 20–1, 47
  and political language 158–61
  and recording 3
perlocutionary acts 151–2
persuasion 2–3, 83, 99, 101, 162
  and convincing 83–4
  in Sir Geoffrey Howe speech 39–40
  and ideology 94
  in Mark Antony speech 109–10
  see also rhetoric
poetics 141–4
poetry, Hausa 61–2, 95, 97
politeness 150–1
politics
  debate 69, 124–5
  language 39–40, 158–61
  see also Democratic National Convention Address 1948; Howe, Sir Geoffrey, resignation speech
Ponca Indians 8–10
power
  and cultural production 92, 162, 163
  and genre 76
  in Hubert Humphrey address 128
  and ideology 93–4
  of silence 18
  in Sir Geoffrey Howe speech 31–2, 39–40, 41
  of the spoken word 17–19, 28
  see also control
power relations 3, 18, 56, 62–3, 130, 161
pragmatics 149–53
praising 57–8, 70, 115
  Hausa 57, 61, 70, 136
  Yoruba 57–8, 65–7
  Zulu 58, 70
presence of communicator 14, 75
private, into public 3, 27–9, 76–9, 91
propaganda 77

proverbs 79–81
  Berba 68–9
  Hausa 60–1, 80–1
  and riddles 82
public culture 4, 76–84
  see also culture
public discourse 115–17
  see also discourse

rap 23–5
reading, solitude of 21
reconstruction 45–6, 72
recontextualization 159–61
recording 3, 72–3, 167
relevance 69–70
repetition 12–13, 113–14
representation, and text 142–3
'residues' 167–8
rhetoric 99–100, 108, 110, 127, 144–9
rhythm, and pattern 33
riddles 82–3
roles 12, 58–9, 74–5
  and language 76
  within speech events 76–7, 90–1
  see also audience; stereotypes

secrecy, Hausa 28
self-referentiality 142–3
silence 13, 18
social contexts 72–5, 90, 168
  see also context
social currents 164–6
social facts 164–6
social position 58–9
socio-linguistics 149
solitude, and reading 21
Somalia, Arabic scholarship 136
songs 136, 137
  see also musical performance; rap
speaker
  and audience 74–7, 85–7
  expectations 48–54
  professional 74–5, 78
speaking
  effectiveness 33–4, 144–5
  ethnography 153–8
  in public 87–90, 145–9
  see also ways of speaking

speech
  categorization 73–4
  economy 69–70
  'expressive' aspect 10–11, 102–10
  linearity in time 12–13
  and power relations 56, 161
  standardized 145, 151
  see also aesthetics of speech; styles of speech
speech acts 130, 154–5
speech community 154
  see also groups
speech events 21–2, 154–5
  and memory 123–4
  roles within 76–7, 90–1
speech-act theory 152
spoken word
  inability to avoid 13
  power 17–19, 28
statements 110–12
stereotypes 101, 118–24
story-telling 67–8
styles of speech 28–9, 168
  see also cultural style; genres
Sunny Delight advertisement 113–14
Swahili, language and gender 75–6
symbolism, Hubert Humphrey address 127

teaching 22–3
text 167, 168
  affectivity 143–4
  and bureaucracy 55–6
  fixity 15, 134, 135, 136–7, 139
  and representation 142–3
  self-referentiality and meaning 142–3
  see also writing
Thatcher, Prime Minister Mrs Margaret, and Sir Geoffrey Howe speech 28–30
Tibbles, Suzette LaFlesche (Bright Eyes), translator 6
Tibbles, Thomas Henry, and Chief Standing Bear trial 4, 8
tone of voice 50

translations 43–5
  Chief Standing Bear speech 6
  Transvaal texts 55–6
Transvaal, orality vs literacy 54–6
Tristram Shandy 86
truth 4, 101, 155–6, 162
  and agreement 99–100
  in Hausa poetry 95–100
  and public culture 4, 77
truth value 96–7, 99, 117
  see also values
typification 79, 83, 117–18, 118–20, 127

understanding 18–19, 75, 105–7, 155, 156–7
  see also agreement
universalization 79, 83

validity claims 79, 155
values 19, 95–100, 110, 162
  see also cultural values; truth values

variability 136–7
verbal interaction 58–9
visual markers, in Sir Geoffrey Howe speech 32

ways of speaking 158, 168
  appropriate 10
  choice 48–54, 70, 152–3
  and expectations 49–54
  see also genres; speaking; styles of speech
writing 26, 138–9
  see also text

Yoruba
  aesthetics of speech 65–7, 70
  praising (*oriki*) 57–8, 65–7
Yucatan, Mayan texts 56

Zulu, praising 58, 70